Testimonials

Unstoppable integrates the fervour, the discipline, and the imagination from the author's experience as an officer in the British forces, and his expertise as a business leader.

Stew expresses his teaching in a way that is both practical and down to earth, and extremely vivid through his personal story. His perspective brings to life a powerful resource that is primal and human in equal measure.

If you want to be a successful business leader, an innovator at the top of your game, and a super-aware human being, read this 'life workshop' of a book, *Unstoppable*!

—**Jean Louis Rodrigue** *is an internationally sought-after acting and performance expert in theatre, film, and television. He has worked with Leonardo DiCaprio, Margot Robbie, Ang Lee, Christian Bale, Josh Brolin, Rachel McAdams, Chris Pine, and many others.*

*

Stew Darling's *Unstoppable: Living Beyond Our Limits* is truly sensational. Knowing Stew and his family, I hold the greatest respect for him. His unique character, forged through remarkable military and life experiences, including life-and-death decisions under pressure, is profoundly authentic; Liz confirms he lives every word of this book.

The book is a life workshop offering practical and down to earth steps for genuine transformation. It empowers readers to "Be Unreasonable," to "Raise our Standards," and to "Determine our Sacrifice".... This guidance changes all; we can no longer complain that we didn't know how to inspire people to live boldly, unreasonably and surpass the highest standards.

Stew has had a far-reaching effect on my life and I will be forever grateful that we met on a buffet lunch line at a meeting where we were both trying to elevate our ability to change the lives of those around us. Stew has changed my life for the better.

—**Markam Rollins III**
Author, The Evolving Man.

*

All children deserve to live *Unstoppable* lives. As children, that spark of imagination along with their tenacity, empowers that 'Unstoppableness'. But for too many children and teens in New Zealand, and across the world, a lack of access to their basic needs precludes this. More importantly, our children often lack a 'north star' to show them the way to living the *Unstoppable* life and living beyond their limits.

In this book, Stew Darling changes all that. We can no longer complain that 'we didn't know how'. Through simple and engaging stories along with exercises and tools, Stew brings to life ways we can all live unreasonably, experience a higher standard and realise that sacrifice is an important part of helping one another.

Too often, we are bombarded with quick fixes and hacks that promise to change our lives but don't. The fact that, after nearly twenty years of KidsCan, our waiting list is longer than ever, and Pet Rescue is already running out of space, are both examples of the glaring evidence of this.

Unstoppable is different and following the KidsCan team's personal experiences from working with Stew, I can say: this works for the long term.

—**Julie Chapman**
Founder and CEO of KidsCan; a national charity dedicated to levelling the playing field for New Zealand children living in poverty.

UNSTOPPABLE
LIVING BEYOND OUR LIMITS

STEW DARLING

Unstoppable: Living Beyond Our Limits
© Stew Darling 2025

First Edition released 2023

Second Edition released 2025

All rights reserved. No part of this publication may be reproduced, stored in a retrieval system, or transmitted in any form or by any means, electronic, mechanical, photocopying, recording or otherwise, without the prior written permission of the author.

Disclaimer: This book is sold with the understanding that the author is not offering specific personal advice to the reader. For personalised advice, you can seek the services of the author. the Lead through Life Framework worked for the author and yet, this may be applied differently when considering diverse personalities and context. Although being a leader is not everything—taking control of your destiny is essential. The author disclaims any responsibility for liability, loss or risk, personal or otherwise, that happens as a consequence of the use and application of any of the contents of this book.

ISBN: 978-1-7640787-2-6 (paperback)   978-1-7640787-3-3 (eBook)

 A catalogue record for this book is available from the National Library of Australia

Printed in Australia

Editor: Marisa Parker

Published by Stew Darling with assistance from Ignite & Write Publishing

For Liz

Every dreamer needs a believer.

Contents

Foreword	xi
The Space in Between	1
A New Darkness	2
Whirlpools and Whirlwinds	3
Faster Than a Homesick Angel	5
The Hole in the Whole	14
Reading This Book	19
Be Unreasonable	19
Raise the Standard	20
Determine Your Sacrifice	21
Part 1: Be Unreasonable	23
Be Unreasonable	25
Here's to the Crazy Ones	25
Is it Really All That Bad?	31
The Odd Ones Out	32
Do You Need a Hug?	37
Ever Had a Brainwave?	44
The Boring Chapter	51
Busy Doing Nothing	52
Count Your Blessings	57
Welcome to the Matrix	61
Finance	62
Health	67
Hobbies	68
Personal Development	70

Mission	72
Friends and Family	75
Intimate Relationships	77
Spirituality	81
The Matrix	84

This Earthly Suit — 87

Stay Social	89
Eat Real Food	93
Positive Material	101
Negative Material	103
Exercise	105
Sleep	109
Don't Stop Believing	114

Belonging in the World — 119

Be Kind; Stay at Home	121
A Path to Belonging	124

Part 2: Raise the Standard — 137

Turn and Face 'the BUT' — 139

That Deep Dive	139
Just Sign Here	144
What Do You Stand For?	148
To Love and Be Loved	151
A Word on Motivation	154
Discipline	157
Do Ethics Matter Anymore?	158
Shedding Our Old Skin	161

Captaincy—The Confluence of Self, System, and Situation — 165

Cocoa Pops, Sir!	168
Going Boldly	170

Leading with Style	173
The Eight Principles of Leadership	174

Communication: Perspective, % Rule, and Team Building Tools — 197

The Words Hardly Matter	200
Shaping the Battle Space	203
Psychopaths and Anyone Who Reads Your Emails	204
Words Come Too Easy	207
Throwing Stones in a Millpond	209
A Team of Teams	211
Looking to the Future	213
Simple Words	214

Participation — 215

Part 3: Determine Your Sacrifice — 219

The Ultimate Sacrifice — 221

Coaxing the Black Bear from Hibernation	221
Scared? Good!	225
We've Done It Before	226

A Seat at the Table — 231

The Dissonance of History	231
The Military Industrial Revolution that Keeps on Giving	234
And Then the Fighting Started	235
Watch Your Language	238
Our Advantage	238
Choosing the Environment	242
Make It Interesting	245
Intelligence Gathering	246
Building Trust	247
The Red Mist	248

This Isn't for Me	250
The Style of Work	250

Ripples in the River — 255

By the Firelight	255
Let the River Run	256
How Could You Not Know?	266
The Baggage We Carry	269

The Evolution Revolution — 271

When Gabrielle Visited	271
Survival is the Exception	275
Dominating the Ground	279
What Next?	282
Waiting for Superman	284

I Am Enough — 287

Discovering Wholeheartedness — 291

The Standard of Man	291
The Unstoppable Muscle	301

A Final Word — 309

A Note from the Author's Wife — 311

With Gratitude — 313

About the Author — 315

Ready for What's Next? — 317

Foreword

When Stew asked me to write the foreword for *Unstoppable*, I was honored; it's not hard to be immediately drawn to his remarkable journey.

As a former NFL player for the Houston Oilers and San Francisco 49ers, I have witnessed firsthand the power of determination, perseverance, and a steadfast commitment to excellence. And the man who penned these pages meets each of these qualities head-on.

Allow me to introduce you to the extraordinary mind behind this book, a man whose story has left a lasting impression on everyone fortunate enough to encounter his wisdom: Stew Darling, a retired British Army officer, has not only experienced the heights of achievement but has also conquered the depths of personal adversity, emerging stronger and more resilient every time.

Throughout his military career, Stew displayed a tenacity and dedication to excellence that elevated him to the rank of colonel. He honed his leadership skills in the crucible of battle, inspiring those under his command to surpass the highest of expectations. But what sets Stew apart is his belief that our potential is limitless and our capacity for growth knows no bounds.

Following Stew's illustrious military career, he embarked on a new path, transitioning into coaching and guiding individuals and businesses toward their highest potential. His approach was not one of conformity or adherence to conventional wisdom, but rather an audacious quest to live unreasonably and break free from the shackles of mediocrity.

In *Unstoppable*, Stew shares the insights he's gained from both his triumphs and his struggles. He deftly intertwines his personal experiences with his exceptional knowledge of human psychology and organisational dynamics.

Having witnessed Stew's unparalleled ability to inspire, I can tell you that this book is unlike any personal development guide you have ever encountered. His insights are hard-won and battle-tested, providing a roadmap to personal and professional success that is both pragmatic and aspirational. This book challenges us to dream bigger, strive harder, and pursue our goals with unyielding determination.

As an ex-football player turned playwright, actor, and speaker, I have seen how storytelling can captivate hearts and spark transformations time and time again. Stew's journey, as recounted in this book, is a testament to the power of the human spirit. His story will touch you deeply, leaving an indelible mark on your soul and awaken the enormous potential within you.

I am honored to have the opportunity to introduce you to *Unstoppable*. Through these pages, you will jump into a journey of self-discovery, guided by a man whose life's purpose is to help others unlock their own *unstoppable* potential. It is my sincerest belief that, like me, you will be forever changed by the wisdom, inspiration, and unwavering resolve that Stew brings to every word he writes.

Prepare to embark on an extraordinary adventure, one that will shatter the limits of what you believe is possible. Prepare to live boldly and unreasonably, to surpass the highest standards, and to give your ultimate sacrifice. Let '*Unstoppable*' be your guide on the path to becoming the best version of yourself.

To embracing the path to being the best.

—**Bo Eason**
Former NFL player for the Houston Oilers and San Francisco 49ers, acclaimed Broadway playwright and performer, and international presence/story coach.

Use this link to receive downloads of worksheets mentioned throughout this book: **https://unstoppableforce.co.nz/worksheets/**

The Space in Between

What is your saddest memory?

Bailey, our second family Golden Retriever. Born with kidney damage, put 'to sleep' within a year of arriving in New Zealand, aged four. Why so sad? She left us too early and as 'dad' it was on me to look after her last moments while also leading my family through those moments and the grief. Oh, and making sure I was okay, too.

A total loss of identity. A sense of being alone, of having nothing to give to this world.

What is your happiest memory?

The moment my daughter met her baby brother. When I heard the word 'baby' uttered by his two-year-old sister, in a yellow summer dress. For the first time, I knew, my family was complete.

I knew exactly who I was—I truly belonged to something. I knew how my life and experiences were to be used for this new generation.

*

Somewhere, between both of these experiences was a power. An *Unstoppable Force* that in understanding the answers to both questions might release me from the constraints and conformity of this world. Every one of us has that Force within us. We all experience grief and joy but seldom do we 'sit' with those moments. Without that sitting time, we fail to use those moments to grow. We lock those sad moments away and await the next moment of happiness—and we lose out on the life in between. The life we were born to live.

Unstoppable was the third, and final, working title of this book. In the time it took to write, I recognised that the story with which it begins, *A New Darkness*, was but another example of me playing small. As I shared in my first book, *Lead through Life*, my military career ended, and we moved to New Zealand. That was ten years ago. In that decade, I had become less and less of myself. Arriving in a new country with a fresh start, a new beginning, I had tried to fit in. With every experience and every failure, I had given myself permission to play smaller. To kill a little bit more of what made me the success that I had been.

It took a rather challenging discussion over dinner, where I was accused of being a 'war criminal', to wake me from this stupor. Two people with no experience of my past had taken a Hollywood-based, uneducated view to damn me. But I was complicit. For too long, I had played around the edges of who I truly am. I had been living an apology. I had not been living the life that God had given me.

Writing this book has been a cathartic experience. It has been a rebirth of the person who I really am. A return to the best of me. An exploration of my faults, and failings. In the end, a realisation that I am *Unstoppable,* and I had been operating, at best, on 50% power.

With this discovery, do I live at 100% every day? No, not yet. But at last, I have a reference point of what 100% feels like and I can always be pointing in that direction.

This book is the documenting of my journey back to me.

It is my hope that, in joining me, you re-find something of yourself. I celebrate you for your vulnerability and look forward to seeing the Unstoppable Force within you continue to rise.

A New Darkness

I drifted into consciousness; I awoke into a peaceful darkness. This wasn't a normal occurrence. Normally, my waking at this time of night was due to the usual stuff; a restless dog whining at the bedroom door, birds squawking in the night, a helicopter transferring a patient from the nearby hospital … a snoring wife!

Something was different tonight; what had changed? This was a new darkness. I hadn't 'started' awake. I had slowly become aware of myself. I felt the warmth of the bedclothes and the softness of the pillow under my head. I became aware of my wife's form next to me. As I opened my eyes, I felt a contentment that had been missing. For the first time in over a year, I felt ready! I felt it was time to get back to some mischief. That was it, I had found 'me' again only one year and two days after the accident: a gliding accident that had nearly claimed my life. As a novice to soaring the 'big blue', the experience of that plane crash had a deeper effect than I could have ever imagined.

During the intervening year, I'd got on with life, not really noticing that I wasn't 'firing on all cylinders'. I'd been on adventures, and started white-water kayaking again, in spite of the ongoing pandemic, business was doing well. We had even started the Podcast and a radio show. All this was hiding a truth—I wasn't myself. The slow creep of chronic pain, those little aches and pains that would not go away. The missing out on gym sessions and running, the weight gain. The lack of focus in my work, a loss of my passion.

Where to from here? I had to take some of my own medicine. It was time to become *Unstoppable*!

Whirlpools and Whirlwinds

Just off the West coast of Scotland lives a terrible monster. I remember the first time I heard of it as a child; it gave me nightmares. As early as the year 908, this monster was described as roaring … amongst the clouds with the steaming volume of a cauldron of fire—yup, most scary. These days, this monster is called the Corryvreckan and is the third biggest whirlpool on Earth. I wonder if it might be the fourth largest ever experienced by humanity.

The earliest surviving account dates back to 1549, in which there is a reference to the monster written by Donald Monro, High Dean of the Isles, in his *Description of the Western Isles of Scotland*. In a manuscript version of his work, Monro describes the whirlpool as 'infinite dangeris'. On one of the earliest maps to show Scotland as a separate geographical entity—as opposed to it being portrayed as a part of the British Isles—the celebrated Flemish geographer and mapmaker, Abraham Ortelius's map of Scotland, produced in Antwerp around 1573, shows the monster in the sea to the east of the Isle of Jura.

The Gulf of Corryvrekan lies between the arms of Scarpa and Jura and, even today, that's a pretty wild place. As the tide enters the narrow stretch of water between the arms of Jura and Scarpa, the water travels at speeds up to 8.5 knots and encounters a variety of underwater seabed features. On the western entrance, a pinnacle rises from depths of 70 metres to 29 metres, and directly in front of the pinnacle is a deep hole in the seabed with a depth of 290 metres. As the water flows into the Gulf, it falls into this hole and then encounters the steep face of the pinnacle, causing a massive upwelling surge of water to rise to the surface. On a flood tide, this surge meets swells entering the Gulf from the west and creates standing waves up to nine metres high. These are not like normal waves as they form directly over the pinnacle, standing still and breaking heavily. Whirlpools also form over the pinnacle throughout the Gulf as opposing water columns meet. These whirlpools can be up to 50 metres wide. It's said that you can hear the roar from the standing waves and whirlpools up to 10 miles away.

A weighted dummy wearing a life jacket and dive computer was thrown into the water close to Corryvreckan and was eventually found several miles out to sea. The dummy had been sucked down an astonishing 200 metres into the abyss and there was gravel in the pockets of its life jacket, which had been severely torn.

Any boat passing through the Gulf of Corryvrekan will need an engine capable of more than 8 knots to ensure it (and the crew) are not sucked into that terrifying vortex.

Imagine a vortex capable of dragging you under, an ever-deepening, darkening experience with little to no way out until your lungs are filled with water or you are crushed by the weight of the water or on the rocks and seabed. An unstoppable downward force.

Have you ever felt that life was a bit like that? In the year after my accident, I hadn't noticed at first but there was a sense of sinking, of being pulled down and surrounded with a sense of claustrophobia, of being dragged under. To start, I felt a wee bit of my identity disappear. Who was I? What had the accident taken away? I stopped talking to people and no longer visited friends—I was ostracising myself from my community. Then, they stopped reaching out to me. Finally, with no one to talk to, I started listening to the voices in my head … you know the ones. The voices that suggest you're not good enough. That it was all your fault.

I had become trapped in a downward crushing vortex. A whirlpool of doom and despair … and this whirlpool is so much more dangerous than the Corryvrekan; this one can 'catch' us anywhere and at any time. The result of being caught can be a sense of fear and foreboding, of anxiety, and a feeling of depression. Surely, this is the biggest whirlpool ever faced by humanity. And it feels like it's getting even more unstoppable.

Faster Than a Homesick Angel

One of my favourite films as a child was *The Wizard of Oz*. I was too young to realise the cinematographic importance of the first colour film, but I did love the good versus evil story and the idea tornadoes are powerful enough to lift a house off the ground and transport the heroine (and wizard) to a different place, without all the 'baggage' of their lives in Kansas.

First used in 1952, the term 'Tornado Alley', describes an area of the central United States where tornadoes are most likely to occur. The rough location of Tornado Alley is from Texas in the south, where the warm dry air of the Arizona and New Mexico deserts push warm dry air North-East and the warm moist air of the Caribbean blows north, through the states of Oklahoma, Kansas, Nebraska, and South Dakota where the tornadoes meet the cold dry air from the north-west and Canada. The jet stream adds energy to the mix as it hooks east from California to Colorado.

These tornadoes are violently rotating columns of air that are in contact with both the surface of the Earth and clouds, sometimes referred to as twisters, whirlwinds, or cyclones. Tornadoes come in many shapes and sizes, and they are often visible in the form of a condensation funnel originating from the base of a cloud, with a cloud of rotating debris and dust beneath it. If not for the dust, debris, and moisture being sucked skywards, tornadoes are invisible.

Not unlike whirlpools, they are one of Mother Nature's destructive powerhouses, an Unstoppable Force. The difference? While whirlpools suck all the debris into the centre to be mixed up and shattered on the seafloor, tornadoes push all the detritus upwards and out; the air inside a tornado is clear and calm. Unlike the seafloor below a whirlpool that is a map of destruction, above a tornado it is calm and clear. All the trash has been removed.

Like the tornado, sometimes, our path to becoming *Unstoppable* is fast, aggressive, and unexplained. However, if all that seems to be too violent as you consider becoming an Unstoppable Force, there is another option …

Sitting in my office, looking east towards the hills, I could watch the gliders from the local club winching into the wide blue yonder and recovering back to the field. It had always been a dream of mine to soar but that was only for the rich. As a child, I had first seen gliders aero-towing out of Portmoak Airfield in Scotland. On our monthly trips to visit the cousins in Fife, on the Eastern coast, we would pass that field and I would watch in amazement at the ability of these powerless white birds, thinking, *One day … one day.*

In my office that day, I decided that today was that *one day*. I called the club and within a week, I had taken my first flight. Three flights captured me—I was going to become a glider pilot, and I was going to soar. I even set a challenge to 'go solo' on fifty flights. The standard 'rule' is that to 'go solo' takes your age plus forty launches—total BS! I was not going to waste the best part of ninety launches before being released, alone, into the heavens. And I was diligent. I rehearsed my pre-launch checks every day, on every run. I bought a simple simulator and practiced launches and landings. I was on the field every weekend, learning everything there was to know about my new hobby. The launch and recovery are the important bits, but the joy of gliding comes in the space in between.

The skill of any proficient glider pilot is to stay aloft as long as possible. While these sailplanes want to fly, to stay airborne—gravity still wins. Finding a thermal is the goal of every pilot. Learning where they might be is an art. Thermals, like tornadoes, are invisible. If you fly too fast, you'll shoot straight through, if your turn is too tight, you'll miss the sense of lift. If you are not monitoring the weather, you'll miss the thermals movements. But when you get everything right, airspeed, angles, and awareness, you will feel that rise, sometimes just a little, yet on the good days, you'll head upwards, faster than a homesick angel … But there are two sides to every thermal, the lift and the drop—there is never a moment to take the thermal for granted and the glider pilot must be conscious and cautious, constantly.

There are clues if we look. Hawks, with wings spread, peacefully climb in the warmer air. When we know the geography of the land we might head back to familiar spots: herds of cattle and corrugated iron roofing are all clues that there might be some thermal activity. We must go there as to miss the first thermal after launch, more often than not results in a short flight.

There is support for any glider learner. In the back seat sat my instructor, patiently guiding me through his years of experience. On the ground, there is a wealth of other experience that I can plug into, assisting me on my way and accelerating my progress through vicarious learning.

To become *Unstoppable*, we have choices. The first is to turn our back on the noisy whirlpool of society that says we are all doomed to a life of control, conformity, fear, and anxiety. The second is to leave our growth to chance. To reap the whirlwind and contend with the violence that might result in our *Unstoppable* Force. Or we can study ourselves and those on the journey. We can become aware of the invisible forces that will carry us to the stars. We can choose to find the thermals, to ride the thermals into our new *Unstoppable* world. The choice is ours, but whichever we choose, we will face both violence and peace as we grow. And, at times, gravity will remind us of her presence.

We can accept the experiences of others and watch for the clues that show we are on the path to reaching beyond our limits.

One day finally, I had made it. It took longer than my planned fifty launches, but late on a Sunday afternoon in December, I was there. The Duty Instructor unstrapped from the back seat of ZK-GPJ (Papa Juliet), a DG-1000 glider, and said, 'Do you think you could do the same again without me?'

Holy Shit, this is it. I had just been given permission to 'go solo'!

Pre-checks were done and the glider with ONLY ME aboard was connected to the launch cable; within a few short moments, I was in the climb. In less than a minute, I was soaring at nearly 2,000 feet over the hills and fields of New Zealand. As there was not much lift—that I could find—on that day, I very quickly made the call to enter the circuit and made a not-too-shabby landing back on the field. Now it was time to learn how to become a true glider pilot and extend my range and altitude away from the field.

'Can I go again?'

'Not today.'

'Bugger.'

The following week, I was back at the club, running the airfield as a class of more experienced pilots took to the skies. Running the airfield entails the responsibility of launching and recovering all aircraft while maintaining a 'safe' environment for all pilots and ground crew. While those pilots were 'on a break', I was offered a check flight which went so well that a different duty instructor asked me if I felt able to go solo again. Nothing was going to stop me.

Pre-checks were done, and with the glider connected to the launch cable, I quickly settled into a 45-degree angle of climb. At 1,800 feet, I felt the cable break away. I only soared for a few minutes. The weather was cool, in my inexperience, I had not found any lift to climb the glider for a longer flight so after those few moments, I checked my altimeter, made the decision to complete my landing check and make the call, and entered the circuit to land. The downwind part of the circuit was fine, altitude, okay, speed, okay, angle from the airfield, good. Turning on to base, I could see a glider below me accelerating into the climb, and before me, the whole field was clear for my approach. Quick check, altitude, okay, speed, okay. I turned onto finals and released the air brake.

Careful to keep the airspeed consistent with the conditions, I descended over the river at 70 knots (130 km/h) and hit an area of sink. I felt the sudden loss of altitude as the glider dropped and my safety harness bit into my shoulders. I closed the air brake to steady my descent at which point I felt gravity force me into my seat, as I hit some lift. By now, l could see trees speeding past and I was still travelling at 130 km/h, my inexperience took over. Rather than opening the air brake, I edged the 'stick' forward pointing the nose of the glider towards the ground causing the glider to accelerate towards Earth.

The trees continued to speed by, but now I was joined by fenceposts as I was still accelerating towards the ground. It all happened so quickly that the next thing, the nose ploughed into the field, and I experienced a rapid deceleration, as my body was thrown forward into my harness. Immediately, the glider bounced back into the air with such force that my head snapped back, hitting the headrest. Then, I hit the ground, once again, and this time caused the wings of the glider to flap and my spine to be slammed backwards into the parachute I was wearing. I felt the ripping of the intercostal muscles between my ribs as I began to lose control of the glider. Despite the crash landing, the glider was on its own path, travelling towards the airfield fence and a row of trees. Fortunately, at this point, I remembered some training and I let the glider land. Glider Papa Juliet rolled to a stop a few hundred metres beyond a deep new furrow in the field that my glider and I had just created.

I became aware that I had been extremely lucky, as a few more knots on the dial and the glider would have flipped over on the nose and killed me. Fortunately, the DG-1000 is a robust beast, and as it turned out, that light aircraft survived the impact in a better state than me.

Through sheer determination, I was back in the air the following day and continued to fly, but the love that had enraptured me was gone. Gravity had beaten me. But, as with every failure, we can learn something about ourselves if we pay attention to the failure. Instead of regret, we must accept it as a learning experience.

There is always a risk when we adventure. As we adventure into an *Unstoppable* world, you will face challenges, even life-threatening challenges, as we are tempted, coerced, and forced back to the comfortable, caged life where most exist. We must see these encounters for what they are. They are temptations to give up on our dreams. It took the best part of a year for me to realise the physical and psychological toll the glider accident had taken. It was a reminder of my military life where, often, death was a constant companion. It was an awakening to how soft I had become.

At that point, it was a clarion call to step back into the fire—into the land of the living—to become *Unstoppable*, once again.

Unstoppable Force is a concept about humanity reaching beyond our limits. Many of us in this world have become just a little bit too comfortable with instant gratification and with everything being there before we even need it.

This book is about all of us who live in that space but believe there is something more. We strive to meet the potential we feel in those moments when we feel *discomfort in our comfort*. Right here we have a choice, but do we? We have tried the gentle approach to improvement. We have got a wee bit better but then our old selves have reacted to the change and before we know it, we are back into our comfort zone. Let's be honest for a moment. That option does not work—we prove it again and again. But where can we turn?

We can take the route that seems the most scary. A route towards the 'Undiscovered Country' where few paths exist. Like Dorothy's departure from Kansas and arrival on the Yellow Brick Road, we must accept that our path will be Unreasonable, it will require us to raise our Standard and, we must commit to giving our Ultimate Sacrifice, every day. And then, repeat. This book is about how we can all do this. It is a book that has been tested in combat using the author as the 'guinea pig'.

If you want to become *Unstoppable*, to become a true powerhouse, forget about settling for mediocrity. It's time to kick things up a notch. I may not have fancy degrees in psychology or psychiatry and I'm no social worker or neuroscientist. I don't have endless studies to back me up. My expertise comes from years of being an absolute badass in the British Forces and rubbing shoulders with elite military folks from around the world. I've also spent a solid decade in the business world, learning the ropes. Everything I've learned is at your disposal, and it's not some pretentious science. It's a primal instinct.

This book is all about tapping into those instincts, facing reality head-on, and ditching the excuses that stand between you and your Unstoppableness. No matter how mind-boggling and unattainable they may seem. Don't let those cynics tell you it can't be done! It can!

This book was not written to tell you how to change because … people don't! I want you to embrace who you already are. Get into that sweet zone where you can shut out all the noise, negativity, fear, distractions, and conformity. Achieve whatever you want. Do whatever it takes to get there. This book and Unstoppable Force workshops, events and courses talk about some juicy topics, and if that makes you squirm, that's okay. Becoming an Unstoppable Force is all about dealing with reality and confronting your inner demons and addictions. The real Unstoppable Forces are those unapologetic, ruthless, yet successful individuals who refuse to be tamed.

If you're aiming to become *Unstoppable*, forget about worrying over whether you'll upset others or what they'll think of you. We're stripping away all that touchy-feely stuff and doing whatever it takes to reach your destination.

From this point forward, your strategy is simple: Be Unreasonable, and make everyone else level up. You're not lowering yourself to their standards. You're not competing with anyone else anymore. It's them who must compete with you.

Our journey through the pages of this book will, at times, seem confronting: awesome! It is only confronting to the 'old you'. Throughout, we will be questioning the status quo and the person you are looking to grow from will react. Watch and feel those moments. The more you feel confronted, the greater the growth opportunity. In those instances, take a moment, put the book down, and do one of the following:

- Pick up a journal and pen and start writing.
- Go for a walk with nature (with no music or phone).

- Meditate.
- Get sweaty!

Each of these activities will settle your overactive brain and your consciousness, and you will sense, through your subconscious, your next step into the person you are becoming. Go with it, trust your gut, and take the step.

Throughout this book, there will be hints and tips along with activities to assist you on this path. There are even some very simple 'hacks' that you can use for a quick boost or confidence builder when the old you roars. But this book is not yet another personal development book to read and cast aside as the next best seller arrives. This book is written as a companion for life. When our choice is to become *Unstoppable*, we cease to go around in circles. We begin to be drawn up, like the warm air in those thermals. We might feel that we are back at the same place, however, if we take time to reflect, we will see that, while the location looks similar, we are more elevated. We have reached a higher realm.

These are the times to return to this book. Each time you sense the tug of the old you, or the drag of society's seemingly endless pull toward conformity and 'the easy life'. When you are under attack from phrases like—What's the point? Or, This feels lonely—it is time to choose which of the three critical steps you can use to refocus. Becoming *Unstoppable* is nothing more, or everything less, than asking of yourself three simple tasks, every day until they become embedded in your subconscious. These are the three critical steps that provided me with a long and successful career in Military Intelligence. My extended shelf-life as a spy was based on the three critical steps that will empower you to become *Unstoppable*. Your mission, should you choose to accept them:

- Be Unreasonable.
- Raise your Standard.
- Determine your Sacrifice.

The Hole in the Whole

If we don't have resilience, fear creeps in and anxiety creeps in. And then suddenly, we start living with anxiety. At Unstoppable Force, I talk to people all the time who say: 'Well, you just have to live with anxiety in the 21st century.' *No, you don't*! You don't at all.

If you're living with anxiety, that's when we begin to use other words; depression, mental health, breakdown; and we don't want anyone to get there. There are folks that, unfortunately, live in that space all the time throughout their lives. Fear, anxiety, and depression can become a habit—we create the neural pathway over a period of approximately thirty days. But if we can catch it when people are just living in a little bit of fear and have a little bit of anxiety, then there's no need for our lives to go down that path.

Unfortunately, if it's not caught within ninety days, then that same fear, anxiety, and depression becomes a part of our personality. Even then, it's not too late. Just as we can create this personality, we can also create whatever personality we choose.

Before the pandemic, 1 in every 8 people, or 970 million people around the world were living with a mental disorder, with anxiety and depressive disorders the most common.[1] In 2020, the number of people living with anxiety and depressive disorders rose significantly as a result of the COVID-19 pandemic. Initial estimates show a 26% and 28% increase respectively for anxiety and major depressive disorders in just one year.[2] While effective prevention and treatment options exist, most people with mental disorders do not have access to effective care. The world can't train sufficient mental health specialists to deal with that sort of number! We've

---

[1] Institute of Health Metrics and Evaluation (2023), *Global Health Data Exchange (GHDx)*, https://vizhub.healthdata.org/gbd-results/.
[2] Geneva: World Health Organization (2022), *Mental Health and COVID-19: Early evidence of the pandemic's impact*.

got to be smart and find different ways to help one another and to stop even more folks from joining that astronomical number. Many people also experience stigma, discrimination and violations of human rights.

Congratulations, you have been smart, as by picking up this book you have chosen to learn how to become *Unstoppable*. You choose to be more for you, your partner, and/or for your children. You chose to teach your family and your tribe a new path so that we don't trip over that fine line between anxiety and those depressive and mental health issues.

Unstoppable Force is about Being Unreasonable and creating self-belief in who we are, building a sense of Belonging in the world through raising our Standard, and giving the Ultimate Sacrifice of our knowledge and experiences to help others discover that path for themselves. As you read this book, realise that your endpoint is someone else's starting point.

But let's back up a little bit. *We have normalised the abnormal and our world is one where it's almost expected that we have anxiety.*

We live in a world where fear, anxiety, depression, and mental health issues are front of mind. A world where celebrities and sports stars are all too desperate to tell the stories of their pain and suffering; of events in their childhood that led to their greatness or, too often, their demise in the public spotlight, which unfortunately leads to a feedback loop. Surely, if our heroes have a 'dark' past then, so must we? We all must have torment in our past, which has led to us, living a life of anxiety or, we can't find that trauma in our past, so we live with anxiety that we are 'odd' or spend our lives self-absorbed seeking that which we just haven't discovered yet.

Our governments have huge budgets for mental health but don't know where or how to spend them for fear of ostracising potential voters; they are more worried about their political legacy than their constituent's wellbeing.

Charities support different mental health issues and different addictions but because each is so niche, they struggle to raise sufficient funds for 'their effect'. They struggle to support the effect, rather than facing the cause. It is the very cause our politicians are all too well aware of but unwilling to face.

Even the words we use are being shifted. We need to be honest! If it is a suicide, then let's call it that. If it is addiction, let's call it that. In not doing so, we are dumbing down, and in doing so, we further normalise the abnormal. We must bring truth to the fore and no longer accept the stories and status quo of the past. Becoming *Unstoppable* requires us to live in truth.

Our world of instant gratification tells us that we must have everything … now! In a world where anything is at our fingertips, we want everything.

We live in toxic relationships; we eat and drink unhealthy foods; we consume vast quantities of toxic substances; alcohol and drugs (illegal and medicated), thinking that we will find the answer to the *hole in the 'whole'*.

Are we all doomed to a future of fear and anxiety—possibly! We will deal with the topic of Epigenetics later in the book to understand one of the reasons why, in the developed world, we find ourselves in this mess. Even with whatever pain and destruction happened within our ancestral lineage, we still have a choice. Too often we hear in the media and across social media that we are being controlled by governments, aliens, and the bright green pumpkin in the sky. The sad thing is, we have heard it so often from the very people claiming our freedom is at risk that we have begun to believe it. Many things in our lives are out of our control, so … where do we start? With the things that we can control! Even if it is just the tiniest action, we must show ourselves how to take back our future.

Is there no hope? Of course, there is hope and while it is certainly no planning tool, by focusing on the cause of the current mess we think we are in, we can better manage the effect.

Is it really that bad? No!! The world is a beautiful place full of wonderful, kind human beings. For the most part, no one gets out of bed with plans to be an asshole. It's just that life gets in the way and the result is asshole-like activity.

That asshole-like activity is born out of uncertainty. Born out of a need to 'be seen'. As we shall see, that need is a part of our sociological make-up and generally shows an individual who is struggling to understand themselves. Any reaction really has nothing to do with 'you' but everything to do with their internal existential battle and, until the battle is won, that individual will always struggle.

How did we lose? We got lazy! We forgot that life is tough, and that toughness is where our personal growth comes from. When life was tough, we celebrated every tiny victory; we lived with enthusiasm. Being lazy, we expect everything to be at our fingertips and complain when it's not. We waste energy on 'stuff' that doesn't matter and in doing so, we lose our identity, feel outcast in society, and become self-absorbed. In short, we enter the whirlpool, the downward vortex towards anxiety, depression, and mental health issues.

In identifying the downward vortex therein lies hope for our future. A future when everyone can find self-belief in who they truly are. A future where everyone belongs rather than being forced to fit in. A world that celebrates every one of us giving our experience and knowledge to create a brighter future. A world where we have become *Unstoppable*.

Welcome to the Unstoppable Force. Once we have an unreasonable level of self-belief in who we are and live to our Standard, we sense belonging which creates balance in our lives, and we begin to feel calm. That calmness and balance create confidence that causes us to choose to participate in the world. We want to share our unique genius and experience—our Ultimate Sacrifice. We choose to share because we are actually part of a tribe that genuinely cheers for us. When this happens, we feel fulfilled. And guess what, when we feel fulfilled, we begin to seek a deeper level of self-belief which, you've guessed it, leads to a higher standard of Belonging and a deeper willingness to give of our Ultimate sacrifice. Balance becomes participation which becomes Fulfilment. And round we go again, ever upwards ... this is Unstoppable Force, not secret sauce, no 'Matrix' pill moment. It is a carefully crafted process you can jive with forever more.

Reading This Book

This book is arranged into three parts:

- Being Unreasonable.
- Raising our Standard.
- Determining our Sacrifice.

It doesn't matter where you start. This is not a list; all chapters are as important as the next or the previous one. Just like the thermals in gliding, wherever you enter, you will be carried higher. When you return to a chapter, you will meet the words as 'the new you' and each lesson will have a deeper meaning. And around we go; ever higher.

Be Unreasonable

Being Unreasonable starts with understanding ourselves. And that's not just ourselves! We must go deeper to become aware of the importance of your lineage. This is how you'll realise how essential it is to understand where you came from and understand what makes us (you) tick. What makes us tick, as human beings, will result in us getting what we need. I'm using the word, need, specifically here. We have needs as human beings that we've forgotten because we live in a world of want and expectation.

Next up, we will count our blessings. We will talk about money, but counting our blessings is the true wealth. We introduce you to the eight pillars of wealth during this part of the book, and as we score that wealth—all eight pillars—you score where you feel you are and then we talk about how to amp that up. How do we begin to amp up all those areas of our lives? We begin to have certainty not only in where we are now, but where we choose to go.

And then we consider our Earthly Suit and all different aspects of our health. To begin to recognise what we can do right now, to extend our health span during our limited time on Earth. Hopefully not too limited.

Raise the Standard

If you don't stand for something, you'll fall for anything. We need to understand our purpose. People have heard me state that I believe we all have a purpose to love and be loved, at specific times in our lives, we have different purposes such as a covert soldier, a nurse and midwife, parent, businessman, coach, etc. You will have different purposes for your life, as well, but we've got to understand what that is. And that comes from understanding our Values.

You can understand and practice values in your workplace (they are normally dictated by the organisation). But you should also do this for your family, as well. Basically, it comes down to leadership. If we're going to go out there to participate in the world, we must understand our purpose and know our values. We've got to understand how to actually lead. Leadership and leaders sometimes get a bad name. In this book, I've chosen to use the word, Captaincy, as leadership is sometimes thought of as a dirty word. However, Unstoppable Force is going to give you the skills and the tools to understand what leadership truly is. And that's leadership from twenty-five years of serving in the British Army, experiencing the different styles of leadership and all that is required.

And then, our last stop on the path to Raising our 'Standard' is the art of communication. We've got a purpose, we know who we are, and we understand how to use the tools to lead people! So, let's communicate.

Too often, we don't communicate in this world, as it is more about how desperate we are to get our next work done. Well, wouldn't it be good to understand that communication is so much more than just the words that come out of our mouths? This is a superpower.

By the end of that chapter, you will have the tools and that superpower to go out there and get your purpose and your mission clearly understood in the world which sets us up beautifully to give the ultimate sacrifice.

Determine Your Sacrifice

From communication, we step into collaboration. We used to call collaboration, conflict negotiation, but as a 'once upon a time' Senior British Military interrogator and hostage negotiator, I realise that conflict can be a negative word; collaboration is far more positive. In this world, you're either right or wrong. It's black or it's white. But here's the truth—neither is the case: the world is full of grey. Wouldn't it be great to have superpowers to win every argument, to get what you want every time? That's the outcome of the collaboration: that everyone gets to feel like they have won, or at least, not to have lost!

And then that leads on to Unwritten Ground Rules—the other side of purpose and values. One of the reasons we get so stressed in the world is because the world is run on Unwritten Ground Rules, the values people use and show in the workplace, not the ones that are written down. But the ones we actually display.

Evolution is what has made us humans, the predominant species on the planet. We can change, we can transition. But we don't actually like it because our egos are saying, I was really quite comfortable just sitting wrapped in cotton wool. But if we didn't evolve, we would still be sitting in caves licking water from the walls. So, we choose to stay the same.

So how do we evolve, and how do we help other people evolve? Because, as we use the skills and the tools to transition and change, this will make people realise it's not scary at all. The scary thing is *not* changing. And that quite nicely links back to a deeper level of self-belief.

*

Through each of the three parts of this book, the three critical steps to becoming *Unstoppable*, you will answer the two questions posed at the beginning of the book.

What is your saddest memory?

What is your happiest memory?

The result will fill another hole in 'the space in between'. Each time you re-read this book or a part of the book, you will gain another opportunity to find and fill another space. This is the *Unstoppable* Pathway.

Part 1: Be Unreasonable

Be Unreasonable

Here's to the Crazy Ones

Right-wing fundamentalists have a lot to answer for. For that matter, so do left-wing fundamentalists. And they are both getting more and more extreme. As most of us sit somewhere in-between, the healthy debate is being stifled. In an article in the May 2022 issue of *The Atlantic* magazine, Johnathan Haidt opined that 'the past 10 years of American life have been uniquely stupid'.[3] Watching from afar, I would concur but add that this is not a uniquely American affair.

The article begins with the biblical story of the tower of Babel. Prior to humanity building the tower 'with its top in the heavens, occupants of this here planet all spoke with 'one tongue'. After the destruction (not by God), humanity spoke in many languages. Haidt suggests that left and right-wing views began to create a similar challenge towards the end of the first decade of this century. The rise of social media in the previous decade led to 'mass democratisation', possibly the best example being the Arab Spring of 2011—the same year that Google Translate 'rebuilt the Tower of Babel'.

Less than a year later, as Facebook planned for a $5 billion Initial Public Offering (IPO), Mark Zuckerberg wrote in a letter to shareholders: "Today, our society has reached another tipping point, Facebook hoped 'to rewire' the way people spread and consume information".[4]

At that point, as they say, the 'wheels came off', as social media has not only changed the way we ingest information but also the information

---

[3] The Atlantic (May 2022), Jonathan Haidt, *Why the Past 10 Years of American Life Have Been Uniquely Stupid*, https://www.theatlantic.com/search/?q=Why+the+past+ 10+years+of+American+life+have+been+uniquely+stupid.
[4] Facebook (2012), Mark Zuckerberg, *Letter to Investors: 'The Hacker Way'*, https://www.wired.com/2012/02/zuck-letter/.

we ingest. The algorithms now feed us similar information to that for which we search, creating an information bias which, in turn, pushes each of us to our extremes.

Without a filter of personal research, it becomes easier and easier to 'go with the flow', accepting more and more 'unreasonable' views … and the share button doesn't help!

In less than five years (from 2010), society had moved from a structure that had lasted, rightly or wrongly, for thousands of years, to the Great 'Awakening' on the left and Donald Trump on the right. Within a few years, this divide spread across the developed world. Even the word 'woke' has been abused and re-interpreted as a part of this division.

The *Hidden Tribes* study, by the pro-democracy group, More in Common, reported that by 2018, the far-right (devoted conservatives) comprised 6% of the US population while the group furthest to the left, the 'progressive activists', comprised 8 percent.[5] In a political sense, the rest of us sit in a relatively neutral position. Some of our beliefs will be slightly more right or left wing but a stable society is enabled by a centrist approach.

When we feel strongly, we will air our views, or grievances, but stop short of an all-out rant because society says, "That's not reasonable." This provides a gap for the fundamentalists and ideologues, and they are filing it. With the expansion of far-right and far-left voices, there has been an increase in violence and unkindness. Look to the 6 January 2022 riots on Capitol Hill in Washington D.C., USA, and, in New Zealand, the occupation of the Parliament lawns in February 2022. Too many get swept up in the 'passion' of these events and many others 'stay home' despite agreeing with much of what is said. Fearful politicians call out extremism as the minority, but this is swiftly becoming the new norm.

---

[5] Hidden Tribes (2018), Stephen Hawkins et al, *A Study of America's Polarized Landscape* https://hiddentribes.us/media/qfpekz4g/hidden_tribes_report.pdf.

There are a minority who move to violence and conspiracy but this masks a view of the majority that society is becoming more and more shattered.

There is nothing wrong with extremist or fundamentalist views. Some of the greatest advances in society have come from this sort of thinking, but we must be free to debate them. It is not the fundamentalist that leads to a breakdown in society, it is the removal of free and healthy debate. Whenever a part of society, or government/governing class takes away this freedom, society begins to collapse, much like the Tower of Babel in the land of Shinar. A quick glance through history shows the demise of the great empires was preceded by a period of social unease.

The Egyptians

The Egyptian Empire spanned several dynasties and lasted for thousands of years. It experienced periods of decline and collapse, as well as periods of renewal and resurgence. However, several factors have been identified as contributing to the eventual decline and collapse of the ancient Egyptian Empire:

Environmental Changes: One of the key factors that led to the decline of the Egyptian Empire was environmental changes. Changes in the Nile River's flood patterns and long-term droughts caused widespread famine, which weakened the economy and made it more difficult to maintain social and political stability.

Invasion and Foreign Rule: The Egyptian Empire faced repeated invasions and periods of foreign rule, which weakened the central government's authority and left it vulnerable to internal rebellions and external threats.

Economic Decline: Egypt's economy was heavily dependent on agriculture and trade. As the empire expanded, it became more difficult to maintain control over trade routes and to keep up with changing economic conditions. This led to a decline in the economy and a weakening of the government's ability to support its military and infrastructure.

Social and Political Instability: Egypt's society was highly stratified and hierarchical, which made it difficult to maintain social and political stability over long periods of time. As the empire grew more complex, it became increasingly difficult to keep the various social and political factions in check.

Cultural and Religious Changes: The Egyptian Empire experienced significant cultural and religious changes over time. The traditional polytheistic religion was replaced by monotheistic faiths such as Christianity and Islam, which led to a decline in the power of the traditional priesthood and the weakening of cultural and social traditions that had held the society together.

The Romans

The decline and fall of the Roman Empire was a complex and multifaceted process that unfolded over several centuries. Historians and scholars have identified numerous factors that contributed to the eventual collapse of this once-mighty empire, including:

Political Instability: As the Roman Empire grew larger and more complex, it became increasingly difficult for one ruler or group of rulers to maintain effective control over such a vast territory. This led to political instability, infighting, and a lack of coherent leadership, which made the empire more vulnerable to external threats.

Economic Decline: Rome's economy was built on a system of slave labour and conquest, which was unsustainable in the long term. As the empire expanded, it became harder to conquer new territories and enslave new populations. At the same time, the costs of maintaining a massive military and infrastructure system began to strain the government's resources.

Barbarian Invasions: The Roman Empire faced repeated attacks from barbarian tribes on its borders, particularly in the 4th and 5th centuries. These invasions weakened the empire's military and infrastructure, making it easier for subsequent invasions to succeed.

Military Overspending: Rome's military was one of the most powerful in the world, but it came at a high cost. The empire spent vast sums of money on building and maintaining its army, which put a strain on its finances and left it vulnerable to economic crises.

Social Decay: Over time, the values and traditions that had held Roman society together began to break down. Corruption, decadence, and social unrest became more common, weakening the fabric of the empire and making it harder to maintain order.

Overexpansion: As the Roman Empire grew larger, it became increasingly difficult to govern effectively. The costs of maintaining a vast empire became too high, and the empire was forced to rely more and more on local rulers and client states to maintain control. This weakened the central government's authority and made it more vulnerable to external threats.

The Soviet Union

Communism aimed to establish a classless, stateless society in which the means of production are owned and controlled collectively by the people. Although the idea of communism was appealing to many people, in practice, it has largely failed to achieve its goals. The fall of the Soviet Union provides several examples of why communism failed:

Economic Inefficiency: Communist economies were often characterised by a lack of economic efficiency and productivity. Central planning, which is a hallmark of communist economies, did not always allow for the efficient allocation of resources and often resulted in shortages and surpluses of goods.

Political Repression: Communist governments often relied on authoritarianism and repression to maintain power, which led to widespread human rights abuses and political repression. The lack of political freedom and civil liberties made it difficult for citizens to express dissent or hold their leaders accountable, which created an atmosphere of fear and distrust.

Lack of Innovation: The emphasis on central planning and collective ownership in communist economies often stifled innovation and entrepreneurship. This led to a lack of technological progress and a failure to adapt to changing economic conditions.

Environmental Degradation: Communist governments often prioritised industrialization and economic growth over environmental concerns, leading to significant environmental degradation and pollution.

Corruption: Communist governments were often plagued by corruption, with officials abusing their power for personal gain. This eroded trust in the government and undermined the legitimacy of the communist system.

The British Empire

The British Empire was one of the largest and most powerful empires in world history. It spanned over a quarter of the world's land area at its height and lasted for several centuries. However, the empire began to decline in the 20th century and eventually collapsed. There were several factors that contributed to the decline and fall of the British Empire:

Economic factors: After World War II, Britain's economy was in shambles, and the country was heavily indebted. The cost of maintaining the empire was becoming increasingly difficult, and the British government began to focus on rebuilding the domestic economy rather than maintaining the empire.

Decolonisation movements: As people in British colonies became more educated and politically aware, they began to demand independence from Britain. This led to a wave of decolonisation movements across the empire, which resulted in many former British colonies gaining independence.

World War II: Britain suffered heavily during World War II, and the cost of fighting the war put a tremendous strain on the country's economy. The war also weakened Britain's global power and influence.

Rise of other powers: The emergence of new global powers, such as the United States and the Soviet Union, challenged Britain's dominance on the world stage. These new powers were better equipped to compete with Britain economically and militarily.

Domestic political factors: Political and social unrest in Britain during the 20th century contributed to the decline of the empire. Labour strikes, civil rights movements, and growing public dissent over the government's policies all weakened Britain's ability to maintain its global influence.

*

Overall, the decline and fall of the great civilizations, as summarised above, is a result of several internal and external factors unique to each. However, all of these examples show that political repression, social decay, and economic inefficiency—all of which we are seeing in the 21st century—were contributing factors to their collapse. It was control and conformity that stifled ideas based on our unwillingness and discomfort to be Unreasonable.

It's not all bad news though. In each of these examples, legacy continues through myth and legend, and language, culture, and legal systems. The end of the Soviet Union brought about a new global environment although we are still to see how that 'lands'. The control that the CIA and KGB held over South America and Africa splintered and new freedoms reigned—along with many teething problems. The current unrest in many of these regions is but a part of each State (and non-State, Kurdistan anyone) as they march to greater freedoms. The war in Ukraine is, much to Putin's chagrin, creating louder dialogues about freedom. The uprisings in Iran are a clamour against the religious fervour of the Ayatollahs.

Is it Really All That Bad?

It is not too late for those of us on the path to an Unstoppable Life. We have the chance, nay, the responsibility, to create lasting positive change and we do this, counter-intuitively by becoming more Unreasonable.

It is too easy to use the excuse of the power of social media. To say that, just like after the fall of the Tower of Babel, our future is too broken to fix. Each of us can make a difference.

Rather than shying away from debate, in case we are considered to be too extreme, we should start. Let's begin within our own communities: let's start talking again. And even without our communities, let's listen to other points of view with anticipation to try and understand. Even if we don't agree, let's use the tension between our understanding so that it becomes a Forming Up Point on a journey to a solution. Let's start thinking beyond the soundbites we are fed by the media. Let's research instead of accepting blindly. Let's take responsibility rather than demand our rights. Let's start being Unreasonable (with kindness) and fix this mess. In getting started, we are already reaching beyond our limits, so let's get started by understanding what makes us unique.

The Odd Ones Out

The Clone Army

The first step to becoming *Unstoppable* is remembering we are unique.

A long time ago, in a galaxy far, far away (I know you are already hearing the opening notes of the 20th Century Fox theme and seeing, in your mind's eye, the four massive flashlights), a single starfighter drops out of travelling at light speed and settles quietly onto the water world of Kamino. According to the *Star Wars* database, Kamino is:

> *"… a planet of endless oceans and storms. Few features mark its surface, save for massive stilt-mounted cities wherein reside the planet's natural inhabitants, the Kaminoans."*

The hero of our story, a certain Obi-Wan Kenobi, is there to meet the chief medical scientist of the Kaminoans and see, firsthand, the operations of the planet's most prized exports—Clones!

A shorter time ago, not so far away, on a Sunday in the summer of 1990, 140 strangers were gathering near the town of Sleaford in Lincolnshire, England. These strangers with ironing boards underarm were willingly gathering to be cloned. We varied in age and knowledge from teenagers to men and women in their early forties; from boys and girls just leaving school, to people who had so much more life experience. With a sense of excitement and awe mixed with just a bit of trepidation, we set forth under the watchful eye of our instructor. Day one at the Royal Air Force College, Cranwell, began with the issuing of uniforms, and over the next six weeks, we all transformed into a cohesive group, drilled to operate the same way, following orders to do their bidding. If some failed to meet the mark, they were sent on their way. To be successful meant a life of servitude, cloned into a form expected by ourselves and society—Royal Air Force Officers. Most of that group were successful and we were commissioned later that year.

Reflecting on this, my 'cloning' began long before my arrival at Cranwell. It began even before I was born. My grandfather had been a member of the Royal Air Force during World War II and my father had been an officer in the Royal Air Force Reserves—the 'light blue' was strong in my family. It was an obvious choice for me to continue that tradition.

From before we are born, we are becoming clones. As mammals, one of our basic needs is to be a part of the herd. But being a part of the herd can mean that we lose ourselves. Blue for boys, pink for girls. In my military days, we all wore the same uniform; we all looked the same. We all wear uniforms, whether we are military, at school, or at work. We even chose to dress the same way or from the same stores as our tribe. All of this creates an illusion that we are all the same. In this way, society has caused us to lose our uniqueness.

Unlike the Clones of Kamino, the British Armed Forces carefully ensure that not all our uniqueness is destroyed in our transition from civilian to military. It is referred to as 'Mission Command'. Mission Command imposes a responsibility on everyone in uniform.

Mission Command tells you what to do, but it's left up to you to choose how to do it. Learning 'how to do it', becomes a lifelong journey. Mission command is a mixture of experience, imagination, and judgement, all mixed up with zest for courageous growth. Mission Command translates to the civilian world as taking responsibility rather than resting on our rights.

My cloning—that had begun so many generations before—was noisily broken less than six years later when I transferred to the British Army. Or to be candid, I'd found some clones that fitted me better. To be clear, anyone thinking that I might have made an error in career choice—not at all. Or that my view of British military training is anything other than that it is some of the best in the world. I was so fortunate to be 'cloned' along with some amazing fellow officers and served with the best soldiers, sailors, and airmen. I do, however, recognise that the success of large armed forces is based on the basic skills common to every individual. This is achieved through a training program that 'clones'.

Our uniqueness is dangerous to some. It is far easier to rule over clones than individuals. Society would fall apart if we didn't have rules and regulations, and communities would be strained if we all chose to 'break the mould'. Driving would be even worse if we didn't drive on the same side of the road or ignored speed limits. If you stood at 'The Kop' Stand in Anfield Stadium in Liverpool, England, wearing anything other than the colour red—the traditional colour of the home team, Liverpool Football Club—you would probably get more than an 'odd' look.

But this does not mean we should conform in all ways. This world needs, and is desperate, for your uniqueness. So where do we start?

We can start by asking three simple questions:

- What do I really need?
- What do I choose in this life?
- What do I dream of?

Grab a pen and some paper. Find a quiet place. Put your phone to silent. Write each of the questions (above) as a heading and write … anything.

As the words appear on your page, you will begin to focus on the subject. Take several minutes for each question and just write. Ask yourself how you feel when creating your answers to each question.

Our research from Unstoppable Force clients, events, and workshops has found that, for the most part, our needs are very similar.[6] These needs are based on our society. A person living in downtown Manhattan will have different needs than someone living in the jungles of the Amazon basin, although some needs will be the same. The most basic of needs are water, air, food, and, as a species, to reproduce.

Moving to the second question. Our wants are an extension of the community in which we live and the stage of life in which we find ourselves. To this point, you've probably found the exercise relatively straightforward. Now take time to think about what you truly dream of. This is the point that you step out of the societal and community crowd. It is our dreams that make us truly unique.

How have you felt in completing this exercise? Talking and thinking about our needs is a low-energy activity … Bumping along the bottom, just getting by.

As we begin to think about what we want, our energy levels increase— this is getting a tiny bit exciting. The moment we start thinking about our dreams is the moment that the magic really occurs. Our energy levels go through the roof, and we truly feel alive.

Now take a moment to consider what state the world is in right now. Do you see a fully energised society or one bouncing along the bottom? It is in talking about and striving for our dreams we really become our unique selves and as each of us grows in our uniqueness, the world will

---

[6] Unstoppable Force (2023), www.unstoppableforce.co.nz.

begin to vibrate at a higher frequency. This is in much the same way as H_2O changes from ice to water to steam as we add more and more energy. We can move from feeling heavy and inanimate to feeling alive and joyous just by living with more energy.

This might seem confronting, but energy can be a useful metaphor for vitality and dynamism. It would be easy to avoid the use of terms such as vibration and frequency, as these can have quite negative associations with the New Age movement. Scientifically-minded readers could, rightly, consider that frequency is only one aspect of wave mechanics and doesn't account for the wave's amplitude, which would have a significant impact on the energy transported by the wave. We are edging into some of the big challenges humanity is currently facing, such as: How do we align traditionally opposing groups? Is there some common ground? Could new scientific hypotheses suggest the difference is maybe not so big? Bruce Lipton believes so.

Bruce Lipton's beliefs underwent significant transformations. After obtaining his BA in biology in 1966 and his PhD in developmental biology in 1971, he began his career teaching anatomy at prestigious schools of medicine.

In the early stages of his career, Lipton's focus was on genes and their role in cellular function, which aligned with the prevailing view of the time—the 'golden age of genes'. However, as he delved deeper into his research and made groundbreaking discoveries, his perspective shifted dramatically.

Sometime during the 1980s, a pivotal turning point occurred in Lipton's beliefs. He embraced a new worldview, rejecting atheism and finding evidence of a higher power through his understanding of cellular function. Lipton became convinced that the complexity and precision with which cells operate were indicative of an intelligent design, leading him to acknowledge the existence of God.

As his ideas began to diverge from mainstream scientific thought, Lipton faced resistance and scepticism from his peers in the scientific community.

The results from his stem-cell studies challenged the prevailing paradigm centred around DNA, and he felt marginalised and disregarded by those who clung to conventional beliefs. He humorously likened them to "lemmings running off the cliff of DNA", highlighting the inertia and reluctance to embrace new perspectives.[7]

Despite the opposition he encountered, Lipton remained steadfast in his convictions. He felt that the importance of his message extended far beyond the narrow confines of academic debates. Realising that the knowledge he possessed could profoundly impact the lives of ordinary people, he made a conscious decision to step away from the traditional scientific system and its restrictive mindset.

Since the late 1980s, Lipton has continued to explore the intersection of biology, spirituality, and consciousness. He has emerged as a trailblazer in bridging the gap between science and spirituality. Through his pursuit of unconventional avenues, Lipton has continued to inspire others to question prevailing beliefs and explore the profound mysteries of life.

Triggered?? Good!! To become *Unstoppable,* we must face the disconcerting and move beyond current hypotheses.

Do You Need a Hug?

In the summer of 1977, I found myself in a massive room; it was so big that hanging from the roof was the 111-metre Saturn V rocket. This was going to have been the rocket for the Apollo 18 mission to the moon. Unfortunately, this rocket never left Earth's atmosphere. At that moment though, standing beneath the 140 tonnes of engineering magnificence, I decided I was going to be an astronaut. Approximately ten minutes later, my hopes were dashed by a tour guide; back then, only American or Soviet citizens could travel to space. Many years later, that dream

---

[7] Bruce H Lipton (2005), *The Biology of Belief: Unleashing the Power of Conscious, Matter and Miracles.*

remains and fortunately, entrepreneurs like Richard Branson, Elon Musk, and Jeff Bezos, are all feverishly working to make my dream come true.

What are your dreams? When did you last share those dreams or ask about a colleague's dreams? Ask a child their dreams and they will share, unfettered, about travelling to school on a sparkly unicorn or playing quarterback for the Houston Oilers, or 'hooker' for the All Blacks. Or being a superhero with powers to fly or have superhuman strength. As we grow, we push our dreams further and further from our consciousness. We trap ourselves in society's reality of needs and wants. At some point, just surviving, and sometimes thriving, becomes enough. What happened to jiving? What happened to our uniqueness?

What happened? We stopped believing in ourselves. At some point, around the age of five to seven, someone, likely a parent or a teacher, said something like:

Just grow up; or,

You're too old to be playing with toys like that; or,

You can't—so … pick a pastime or skill you still block.

The first time it was said, you didn't think much of it but over time you began to believe the statement, and even worse, you started to tell yourself that it was true. Once we start telling ourselves we're not good enough, we lose our uniqueness and spend the rest of our lives trying to fit-in wondering why life is so 'stressy'.

We focus on our needs and what society 'says' we want. That bigger car, nicer house, more exotic holiday. Focusing on what we want does nothing but create a life of scarcity and lack.

Worse, in the developed world of the 21st century, most of our basic needs are met but we still feel out of balance, lacking participation and fulfilment.

It's less than 100 years since Abraham Maslow proposed his *Hierarchy of Needs*.[8] When written in 1943, the world had celebrated the exploration and invention of the Victorian era, survived the terror of World War I, struggled through 'The Great Depression', and found itself mired in World War II. This was also a period of massive acceleration in technology. In the 100 years before, industrialisation had opened up trade routes and introduced new technology. Schooling was 'invented' to prepare our children to enter the factory/mining workforce—if you struggle with that idea, ask yourself why the school bell was created. The answer: to mimic the sound of the factory hooter that started the workday. Electrical lighting became the norm so we could see before sun-up (and work longer hours). Industrial-scale production lines were required to build locomotives, main battle tanks, cars, and weaponry. Processed food was manufactured on a scale never before seen to feed the troops deploying far from home for extended periods.

Our lives and brains, which had been very comfortable—thank you very much—with the pre-industrial norms of waking at sunrise, working in the fields to grow sufficient produce for ourselves and our communities, and then, heading to bed as the sun sets. Suddenly, we were expected to change in less than a few decades. But that acceleration never stopped, it continues to this day … and shows no sign of slowing down.

Our bodies and brains that had slowly developed from the dawn of humanity, now all of a sudden, had to deal with a new stress! A stress caused by the march of greed and expansion. We have all that we 'need' but still we feel inadequate. We can have all that we want but still, it is not enough. We expect so much more.

---

[8] Cambridge University Press (2018), Abraham H. Maslow (1942), *A Theory of Human Motivation*, https://www.cambridge.org/core/journals/the-british-journal-of-psychiatry/article/theory-of-human-motivation-by-abraham-h-maslow-1942/519D-1FAFADE96014EC0C3CE52FC1698F.

Maslow's *Hierarchy of Needs* is still true today, but society has become trapped in our world of want and expectation. At a time when so much is available, we want more. Here is the kicker, when we want something, we are telling ourselves that we are living in lack. Living in lack means that we feel insecure. That feeling of insecurity means we are stuck on the second level of Maslow's hierarchy. Being stuck on the second level means we struggle to reach the third. The third level of Maslow's hierarchy is Belongingness and Love. And we wonder why we are so stressed. We might want for so much when all we really need is a hug. That hug opens a myriad of opportunities: there is a confidence to be ourselves, a willingness to share our experiences, or simply put, we find self-esteem (Maslow's fourth level). Through that self-esteem, some will go on to question and learn, and in time, a few might even self-actualise. Through self-actualisation, society begins to move forward once again and as individuals, we can celebrate our uniqueness.

Organisations can do this too. As businesses and communities mature, they also rise up the order of Maslow's identified needs. As a start-up, businesses often struggle with available funds and the number of hours in the day to just get by. There is a constant feeling of lack and that can quickly become the death of the dream. Even once that business moves into 'Stay up' it can stall without the proper technology, people, and processes. It is these factors that enable the business to feel secure and, therefore, mature to the 'grow up' stage. At this point, the business understands itself and becomes more relaxed about its place in the market. As such, the business and its people become a part of the community of business, and a few go on to Self-Actualise. Those are the businesses that we all know and love—those businesses 'just are' (think Nike or Apple). Whether those businesses are within our local communities or industry giants, they are a part of our lives, our confidence.

So, it all starts with a hug. But when does it start? Science is now revealing that the need for a hug; that Certainty, begins at the moment of conception; the count for the first 1,000 days of a baby's life starts then. The certainty provided in the womb, the nutrition and warmth.

The sense of being a part of something. The sounds of love and laughter from the parents are the first 'hug' all mammals need. On leaving the womb, a baby already feels loved, they are born into Certainty. This is the first step of a balanced life. A life in Certainty causes us to seek Variety. The natural process, too much Certainty, breeds a feeling of boredom, so we go exploring. We try new foods, we get up to mischief, and we meet new friends. At some point, that Variety gets a wee bit scary; perhaps we stepped too far into the 'Zone of the unknown'? So, we return to 'the Certainty'.

Working with parents of teenagers, I sometimes receive calls from bereft mums (it's usually mums) wailing about their little cherub's behaviour and struggling to understand how everyone else thinks their child terrorist is an amazing human being. I listen patiently to the list of messy bedrooms, answering back, staying out late, hanging around with other children who 'Mum's not happy with'. My response every time is:

"Congratulations, you must be an amazing parent."

Throughout that child's early years, those parents continued the loving Certainty that was created in the womb. Their 'little darlings' know they can get up to all sorts of mischief and messiness, safe in the knowledge whatever 'Variety' they get up to, there will always be the Certainty of family love, even when they go too far.

This is the first paradox: once we have Certainty, we strive for Variety.

Our first challenge in maturing is to find where we are comfortable on the continuum between Certainty and Variety. A child born into a loving environment where the right sustenance was available in the womb, where there were few loud noises, and no violence, has a far greater chance of establishing a healthy place on this continuum than a child born into a less balanced world. A child conceived into a world of anger and violence where possibly drugs and alcohol are a part of their daily nourishment in the womb will arrive into the world with un-Certainty. That child's #1 goal is to establish Certainty (or dull the pain of the unCertainty). Until that Certainty is established, they are unlikely to grow into an active or successful member of their tribe and society. Seeking Certainty, wherever it might be available, leads to children who feel like they don't fit in. This imbalance in their need slows their movement toward the next paradox.

We have all seen our children (or other parents' children) throw tantrums; generally, on the floor of a supermarket for all to see. This is an early example of a child seeking to be different, to be noticed. A child seeking to be Significant. Words such as my, mine, or no, creep into the vocabulary as they 'find themselves'. Of course, those tantrums and arguments don't last long, as the little one wants to feel loved. This is the first expression of a child experiencing the second paradox. As human beings, we need to show our individuality but if we take that individuality too far, we ostracise ourselves from the tribe. Through experience and loving guidance, our task is to become comfortable somewhere on the continuum between Significance and Belonging.

These examples are based on early childhood experiences, but unfortunately, we are unlikely to establish our place on each continuum for it never to change. Every day and in every situation and relationship, our place on this continuum will be challenged. In seeking and establishing our uniqueness, we find balance within those situations and relationships; this is called living in Community.

These needs and paradoxes are based on the work of Cloe Madanes, a renowned family therapist and co-founder of the *Strategic Family Therapy* model.[9] In her work, she explores the fundamental aspects of human behaviour and the driving forces behind our actions. Madanes' research is grounded in the belief that all human beings have six core needs that must be met in order to lead a fulfilling life. These needs are Certainty, Variety, Significance, Love and Belonging, Growth, and Contribution.

---

[9] Cloé Madanes (1991), *Strategic Family Therapy*, Jossey-Bass Publishers (John Wiley & Sons Network).

Madanes posits that when these needs are met, individuals experience a sense of fulfilment and happiness. However, when one or more of these needs are unmet, it can lead to feelings of dissatisfaction, frustration, and even depression.

One of the key insights of these studies is the concept of 'competing needs'. This refers to the idea that sometimes, fulfilling one need may come at the expense of another. For example, pursuing a high-powered career may provide a sense of significance but may also limit the time available for building deep connections with loved ones. In such cases, individuals must find a balance between meeting their various needs in order to achieve overall wellbeing.

Madanes' work also highlights the importance of understanding our own needs and the needs of others in order to foster healthy relationships and personal growth. By recognising and addressing unmet needs, individuals can work towards creating a more fulfilling life for themselves and those around them.

What we are seeing in the post-pandemic world is a re-working of those paradoxes whether it be at the individual, family, country levels, or on a global scale. My suggestion to us all is to hug a wee bit more and in doing so we build a new certainty for ourselves and our community.

Even this creates a challenge, as we are all so stressed that we struggle to let our defences down enough to reach out and hug one another. Living in 'survival' mode is stopping us … living! Once upon a time, we needed survival mode: the world was a dangerous place with sabre-tooth tigers behind every rock and giant Haast eagles soaring overhead waiting for our ancestors to pop their heads out from cover. Our reptilian brain was handy back then for our very survival, but not so much these days. For the most part, we live in a relatively safe environment. Most of the 'danger' is in our heads—we create fear or listen to the fear being promulgated through social media and the mainstream. How did we get to a place where we live in constant panic; and can we change?

Fortunately, we now understand how we got here and how every one of us can create a far less 'panicky' view of the world. With less panic and stress, we can return to a place where 'a hug' is natural. A place where we no longer 'want'. By living less stressed lives, we will heighten our awareness, and in so doing, we will be ready when real danger threatens. It is *our task* to live less stressed lives and in doing so return to our uniqueness. It is time to understand our brains in greater detail.

Ever Had a Brainwave?

Have you ever noticed that people change? Have you ever noticed that children go through stages? Have you ever wondered about that?

Science is now showing that, as we mature, our brains operate with an increasing range of frequency. The brainwave activity in the human brain may hold the answer to many of our behaviours and stages of growth as Table 1 shows.[10]

Table One: Brainwave Activity Related to Age

Wave	Age (years)	Frequency (Hz)
Delta	0–2	0.5–4
Theta	2–6	4–8
Alpha	6–12	8–13
Beta 1	12+	13–15
Beta 2	12+	16–22
Beta 3	12+	22–50
Gamma		100+

---

[10] Dr Joe Dispenza (2012), *Breaking the Habit of Being Yourself, How to lose your mind and create a new one.*

From birth to around twenty-four months, our brains don't show much brainwave activity. New babies don't really do much; they eat, sleep, poo, and scream. However, their subconscious is soaking in every sensation and noise. They will eat whatever they are given and accept whatever behaviour they experience as 'normal'. At this stage, even if they were to reach out and grab a red-hot radiator, while they would 'feel' the sensation of heat, they may not understand it was harmful.

At this stage in life, babies experience Delta-wave brain activity.

Around the age of two, there is an increase in brain activity. You have probably seen this if you spend any time with two-year-olds. Overnight, they may stop enjoying food that they have always eaten—what's wrong with pureed parsnip and avocado? This is the age that those words—me, mine, and no—arrive. Suddenly, they don't like this or that. Our placid little ones become 'terrible twos'. Around this age, they also become sensitive to pain. Grabbing that hot radiator or sipping a very hot drink at this age will elicit screams of pain.

Our toddlers are experiencing Theta-wave brain activity.

In New Zealand, children start school on their fifth birthday. This is reflected across the 'developed' world with children commencing full-time education between the ages of 5-7 years. Science is now showing that around this age, there is yet another acceleration in brain activity. (Please remember that each stage of acceleration will happen at a different time for every child. This is why some children are 'ready for school' while others are not). At this age, our children are beginning to think for themselves. Not only are they asking 'why', but they begin to find their own answers.

Our children are now experiencing Alpha-wave brain activity.

This transition, from Theta to Alpha, is one of the most significant of which to be aware of as this is the transition from Subconscious brain activity to Conscious brain activity. Up until now, those brains have been sucking in anything they see, hear, or experience. Often this is the age where many of our deepest beliefs in ourselves stem—the age when those comments of 'just grow up' creep in.

Beyond the age of twelve years, our brains are capable of functioning within the Beta-range of brainwaves. At the lower levels of Beta-wave activity, we are capable of analytical thought.

Imagine you are in a conference room listening to an amazing, handsome, blue-eyed speaker. He describes how the brain develops and how brainwave frequency increases over the first decade of life (sound familiar). You are immersed in the lilting sound of his mild Scottish accent and your brain is absorbing the fascinating subject. You are comfortable that, even if the presenter was to ask a question, there are plenty of other willing souls in the room to provide the answer. It's most likely that your brain is operating in the low-level Beta frequency (Beta 1).

Fortunately, our brainwave activity doesn't stop at low-level Beta. From the age of twelve upwards, we become capable of deeper analytical thinking. Ever had to do a presentation at work or sit an exam? I bet even just reading these words has caused you mild discomfort; certainly, writing these words did. This is mid-level Beta (Beta 2). We are using that discomfort to focus our brainwaves and deliver an outcome. We feel the butterflies in the tummy, we might experience nervousness. Congratulations, you are in the growth zone. Once the exam or presentation is complete and the standing ovation has settled to a dull roar, you take a deep breath, and that deep breath returns you to Beta 1.

But we are not finished. There is another Beta level we have yet to experience. Welcome to Beta 3—the highest level of Beta brainwave frequency and the one that covers the greatest range of frequencies. Imagine for a moment, you are about to start that presentation and your laptop dies, the CEO has just entered the room, and for good measure, you pour a cup of coffee down your front. How do you feel right now? Or you turn over that exam paper to find the question you had studied so hard to answer doesn't appear anywhere on the paper.

Welcome to Beta 3—or to put it simply—blind panic!

By the time we reach adolescence, we are capable of experiencing every level of brainwave frequency, and we do so, every day. The effect of lower-frequency brainwaves on the body and mind can induce a state of deep relaxation, reducing stress and promoting overall well-being. Our creativity can increase, and they are linked to improved learning, memory consolidation, and information retention. Lower frequency brainwaves can help reduce stress and anxiety, so promoting mindfulness.

Unfortunately, most of the time we are operating in Beta 3. The world is so rushed, everything is a competition and our fascination with devices is making it worse. We plonk our kids in front of the TV or allow them screen time just to get a few moments of peace and, in doing so, introduce them to higher levels of brain frequency before they are ready. The world of now, Now, NOW! Our sleep time is reduced, our quality of sleep is worse, and our food intake is less natural than it was once upon a time. We are learning to live with a pandemic and there is a fear of the next virus … Monkeypox anyone?

Is it no wonder that we feel incapable of hugging. Health protocols even forbade human touch for a while … removing this most basic of human needs. Is there no end to this panicked life we lead?

Sadly, for many, the answer is no. Many have found Certainty in this madness. The madness of conforming to society's limits and beliefs. They would rather remain in this toxic relationship than find a way out. A way out of that conformity to an exciting journey towards our uniqueness. We can seek Certainty in conformity or anything material, but we are looking in the wrong direction. Certainty can only truly come from one place. It comes from deep inside us. Our self-belief is therefore the gateway to our uniqueness. An access point to that gateway is simple. There are three simple activities we can all undertake, right now to begin our recovery. To break out of this toxic relationship with stress. To find our way back to having the confidence to give and receive hugs. To rediscover a place where we can feel our own uniqueness.

A Return to Us

Better Sleep: Remember when you were young, and you fought against bedtime? Remember, as a teenager, you were left to sleep late? In our younger years, hopefully, our parents had a bedtime routine for us. Where did that go? We go to bed later, just to squeeze in another episode of our favourite show. Our alarms are set even earlier to ensure we get ahead of the traffic. Current advice is we need at least seven hours of quality sleep to ensure we get sufficient time in each of the three sleep levels. To summarise from Table 1 (above):

> **Alpha waves** occur during the early stages of sleep when a person is transitioning from wakefulness to drowsiness, as well as during light sleep.
>
> **Theta waves** are commonly observed during REM (rapid eye movement) sleep, which is the stage of sleep associated with dreaming.
>
> **Delta waves** are most prominent during deep sleep stages. During this stage, the body and brain are in a state of restorative rest, and it is essential for physical and mental rejuvenation.

We will return to the subject of sleep in the chapter titled, *This Earthly Suit*, but in simple terms, we all need to sleep more.

The 50-minute hour: Every hour, leave your desk, find somewhere you feel safe, close your eyes, and take ten deep breaths. Even just the act of closing our eyes removes 80% of the stressors we experience. Those ten deep breaths activate a greater percentage of our lungs and release the 'good' chemicals in our brains. Also, 'take on' some water and do some light stretches.

When this subject comes up in workshops and coaching calls there is always someone who is too busy to spare those ten minutes—to save their lives—and I stress that it is all about priorities! To be fair, there are some roles and occupations that do not afford that luxury. I might be rather upset if the flight attendant suddenly stopped serving drinks just before getting me so they could keep to their 50-minute hour schedule. Surgeons and nurses are unlikely to stop a procedure. However, everyone has time to stop, close their eyes, and take a deep breath. Just this activity practiced frequently will empower you to move from Beta 3 brain activity to Beta 1. You are no longer in panic mode.

Meditation: The number of times I ask, "Who mediates?" and receive the response, "I've tried but it's too difficult," amazes and confounds me. It doesn't even have to be the traditional image of sitting cross-legged in the lotus position chanting, "Ohm." There are many ways to meditate but they all take practice and commitment. There are even free Apps to help you get started. Meditation can move our brain frequency from Beta 3 to Delta wave activity to become a deep subconscious healing. Take time to practice mediation. Start with five or ten minutes but please start. Walking in nature, watching the stars at night, listening to the ocean or a babbling stream are all ways of 'meditating'.

*

Those of you who are reading (and thoroughly captured by the content of) this book (Beta 1 brain activity) are probably thinking by now that I have forgotten to discuss Gamma wave brain activity. Intentionally, I have left this to the very end, as it is the frequency that few of us often ever experience. From Table 1 (above), you will see the frequency is so much higher than even Beta 3: 40–100 Hz! Gamma waves are associated with elevated states of compassion and happiness, even increased consciousness.[11] In Maslow's terms, maybe we reach Gamma wave frequencies when we become self-actualised.

---

[11] Beverly Rubik (2011), *Neurofeedback-Enhanced Gamma Brainwaves from the Prefrontal Cortical Region of Meditators and Non-Meditators and Associated Subjective Experiences.*

Unlike the unfortunate scientist, Dr David Banner (yes, David—I'm a child of the 70s) a quick blast of Gamma waves is not the answer to elevated strength or hint of Verdigris.

In the history of history, there will only ever be one of 'you' created. You were created for a life at this point in galactic time. You have something that this world needs and is desperate for you to give. Unfortunately, society wants the very opposite. Society has decided that you must conform. That conformity will destroy your (and everyone else's) uniqueness unless we choose otherwise. We can choose to seek our uniqueness through living towards our dreams, and by balancing our place on the continuum between Certainty and Variety, and Significance and Belonging. When we choose to calm our brains to lower brainwave frequency, we can see how unique we really are, and even by just glimpsing that uniqueness we move closer to true self-belief and becoming *Unstoppable*.

We have always been taught that being the 'black sheep', the odd one out, is a failing. But we are all the odd ones out. Our Uniqueness confirms this. As we shall see, harnessing our uniqueness and applying ourselves to our one unique time is what the world needs. Conformity is the easy route and look where it has got us. Uniqueness will enable us to find our tribe. That tribe will celebrate us and our ideas. The energy of that celebration will see our generosity expand across our relationships and we will selflessly be a part of creating a world in which we are all worthy of living.

Strike that path towards uniqueness. Take some time to consider your dreams. Be mindful of your place in this world and, using your dreams, move towards that destiny.

The Boring Chapter

We were meant to be bored. For millennia and generations of humanity, we had nothing to do and were happy with it. We hunted, gathered, and collected water from rivers and watering holes. We watched the stars and planets move across the sky and wondered at the rising and setting of the sun and the waxing and waning of the moon. We shared stories passed down by our ancestors by firelight and got bored. Of course, we didn't consider it boredom back then, it was life. Our brain accepted that unfocused time and it was good for us. Boredom causes reflection which breeds imagination. Imagination, in turn, causes invention, failure, and improvement.

Now, our days, weeks, and months are filled. We have become afraid of boredom. It has been trained out of us. Even in my own lifetime, I remember boredom. As a child, we had access to but three TV channels, and even they stopped after a rendition of 'God Save the Queen' before midnight. Imagine, those hours of darkness with no screen time!

Over the last decade, as 'screen time' has become more and more available, our opportunity for boredom has decreased even further. A recent US survey concluded that the average adult touches their smart phone over 2,500 times per day[12] and, for most of us, that's only one of the screens we use on an hourly basis. We have created a world with no 'spare' time. Even that word suggests we should fill those 'spare' moments … if we could find them.

We stop at traffic lights and check our phones. We wait for our coffee and check our phones. We wait for the kids at the school gate,

---

[12] Dscout Inc. (2016), *Mobile Touches dscout's inaugural study on humans and their tech*, https://pages.dscout.com/hubfs/downloads/dscout_mobile_touches_study_2016.pdf?_ga=2.180416224.67221035.1650551540-199217915.1650551540.

and we check our phones. We go on dates and check our phones. In the moments when we are not checking our phones, we are frustrated by the people who are checking theirs! This behaviour is passed on to our children, they are restless, and that restlessness becomes mischief and then the most restless are labelled as problems or their parents informed, they are in need of medication. Is that restlessness not just the early stage of reflection, is that mischief not just investigation?

Our aversion to boredom is creating a generation of automatons who, through screens, our comments, behaviours, and medication are being controlled even more than the current generation.

Being bored is considered a waste of time, of being unproductive. We eat at our desks and eat on the run. We buy fast-food because we don't have time. We angrily speed our cars home from work, the grocery store, and everywhere else to fill our time binge-watching. And here is the kicker; you cannot become *Unstoppable* without boredom. Doing nothing is an important part of Unstoppableness.

Busy Doing Nothing

The seconds

The very next time your hand drifts towards your pocket to grab your phone—don't! Stop yourself. Leave it alone. You probably checked in the last fifteen minutes; the world won't grind to a halt on its axis. Instead of looking at your phone, take some time to be aware of your environment. Listen to conversations. Look (don't stare) at the people around you. Look at the scenery. You might be surprised at the power that almost overwhelms you to pick up your phone; don't worry, that's natural. It has become a habit. It has become societal. Be the difference. Every time you feel the need to look at your device, take 60 seconds before you do. Build it up to 180 seconds and become conscious of the world around you.

The minutes

You've already read about the 50-minute hour. At least once a day, take twenty minutes and head outside. Even if you are in a concrete jungle, there will be some green space or at the very least a glimpse of the sky. Leave technology behind and allow yourself to be 'bored' for twenty minutes. At first, this will feel scary, you have left your security blanket behind—Fear of Missing Out (FOMO) will punch you straight between the eyes. Take a breath, you've survived worse, experience JOMO (Joy of Missing Out). Just walk, for at least twenty minutes, most days, and let your mind wander. Listen to the arguments going on in your head; they are fascinating.

If you can, take your walk with nature. Away from the noise of the city. Maybe give yourself permission to get home twenty minutes later to give yourself that twenty minutes of boredom.

The days

Even the tranquillity of New Zealand can get too much. Human beings need to return to nature and do so for longer periods. Our ancestors lived, for thousands of years, as a part of nature. It is only in the last few centuries that humans have migrated toward cities. The ease of living is killing our Unstoppable Force. Studies show that three days in nature, away from technology, is sufficient time for a brain reset.

In the southern hemisphere winter of 2021, New Zealand was still the biggest prison on Earth. Our borders had been closed for over a year and our 'Great Walks' were suffering. For years, visitors had travelled to New Zealand to walk in some of the most beautiful scenery. The Milford, Routeburn, and Abel Tasman might be the more famous but New Zealand boasts many great walks and, in 2021, they were all empty. One of the least known of these tracks is the Waikaremoana, deep in the northeast of North Island.

I had taken a few days to get back to nature. The walk is just less than 60 kms but due to the time of year, and disputes between the government and the local Māori Iwi (tribe) the boat that should collect you from the end of that walk was not running, maybe.

"We might be there to pick you up, but we can't confirm that and there is no phone reception."

The simplest option, I decided, was to walk there and back. My three days became five. The track hugs the edge of Lake Waikaremoana and begins with a 1,200-metre climb up the bluffs to the hut that would be my first night's accommodation. My backpack was full and before I had even reached the hut, the voices in my head were screaming abuse. Even in New Zealand, 1,200 metres of altitude in winter promises a cold night … and then the snow started.

For the next five days, it rained torrentially, and I met not one person. I was alone, without phone service, and miles from my car, which was miles from the nearest habitation. This is what our brains need. Although we're not that keen on it, initially.

During the first day, we miss our phones and worry about getting lost or being lost. We jump at every strange noise; we fight the expanse of nature. By day two, we begin to notice our surroundings. We stop missing our phones we begin to enjoy our surroundings. Our senses become more attuned to the sights, sounds, smell, and touch of nature. Even the rain becomes a part of the experience. I was wet, soaked through, for most of my waking hours for those five days and, after the initial 'joy' of putting on wet, cold gear each morning, I hardly noticed. We slow to the pace of the world around us.

By day three, we have reset. No longer do we care about our phones, or about the world outside of our direct need. Everything I needed was on my back; I had not a care in the world. On day five, I returned to the car and drove back into the 21st century and even the first small village was an assault on the senses. Noise, smell … humans!

Even the thought of a 3-day trip to nature might seem frightening, of course it does, we have been 'trained' to believe that nature is where poisonous, dangerous beasties live. The wilderness is the domain of the murderer, rapist, and weirdo. Even the map makers of old got in on this fearmongering by stamping 'here be dragons' across the unexplored oceans. But three days, in the woods, once a year, is necessary for us to thrive in modern society.

Start with the 180 seconds away from your phone, move to the twenty minutes outside, and when you are ready, step courageously back to nature. Get comfortable with your return to nature. Set yourself the challenge of spending three days, disconnected from technology and the rest of humanity. Re-find that comfort in your discomfort. Be an Unstoppable Force.

Boredom, like meditation, allows us to settle into the pace at which humans have lived for most of our existence. It is only in the last few centuries that we have left mother nature and created this frenetic, panicked, anxiety-filled life. In the developed world, the abuse of capitalism has led to a greedier, more divided society. The next step in our path to living an *Unstoppable* life is to consider what makes us truly wealthy.

Count Your Blessings

What is wealth?

Sometimes, when we reflect on such a massive question, it is worth considering it through a global lens. A view that causes us to look outside of our ourselves, our families, and even our communities. When we consider that wealth could be so much more than just the state of our bank account, it becomes the lens through which we may consider humanity's approach to humanity.

Following the abolishment of their monarchy at the end of World War II, the country of Yugoslavia, a communist state modelled on the Soviet Union, was led by Marshal Josip Bros Tito, until he died in 1980. The end of Tito's autocratic rule brought about a decade of economic and political crises and, along with a rise in nationalism caused Yugoslavia to fracture along historic borders causing the creation of six countries: Bosnia Herzegovina, Croatia, Macedonia, Montenegro, Serbia, and Slovenia. By the early 1990s, the countries of the Former Yugoslavia descended into what history remembers as 'the Yugoslav Wars'.

Over the following years, the United Nations deployed troops in the peace-keeping role in an attempt to quell the fighting and establish a lasting peace in the region. Looking at the region from our 21st century viewpoint, it has moved on from that dangerous period however, throughout the 1990s, the peoples of the Former Yugoslavia endured bitter fighting and, in some places, even genocide.

As the Former Yugoslavia began to disintegrate along historic boundaries, the people of Bosnia Herzegovina voted for independence—the minority Serbian representatives were against independence and boycotted the referendum—and independence was granted and recognised by the European Union and the United Nations in 1992. Unperturbed by this, Bosnian Serb Forces attacked the Republic of Bosnia Herzegovina.

In the subsequent fighting, the Bosnian people, especially along the Serbian Border, were subjected to ethnic cleansing.

The Srebrenica massacre in July 1995 was one of the most apparent instances of this ethnic cleansing which, later, the International Criminal Tribunal for the Former Yugoslavia recognised as genocide. The killings were carried out by the Bosnian Serb Army, under the command of Ratko Mladic. In the months before the killing, the UN had established a 'safe area' around the enclave of Srebrenica and deployed a lightly armed Dutch military unit to provide protection. The UN failed, the Dutch were unable to prevent the town's capture, and over 8,000 Bosnian men and boys were killed, and their bodies dumped in mass graves.

The suspected orchestrators of this, and other atrocities were Slobodan Milosevic, President of Serbia within Yugoslavia, Radovan Karadzic, the war-time President of the Serb Republic and Supreme Commander of its armed forces, and Ratko Mladić, the Commander of the Army. In time, they would be found guilty of genocide and sentenced to life imprisonment. Milosevic died in prison before sentencing. Back in late 1997, the hunt was on to bring Ratko Mladic and his commanders to justice.

This is the point at which a dashing, young British military intelligence officer enters the scene. Having recently completed my transfer from the Royal Air Force to the Intelligence Corps, I was in the final days of completing my junior officer training. I had been very politely asked by a senior officer if I might be interested in deploying to the Former Yugoslavia. Arrogant, even back then, I informed said senior officer that I'm sure I would love the opportunity, "But, you see, sir, my wife is pregnant so I could only possibly deploy for up to four months." (The usual being six). Unbelievably, I received orders for a four-month deployment and off I went to command my very first Human Intelligence (HUMINT) detachment in North-East Bosnia Herzegovina. My mission, along with many others—find Ratko Mladic!

The thing was, Mladic didn't really want to be found. We spent months building an intelligence picture of the area around the cities of

Doboj, Tuzla, and Zvornik, and established several strong agents and relationships but, frankly, we were not welcome. It didn't help that, after years of economic turmoil and war, the locals were very fearful of strangers. As soon as our vehicles rolled into town, the locals would 'go to ground' - very few would speak to us.

Building an intelligence picture through HUMINT is often explained using the analogy of a slice of an onion—the goal is to engage with the very centre of the onion, in our case, Mladic. Unfortunately, our work involves working our way, away from the centre until we find someone, anyone, willing to speak to us. At that point, we change direction and start working back towards the centre through relationships that those 'agents' might have or could cultivate. We had to travel a long way from the centre of 'our onion' before people began to speak.

We found that to stand any chance of meeting the townsfolk of Srebrenica, it was a good idea to stay off the main roads. This led us to travel the narrow, windy mountain tracks, resulting in us spending time in the farming hamlets with the subsistence farming communities. Meeting these Bosnians resulted in introductions to their families who did still live in the towns, so not all was lost. These communities had lost everything. Over forty years of communist rule; families lost to war; the ongoing uncertainty had broken communities and the poor mountain soil made even subsistence farming a struggle. These were people who were barely surviving, but they were some of the kindest and most contented people I have ever met. Years later, I would have similar experiences with the 'peasants' of Iraq and Afghanistan.

The locals would serve us the only food they had, on the best plates they could, and they would sit and watch us eat and go without. Their blessing was that we were taking time for them and their families. We always took food and drink with us as gifts but even this was only accepted when we explained it was for their children. Proof, if we ever needed it, that a wealthy life is so much more than just having access to money.

Too often the word, wealth, is only used in reference to money. If we have money, we are wealthy, if we have insufficient money, we are unwealthy. As you will see, money is a part of wealth but only a small part. Wealth has also been described as the length of time you might survive with no 'new' money arriving each week or month. If you lost your job but had savings of $100,000, with monthly outgoings of $10,000, you would have wealth to last you 10 months. Unfortunately, this example still focuses on cash.

Using money as the only metric for measuring wealth creates a very binary view of our world; if I have money, I am wealthy, if not, I am poor. Continuing this binary view, if I have money, I have no need to be anxious, if I lack money, I introduce fear and anxiety into my daily habits thus entering the top of the downward spiral. I get trapped in uncertainty. But this binary metric fails to take other factors that could bring wealth.

Reflecting on my experiences in Bosnia, the Middle East, and more locally, wealth is so much more than just money; becoming Unstoppable requires each one of us to understand what wealth means to us. For this reason, we created the Unstoppable Force Wealth Matrix which enables us to measure where we stand in our journey to certainty. Use this link to receive downloads of worksheets mentioned throughout this book:

https://unstoppableforce.co.nz/worksheets/

Welcome to the Matrix

As a wee boy, along with my sister, every few months we'd get loaded into the car for the trip from home to the Scottish Borders. Back then, that was a good three hours in the car, and, as it was only a day trip, another three hours back again. But it was always worth it. We were heading to the border town of Melrose, heading to the home of one of our great aunts, but not just any old great aunt, and even back then, she was old. Aunt Celia was the matriarch of our family. It was always a joy to visit her. She and Uncle Bill lived in an old house with a huge garden with fruit trees and plants and vegetables, and plenty of places for young children to run. We spent the afternoon with them and always had a 'cakey' tea. A 'cakey' tea started with sandwiches and scones, and then various cakes, culminating with a huge sponge cake decorated with thick, thick buttercream icing.

At the end of the day, as we were tiredly being loaded back into the car for the journey north, we were always handed lucky bags. The lucky bags had been filled with sweets and toys that had been lovingly bought individually for me and something different for my sister. But the 'cakey' tea, the garden, or even the lucky bags were never the highlight of that trip. The highlight of the trip was the climb up the ladders to the attic and there, with a pencil in hand, our height would be measured off against one of the roof frames.

On every visit, our height would be measured. And for the most part, we'd gotten taller. We got to see how quickly our cousins were growing. It was a sort of competition to see who could grow the fastest, but it was also a competition with ourselves to see how much we were growing, growing away from childhood into adulthood. Three or four times a year, we measured our height. The excitement of hitting a new milestone or overtaking a cousin was palpable. That excitement was shared across the three generations present. It got us talking about how much taller we might grow, about the (friendly) competition in which we were involved. I remain convinced after all these years that the energy of 'the measuring' made us all stand a few inches taller.

We spend our lives measuring things. We measure our weight when we stand on the scales. We measure the flour before we bake something, we measure our ability against other people, and we measure our riches compared to our neighbours. Always measuring things, measuring ourselves against friends and acquaintances, measuring ourselves against superstars and celebrities, measuring ourselves against other business leaders. But do we actually do the measuring that counts? When did you last measure your life? When did you last consider where you're headed in life?

The 'Wealth Matrix' that my team and I have created not only considers Finance but also measures how we feel about seven other areas of our lives: Health, Hobbies, Intimate relationships, Friends and Family, Personal Development, Mission, and Spirituality.

Using the Wealth Matrix, we can measure these eight different areas of life. Doing so frequently, we can see how we are tracking and so be in control of our lives, our environment and our path to becoming *Unstoppable*. We can see that we're moving forward, and we understand where we are content. This is awesome and we should celebrate that we have come to a place of contentment, but there might be other areas of our lives, where it's just not happening. Putting a score against those areas of life allows us to measure ourselves against the person we choose to be, the self we are growing into. These metrics also show us where we have momentum and, just like a bicycle, when we have momentum, we create balance. Where there is no momentum, we feel wobbly.

Finance

Of course, the amount of money we have is important, especially in the developed world of the 21st century. Whether that 'money' is considered in notes and coins or seashells and camels' this money enables us to buy the things we need to live. We use it to buy our clothes, the food we eat, and our shelter. But is there a figure of 'enough' money? An amount where it becomes superfluous? The answer is not to compare yourself with others or to blindly try to keep making more (there will always be some shiny, new thing to covet). The answer is to take a hard look at your own financial realities and aspirations and come up with a goal number. How much money is sufficient for you?

It's likely that the number will be different for everyone, depending on your circumstances and values, but science can give us some sense of how much money might be "enough." An article in Inc. magazine[13] suggests that approximately US$75,000 dollars a year, (if you live in the US) give or take a bit depending on cost of living, will keep you content enough. Money has a big impact on both day-to-day happiness and life satisfaction.

Below this level, making more will probably make you significantly happier. Above the US$75,000 figure, each additional dollar adds a little less to your life. There is a level of wealth way before the Elon Musk or Warren Buffet level that trading more effort and time for more money ceases to make sense.

But whatever figure you land on as 'enough', money is still a huge stress. One of the principal reasons for this is our parents. Ever heard one of the following phrases:

"Money doesn't grow on trees!"

"He's filthy rich!!!"

"You are greedy!"

"Do you think I'm made of money?"

---

[13] Daniel Kahneman and Angus Deaton (2010), *High income improves evaluation of life but not emotional wellbeing.*

All these phrases, and many more alike, suggest that having money is a bad thing and that 'getting' money is difficult. In her amusingly titled book, *You are a Badass at Making Money: Master the Mindset of Wealth*, Jen Sincero, rebukes these claims and, instead suggests that we should change our view of money. [14] We should change our relationship with money to one similar to a relationship we might have with our partner. And it works. If you love money and show it respect, use it wisely, and know where it is and where it is being spent, money becomes so much less stressful.

How do we begin to do this?

Do you know where your money is? Do you know where it goes?

A few years ago, we were building a house on a five-acre plot of land. The build was taking a little bit longer than planned so the rental property we had planned to live in for about three months was still our home over a year later. We had begun to loathe that place. We were desperate to move into our beautiful new home and were finding every excuse not to be in that rental property. So much so, that we were spending more and more time in coffee shops and restaurants. When we reviewed our finances during our penultimate month in the rental, we had lavished over $1,500 on coffee and cakes. We were not respecting our money and it was disappearing rapidly. I say, disappearing, but I think it re-appeared on my waistline.

In the book, *The Richest Man in Babylon*, the author, George S Clason, proposes learning to live on 70% of your (after tax) income.[15] I completely concur, however, Clason suggests that the split of the remainder is as follows; 20% to pay down debt and the other 10% to saving, I propose a slight amendment. Once the debt is paid down—and much stress removed—the 30% could then be allocated in five ways: savings, capital investment, education, fun, and charity.

---

[14] Jen Sincero (2018), *You are a Badass at Making Money: Master the Mindset of Wealth*.
[15] George. S. Clason (1926), *The Richest Man in Babylon*.

Savings

These savings are an 'insurance' for the more fallow periods of life. Remember the 'luxuries' of life still come from the 70% 'spending money'.

Capital Investment

Save this money until you can buy or invest assets to hold for the long-term; shares or investment properties fall into this area.

Education

To become truly *Unstoppable*, we must embrace a continuous pursuit of knowledge. Learning from individuals who have already achieved unstoppable success is key. I have found that the greatest impact on my own journey came from those who were not just self-proclaimed experts, but individuals with tangible real-world accomplishments to support their claims.

If you were preparing to climb Mount Everest, would you entrust your adventure to Bob, whom you met at the pub, or would it be wiser to seek out a Sherpa who has summited multiple times and understands what's needed for success? Exercise caution in selecting your sources of knowledge and guidance; even if someone labels themselves as a consultant, coach, or planner, if they lack the experience, be mindful of learning from them.

A capable, experienced coach will keep you focused on the path you desire to follow. It is crucial to investigate the background of potential coaches and ensure their proven success aligns with what matters most to you.

This is why the Unstoppable Force Mastermind, the workshops, and this book exist, for folks who are seeking to become *Unstoppable*. Whichever direction you take, I strongly urge you to allocate a percentage of your income specifically to education. Use these funds for courses, books, podcasts, or any other means of self-improvement that resonate with you, whether it be through formal education systems, coaching programs, or personalised one-on-one coaching. Regardless of the method you choose, dedicating these resources will ensure you always possess the means to learn and grow.

Remember, the pursuit of knowledge is an indispensable ingredient in the recipe for becoming *Unstoppable*. Embrace learning from the masters, exercise discernment in selecting your mentors, and commit to lifelong education. By doing so, you will empower yourself to overcome any obstacle that stands in your way.

Fun

Don't forget to allocate some funds for fun. This is not money to be frittered away. Have a plan for how you will spend it. Do you enjoy fine dining? Is an exceptionally good St Emilion Grand Cru your tipple of choice? Do you enjoy completing jigsaw puzzles or Lego? Whatever is your thing, spend some money every month and reward your hard work.

Charity

Giving to the community and those who need assistance. Start early and give often. Often, we can increase this giving through our time.

*

Many years ago, we had gotten into the habit of reviewing our finances every month and I hated it! It was a chore. I had to be dragged to the table, coerced by coffee and croissants. Despite taking responsibility for reviewing the finances, I could hardly be described as in a loving relationship with money.

That is the shift we must all make with money. However little, or however much we feel we have; we must love spending time with it. Respect it for what it does in our lives. Always remember that there are two ways to have more money. Either we can make more, or we can spend less. A monthly review of our finances will enable us to see firstly, where we can maybe 'tighten the belt'—coffee and cakes in my example above—or secondly, if we need to be looking for that raise or a side hustle. By creating a loving relationship with money, this task will become so much easier as we will see in later chapters when we discuss energy.

The real joy we should all find in money is in spending it. Once we reach our 'enough' figure. Money becomes a vehicle to share joy. Likely, that joy is initially shared with family and friends, but there comes a time when we realise that true joy comes from freely giving to causes that are important to us.

Nowadays, I look forward to the monthly gathering to discuss our finances. We not only manage our private finances but also the business and we hold true to the 70:30 rule in that too. We save money to ensure the business can cope if we miss sales targets, and we reinvest the profit to grow the business into the future. Most importantly, we ensure that 10% of our revenue is 'gifted' to our local and national charitable partners, through the Unstoppable Force Foundation, supporting others less fortunate on their journey to becoming *Unstoppable*.

This is the blessing of money.

Health

Health is so important as we grow to become *Unstoppable*. Without health, we run out of the time and capacity we require to become truly *Unstoppable*. For that reason, Health gets its very own special place in the *Unstoppable* framework. For now, ask yourself, what would you do differently if rather than thinking, *I'll do that later*, about our health, we thought: *It's not a priority*. I hope thinking the latter re-enforces the point that we only have one life and, to live it in an *Unstoppable* way, we must prioritise our health practices. We will return to this in so much more detail in the next chapter.

Hobbies

For twenty-eight years of my life, I had but one hobby. I tried others but none of them stuck. Only now am I truly discovering the importance of the 'past-time'. Although, I prefer the word hobby to the phrase past-time. A hobby does enable us to 'pass-the-time' but this minimises the importance of taking time out. My hobby for all those years was drinking … and I was an expert. I have shared the story previously, so will not do so here other than to say that from the ages 18-46 (unless I was deployed on operations), I drank heavily almost every night. Not only did this rob me of time for hobbies, but it also robbed me of the necessary finances.

On top of the drinking, I had a full-time military position; this cannot be described as a 9-5 job, and I was a dad to two children. When would I have time for hobbies? I've heard this same excuse so many times, from so many students when they complete the Wealth Matrix. What is this excuse? It is a de-prioritising of ourselves. Subconsciously, we are telling ourselves that we are less important than anyone else!

Other excuses: I've got young kids, I need to spend time with my partner, and after a busy day I have no energy … These are yet more messages to our subconscious that we are not important.

Is it *not* a good idea to let our children know, "This is Mummy's special time," or that, "It's Daddy's turn to play with you." As we will cover later in this chapter, a healthy intimate relationship is one where we both provide time and space for the other to grow. In doing so, we both know the relationship will be all the stronger.

On a good day, I weigh about 85 kg. Using Einstein's famous equation, $E=mc^2$ means I have a similar amount of potential energy as eight of the atomic bombs that exploded over Japan in the closing days of World War II. Whatever you weigh, your potential energy will be similar, so the excuse of 'I don't have the energy' doesn't wash for any of us. The truth is, when it comes to hobbies, we are a mixture of two things: disinterested and frightened.

Our disinterest comes from the repetitive nature of life. Our disinterest is the certainty for which we strive from our earliest days. Once we have that certainty, our boredom will grow until it is uncontainable at which point, we are likely to go mad, buy a motorbike, take up an extreme sport, or do other less healthy activities.

Our fear is based on those stories we were told when we were young; you're not good enough, you can't (insert your own activity here). Over time we began to believe the voices in our heads and lost just a wee bit of our identity. We now sit at home, daydreaming but always stopping short of action. We have created a hobby of tedium and fear.

Fortunately, we can change that habit. Neurologists have proven that we can actually change our minds. Gone are the days of believing that if we are born with certain skills we will die with those skills and no more. It turns out, you can teach a dog new tricks.

In the early days of the space-race, NASA scientists designed an experiment to help astronauts focus while in space where they would have no reference point for the horizon. Each astronaut was provided with a pair of spectacles that inverted their vision. Half of the astronauts wore the spectacles for 30 days while the others were allowed a break after twenty-five days before continuing with the experiment. At the end of the 30-day period, those spacemen who had worn glasses for the full time could invert their vision on command; the remainder could not. NASA, and their human guinea pigs, have proven that we can create new neural pathways in our brains. We can do the same—in approximately thirty days.

The first step of seeking greater wealth in this space is to reflect on hobbies you used to enjoy, or maybe ones you hear friends talking about. Maybe you have seen something on TV that has interested you. The next step is to have a go. You're not going to like them all, but you are creating variety in your life. Trying new things is a hobby in itself until you land on those activities that give you a break from yourself and your daily routine. As I write this, my wife, Liz, is out in the shed painting. An activity that for years, since her early childhood, she was told she was 'rubbish at'. Having discovered that the voice was wrong, she now spends hours, at peace, creating (and now selling) art.

What hobby are you going to try? I am an active relaxer, so cooking and baking in the kitchen, getting with nature, running and reading are my go-to activities.

Personal Development

One of the questions I always ask attendees of Unstoppable Force workshops is, "Have you ever undertaken any personal development before reaching out to me?" For the most part, they will talk about other coaches they have worked with or workshops and seminars they have attended. Others will flatly state that they have never done any personal development. The question is loaded. Of course, we have all undertaken personal development. Unfortunately, for most of us, that personal development was undertaken subconsciously. We never thought of it as personal development, it was just reading, watching, or listening.

Personal development is a necessary part of human progress. Think about the very first meal you prepared. Now think about the most impressive invention to ever have come from the kitchen (on your watch). I'm really hoping the slice of buttered toast has developed into at least beans on toast. You have undertaken personal development. Watching a baby struggle to move, progressing to crawling and walking is another example of personal development.

For many of us, our personal development ends when we finish the traditional schooling system. Most of us only read 1.2 books a year and, a wee bit like our excuses for a lack of hobbies, we complain that we 'don't have the time'. Of course, we have the time, we just fail to prioritise it.

Imagine what would happen if we committed to our personal development and read a chapter of a book every day; that's 363 chapters in a year (I gave you Christmas Day and your birthday off). Instead of listening to music on the journey to work; listen to a podcast (Unstoppable Force TV is awesome) or an audio book. We've already spoken about new hobbies, so how about finding a new hobby that really challenges you mentally or physically? This is all personal development.

A by-product of personal development is that our children see us learning. Not only will they learn from what they are hearing, but they will also learn that learning is fun—Daddy does it, so it must be. Our tedious lives become interesting again as we explore, with an open mind, places and subjects that are new to us. Our relationships improve as we communicate what we are learning. Our employment and promotion prospects improve as we grow in knowledge. There is no downside to personal development.

Take some time to consider where you are subconsciously engaged in personal development, and 'lean in,' and start learning consciously. If, after reflection, there ain't much happening, take some of the ideas above and put one of them into practice. The fact you picked up this book not only suggests you have epic taste in literature, but also that you are conscious about your own personal development.

If you are looking to extend that personal development, look at longer courses for which you can sign up. We live in a world where we have access to more information than ever before in the history of humanity.

Harness that and use it as an opportunity to go deep into your own progress.

Newsflash: personal development comes with a warning.

As a little boy, I watched my dad play his 12-string guitar. It was far too big for me to handle, but I'd always wished to be big enough to start playing. On one birthday, I received my first guitar and some guitar lessons. That was it, by the following Tuesday, I would be a guitar virtuoso. It didn't quite work out like that. After many years of practice, or not, I achieved what I'd set out to do. Twelve years after that birthday, I was finally playing a Grade 8 piece of classical music—*Cavatina*, the theme to the Academy award-winning film, *The Deer Hunter*. Maybe not to the standard of John Williams, but recognisable all the same. Personal development doesn't stop. We never achieve that nirvana. Once we set out on the journey, there will always be more out there to learn and experience.

With that caveat, start or recommit today. The world needs learners. The world is crying out for those of us who are breaking the mould of conformity. Those of us who are not only screaming the question, "I wonder why?" but are also courageous enough to seek the answers.

Mission

In the British Army, a mission is defined as a task with a culminating purpose. In simpler terms, it is the what and the why. There is no 'how' in a military mission statement. The concept of Mission Command leaves the 'how' to the commanders on the ground. With trust, delegation, and focus on the higher headquarters intent, Mission Command is a highly successful means of creating success in any field, not just the battlefield. A mission is important in life and business as it provides a roadmap for success, it instils a sense of purpose and direction, and guides your decision-making. It aligns your actions with your values and long-term vision, while also fostering resilience, focus, and cohesion.

What is *your* mission? What is your what and why?

When creating the Wealth Matrix, I thought about calling this pillar 'employment' but that didn't really get to the depth we should all explore.

The question is really: Why do you do what you do? Your employment is probably just a means to an end—to pay the bills—unless you are fortunate enough to have found a job in a field you are truly passionate about. In a recent study, only 11% of Americans said they loved going to work which suggests we only do it for the financial, extrinsic rewards.[16]

After leaving the British Army, I really struggled to find my mission. It wasn't until I took some time to look back on my military career that I realised my mission was the coaching and mentoring of others. As much as I had been involved in very exciting and fulfilling exploits, the thing that really got me engaged was seeing my soldiers, sailors, and airmen growing into their best selves. The highlight of my career really was my final posting where I had the honour of seeing over 10,000 students graduate during my tenure as Commanding Officer of the Defence School of Intelligence. Since this reflection, my mission has become very simple; to positively impact 10 million lives in ten years.

I tell this to help you see that our mission should be out of time and too big for us to achieve alone. Simon Sinek describes this, in his book of the same name, as *The Infinite Game*.[17] Any less and life runs the risk of getting tedious again.

Our mission is different from our purpose. Too often, I hear the question: What is your life's purpose? And people look perplexed. I understand that completely. As human beings, all of our life's purpose should be the same: to love and be loved. Imagine what that would feel like! Beyond that, our purpose changes with time. A long time ago, my

---

[16] Jane Their (2022), *American workers hate their jobs so much that nearly half of them wouldn't wish it on their worst enemy.*
[17] Simon Sinek (2020), *The Infinite Game.*

purpose was to attend school and (as a Boy Scout) do my best. Later in life, my purpose was to successfully prosecute military operations. Concurrent to that purpose, I became a husband and father. Now I am an entrepreneur, author, public speaker, and coach.

All of my purposes up to now were a part of my mission. It has certainly not been a straight line from there to here but, looking back I can see that every single one of my purposes has led me to this point—even the ones that didn't seem important or fun at the time.

Now it is your turn. What is your mission? What is that personal legend, as Paulo Coelho describes it in his book, *The Alchemist*, that is still nagging away at you? [18] Sometimes, we go for months, busy with the day-to-day, but every once in a while, that still, small voice calls out to us, reminding us of something bigger. Our mission!!

Our mission can often be aligned with our dreams. During Unstoppable Force workshops, when I'm proving to everyone in the room that they are unique, we share our dreams. For some, it is an exotic holiday or to live in different locations across the globe. For others, it is to open an animal sanctuary, or foster children, to be in a position to remove some of the pain and suffering from the world. These dreams open another lens on our mission. Our mission, our Infinite Game, will be other people-centric. How could our mission be infinite if we were only considering ourselves or our families—even limiting to our community is playing it small.

Here are some questions that might help you as you get started.

What am I doing?

Who am I helping?

Where am I doing it?

---

[18] Paulo Coelho (1988), *The Alchemist*.

What is my time frame?

Why am I doing this?

Don't worry too much about the 'How do I do this'? The key to any mission is to get started. I have no clue how I will positively impact 10 million lives in ten years. Maybe I will fail, but in the decade-long journey towards 10 million, I will learn, and I will positively impact some lives. The 'how' is a bit like shining a torch on a dark stairwell—you might only see the first step. Take that first step, the second step will emerge through the gloom, and trust the process.

Friends and Family

We spent three years living in Ottawa, Canada, for at least four months of the year it is so cold that when we opened the door and took a deep breath, all my nose hair froze and shattered. Unless it is for fun, like for winter activities, most Canadians will do anything not to venture outside, with the exception of clearing snow from the driveway—the cause of most heart attacks in Canada. Every winter, cars move carefully down the street, break quietly, and turn into driveways. As the car turns, a small button is pressed by the driver and, as if by magic, a garage door begins to rise.

The vehicle and occupants ride into the darkness of the garage and the electric door rumbles closed behind them. In this way, residents who live just a few metres apart can go for months without talking to their neighbours. In many other ways, technology is making hermits of us all. Chairs and couches moved to make watching TV easy. Screens with engaging content interrupt the conversation. Parents choose to wrap their children in 'cotton wool' for fear of the boogieman. Smaller family units and more peripatetic lifestyles all make it more challenging to make long and lasting friendships. Pre-COVID, the world was so small we could travel to most places on Earth in less than two days—despite this, relationships moved online.

During my research for this book, with my military background, I was interested in understanding loneliness for veterans. Every now and again, there are stories in the media of an 'old soldier' dying with no one to attend their funerals. Fortunately, a by-product of two decades of conflict, there is a robust military family of regimental associations who can be called upon to 'parade' at the cemetery. But what about people who don't have that backup?

It takes effort to maintain relationships including those with family and friends. If we leave it too late, who will be there for us as we grow older and need that sense of belonging? If we don't recognise that those days will exist for all of us, might we leave it too late?

As with many reality TV shows, I take a brief look and disregard it as a waste of time. However, recently I caught a few minutes of a UK TV program called *Lodgers for Codgers*.[19] The concept is that impoverished young folks looking for accommodation are paired up with older people with spare rooms. The youngsters get a bed and the more mature 'codgers' get some company. This TV program is loosely based on a UK organisation called Homeshare.

It is different from the TV show, as Homeshare is not a commercial arrangement with a 'landlord' and 'tenant' relationship. The householder is usually an older person who has a comfortable spare room and is looking to offer it to a younger person (a homesharer) in exchange for some company and practical help around the house. No rent is exchanged but both have something to give and something they need.

Homeshare matches are based on mutual respect, and shared interests, and this lasts for as long as people want. All Homeshare matches are arranged and facilitated by a third-party Homeshare organisation, which carefully vets and matches each party for safety and compatibility.

---

[19] Channel 4 (UK) (2020), *Lodgers for Codgers*.

They are given time to get to know each other before moving in and the match is monitored and supported on an ongoing basis, to ensure continued safety and security.

When we think about the importance of friends and family, while Homeshare is different from the TV show, the overall concept of *Lodgers for Codgers* is the same; two groups of people that are facing challenges but have plenty to offer each other. The householders have spare rooms in nice, comfortable, safe houses, but maybe they are living alone and need companionship, a friendly face, or an extra pair of hands. Loneliness can be an issue for people of all ages, and the pandemic and social restrictions have only exacerbated this. So, all things considered, using the existing housing assets we have and creating real solutions seems like a no-brainer!

Lodgers for Codgers is a fairly safe TV experiment and is not unpleasant viewing. It is raising awareness of a genuine issue we might all face. Homeshare is a great concept; what will you do today to ensure you have friends and family around when it's your turn?

Focusing on friends and family enables us to feel a wealth of emotion and realise that we are not alone in this world. A feeling of community is so important to the 'herd' animal that is a human. Community is wealth.

Intimate Relationships

Before we dive too far into this one, there is a need for clarity. The word, intimate, can be confronting to some. If that is you, sit with it for a while and ask yourself why you are confronted by a word, as defined by the Merriam-Webster dictionary:

> *… marked by a warm friendship developing through long association, suggesting informal warmth or privacy, of a very personal or private nature, or belonging to or characterising one's deepest nature.*

Unfortunately, too often we focus only on the 'sex or sexual relations' bit of the definition and become embarrassed. We become embarrassed about the very act that created every one of us.

As you can see from the definition above, there is so much more to intimacy than just the 'messy stuff'. And now, with that definition, we can move forward.

In 2021, my wife and I celebrated our silver wedding anniversary. Liz maintains that to this day, it was only achievable because I spent so much time in one war zone or another. Nevertheless, celebrate the milestone we did—on Waiheke Island in the Hauraki Gulf in New Zealand. We were meant to be in the Cook Islands, but COVID happened.

What does it take to survive (oops, thrive) that long in an intimate relationship?

The truth is, and anyone who has enjoyed marriage for any length of time will recognise this, you will never be good enough and that's ok because she will never be good enough for you.

And that is the merry dance of every relationship.

I've heard people say, "My partner makes me whole." No, we are already whole. By now you should be recognising that you are unique and perfect, and so is your partner. We do not need one another to be whole but, when two souls come together and already understand how unique and perfect each of us is, there is a basis for a truly loving and intimate relationship.

In my opinion, the only way that long-term relationships endure is through recognising that a true and loving marriage/partnership is the meeting of two wonderful human beings who are complete within themselves but so much greater when they come together. It is that blending of history and individuality that creates the relationship that enables both to grow, independently and as a couple.

So that's the getting together bit of the relationship, the firm foundation. What happens over time? Over time, both parts of the relationship continue to grow and mature. Often, this growth happens at different times, and this can create tension. If this truly is 'the one' and both are committed, isn't that enough? You won't be surprised to hear me shout a resounding, "NO!" Long-term relationships are tough but so worth it. The key here is understanding and respecting one another and communicating—often. When we don't say what we feel, how can our partner understand how to support us? When we are in the dark about their moods and mood swings, how can we support them if we have not asked the right questions?

During one of our online programs, the penny dropped for one of our clients. She had really embraced the concept of the Wealth Matrix and was working hard to improve her life in each of the eight pillars. However, she was struggling with this one. She had scored what she thought was a low score and was committed to doing something about it. The challenge she had was that, unlike every other pillar, this one had to involve someone else. And not just anyone else; this one requires input from 'a significant other', in this case, her husband of many years.

So, the die was cast. That evening, when her husband returned home from a busy day, she sat him down and, quite matter-of-factly, informed him that she needed to work on her intimate relationship. She then went on to demand that he share the details of his day, and she in turn shared hers. She was somewhat surprised when the conversation descended into a heated discussion about why she wasn't happy. How could he do anything about it when the first he heard about it was 'right now'?

Our client came back to the next live session and explained her predicament and we didn't laugh, but asked how she thought it was likely to go. How would she feel if 'the shoe was on the other foot'? At this point, she realised that this was actually the basis of the lack of intimacy in their relationship. She had been under the misapprehension that it was all on her. Any relationship, especially our most intimate one, is a two-way thing. We are both guilty of all the successes and all the mistakes. By communicating, little and often, we not only stop the big blow-outs happening but also grow closer to one another.

Why is this important? Because the more we practice communicating honestly, a little and often, it comes to define our relationship. In defining and practicing every minute of every day, it becomes a part of who we are, a part of our relationship, and other people see it.

When our daughter arrived at (one of many) of her new schools, her new friends were so inquisitive about this 'new kid'. As they got to know her, they found it 'cute' that her parents were still married. When I was young, that was the norm. I realise that there are many good reasons why relationships end but there are also many sad reasons why relationships end. Often, the saddest reason is that moving on is easier than going through the pain of growth and creating the space for our partner to grow.

The saddest reason for relationships to end, that end to intimacy, is that there are too few couples out there, who are so comfortable in their kinship, that society sees the beauty of a truly intimate relationship. That couples, are so excited by the prospect that they, are willing to do the 'hard yards' of truly loving their partner and are sufficiently vulnerable to being loved. That sort of relationship is available to every one of us, and to be clear, it's so much more than sex.

So, what can you do to increase your intimacy? Here are eight suggestions:

- Listen more, you know, two ears, one mouth. Hear what they are saying rather than preparing your response. Ask if they want comfort or solutions.
- Tell them what's bothering you, even if it's difficult. Try using this sentence. "When you/they (do that thing), it makes me feel (insert emotion)." I choose to share this to find a solution.

- Compromise but don't cross your red line. We talk about red-lines later in the book but for now—what is your non-negotiable limit? Maybe they have feelings on the subject too and this is a relationship to work together. There is more on this in the chapters on communication and collaboration.

- Be kind and useful. No one gets out of bed with plans to be an idiot. It sometimes happens though, so be useful and solve some of their minor niggles.

- Share intimacy. It doesn't always have to be the 'sexy stuff'. Shared stories, experiences, and humour are great reminders of why you are together.

- Spend time together and make it quality time. Streaming services and screen time do not count. You must value that time together. Remember, the next time they leave the house might be the last time you ever see them. Hold that thought in your heart and just as we shouldn't go to bed in an argument, we shouldn't say goodbye with anything less than a feeling of that most intimate love.

- Laugh and giggle together; it lifts our energy levels. This is about laughing with one another not at one another.

- Plan the future. You're reading this book, and this is about personal development; make it about intimate relationship development.

If all eight of those identified above are too much, do this one thing: be consciously present.

Spirituality

This one topic—spirituality—either causes utter silence or a heated discussion! Often, people struggle to even define spirituality. Before we even get close, someone will mutter, I don't believe in God, or religion it is guilty of so much pain for humanity.

How did we get off topic so quickly? Neither God nor religion had been mentioned. Unfortunately, the latter, religion, has shaped much of our thinking about spirituality for centuries. The church has been running the narrative for so long that God, religion, and spirituality have morphed into one. Worse, spirituality has become the domain of hippies, of the New Age. To talk of spirituality in today's society can lead to the rolling of eyes and comments like, "Oh, you're one of them now." One of who?

Our challenge here is to uncouple God, religion, and spirituality and begin to understand again. As I wrote in *Lead Through Life*, my faith is important to me, but that faith has little to do with religion. In fact, it was religion that saw me disengaging from my traditional Christian upbringing to seek to understand a deeper relationship with my spirituality and, in time, with God.

This pillar of the Wealth Matrix is offering you the same opportunity: go deep within and meet your spirituality … it's there. It might be blocked off or even a wee bit dusty, maybe. It might have even been hidden by your ego because rediscovering our spirit is scary for our ego. The ego needs control, our spirit thrives in freedom.

So how do we 'find' our spirituality? How do we rediscover it? By recognising our spirit is linked to every other being and 'thing' in this universe. We live such cluttered lives with constant noise and commotion, we give little thought to spending time in peace. We are constantly on our devices; we are constantly moving to 'the next thing.' It starts in childhood, our kids are always busy, schools, clubs, parties, sports; where is the space, the peace, where is the time for silence? It is in those moments that we will re-meet our Spirit in: *The thin places when the wall between humanity and divinity is thin.*

This can be a scary place to tread! What will we find? We will find our true nature. The ego, our belongings, all stripped away; sitting in that space truly is peace. When we sit in peace with our spirit, we realise that, while important, the other seven pillars are all the lesser to this most ignored one.

If this is still not resonating, try this. I was fortunate enough to watch as someone consciously experienced spirituality for the first time. It happened high on a mountain (well, of course it would) in Scotland. I had been climbing with my two young children. Andrew was used to the mountains, as this was to be his fourth summit, however, this was Rachel's first. We had been climbing the steep rocky path for a good length of time and I'd be lying if I said there had been no cross words. There was little to see as we worked our way up the deep ravine and then, in a moment, we stepped onto a ridge and the whole of Scotland, it seemed, was below us. The 360-degree views were jaw-dropping. Andrew and I took all this in our stride, probably to our loss. As Rachel crested the ridge, her eyes filled with tears. Thinking something must be wrong, we both dashed to her side. Her response?

"It's so beautiful, I don't know why I am crying."

Poets and philosophers have long tried to describe spirituality; for me, I find myself closest to my spirit when I return to nature. These words by the poet, Nancy Newhall, from the 1960s book, *This is the American Earth*, sum it up perfectly. [20]

To the primal wonders no road can ever lead; they are not so won.

To know them you shall leave road and roof behind;

you shall go light and spare.

You shall win them yourself, in sweat, sun, laughter, in dust and rain, with only a few companions.

you shall dare, delighting, to pit your skill, courage, and wisdom against colossal facts.

You shall live lifted up in light; you shall move among the clouds.

---

[20] Nancy Newall (1992), *This is the American Earth*.

You shall see storms arise, and, drenched and deafened, shall exult in them.

You shall top a rise and behold creation.

And you shall need the tongues of angels to tell what you have seen.

Welcome to Spirituality. We often first meet spirituality after a physical struggle when 'the self' is either too tired or so calm, it doesn't get in the way. Fortunately, there are easier ways than climbing the high peaks to make that first approach. Here are a few:

- Stand on the early morning dew-covered grass in bare feet and feel the earth below your feet.
- Watch the sunrise of a new day and feel gratitude for your life.
- Stand under the stars at night until you see a shooting star; don't look for one, just be aware of the heavens.
- Sit quietly and listen to nature, the wind in the leaves, the ripple of a tide, the babble of a flowing stream.

Since Einstein's famous equation, $E=mc^2$, scientists now understand that the universe is all energy. Maybe a different way of seeing the universe is that it is all Spirit. Try each of the approaches above and come to your own conclusion.

The Matrix

In the film, *The Matrix*, our hero, Neo, is offered a choice by the character Morpheus. The choice represents a pivotal moment; the decision between accepting the truth or remaining in ignorance.

Regarding the Wealth Matrix, now that you are aware that wealth is multi-faceted, will you continue to live in a state of ignorance or denial, or will you question societal norms and seek a deeper understanding of what wealth means to you (even if it's harsh or uncomfortable)?

Is money the most important thing in your life or has society duped you into thinking like that? Maybe your quest for more money in the bank account has caused you to lose sight of what you feel makes you truly wealthy. This is a very personal consideration and a part of what makes you unique.

Now that you have completed this chapter, has your view changed? Once you have completed the Wealth Matrix, you will identify pillars where you are content and others that you feel deserve attention. Give those pillars that attention. What would it take to increase your 'score' in that pillar? It only has to be a small shift to see a change. Once that change is locked in you are likely to see shifts in other pillars too. Repeat the exercise each month (or week to begin with) and see how your relationship to wealth shifts. As with many of the shifts you will experience as you become more *Unstoppable*, don't be surprised if it is your friends, family, and work colleagues who see it first.

This is a part of your growth and shifting energies, it is the *you* that you are becoming, and it feels natural. For those who are yet to join this *Unstoppable* path, they may be challenged, and in some cases confronted, by the new you. For those of us who are already on the path, we will look for other ways to continue our growth. It is now time to consider how we can extend the warranty of the Earthy suit we inhabit during our time on Earth to allow us the longest possible time to experience this Unstoppable Force called life.

This Earthly Suit

When Abraham Maslow wrote his *Hierarchy of Needs* in 1943, he proclaimed, rightly, that without the base level of physiological needs, humanity would cease to exist. As a reminder from earlier, our physiological needs are food, air, water, and, as a species, reproduction. Our physiological needs remain the same, however, the world has moved on exponentially in the last eighty years. What we describe as food has changed. The air we breathe is so much more polluted. Over 25% of humanity lacks access to clean drinking water; in New Zealand approximately 20% of the population does not have access to drinking-water that meets all three standards for compliance.[21, 22]

These shifts have had a direct effect on our Earthly Suit's ability to protect us from our environment. We must become more conscious of how these changes are affecting our lives. Becoming *Unstoppable* is impossible if we do not deeply consider what we can do it improve our health.

To become *Unstoppable* in the world means we must look after everything about ourselves. It is no good to 'run' at a million miles an hour and expect that we can continue ad infinitum. In the British Army, it is called 'Rest and Recouperation': we must all take time to recharge the batteries. However, there is another side to it. Imagine if we recognised that those times of stress and weariness are going to happen, they are a part of life. With that acceptance, we can plan. We can ensure that we live a life that minimises those stresses on our bodies enabling us to continue operating at that *Unstoppable* level for longer. And not just longer each day, science is now showing that, with a few shifts in

---

[21] World Health Organization (2022), *Drinking Water Fact Sheet*, https://www.who.int/news-room/fact-sheets/detail/drinking-water.
[22] New Zealand Ministry of Health (2021), *Annual Report on Drinking-water Quality 2019-2020*, https://www.health.govt.nz/publication/annual-report-drinking-water-quality-2019-2020.

our habits, we can actually extend our lives and, wait for it, the lives of generations yet to come.

So, what is health? The World Health Organization's definition of health is 'a state of complete physical, mental and social wellbeing and not merely the absence of disease'.

Not merely the absence of DIS-ease. A healthy body should feel at ease and that 'ease' enables an Unstoppable Force.

This Earthly Suit …

We now live longer than previous generations, but the incidence of DIS-ease has also increased so many people are living longer but not necessarily in a healthy state. Not able to enjoy or get the most from life. We only have this life and one body in which to live it. In this chapter, you will learn why many of the health 'experts' are now admitting they got it wrong and what we can start doing 'right' to help ourselves and our families live healthier lives. As human lifespans increase, current advice means we will spend longer periods of it being ill. So, here are some tools that, if employed will not only potentially extend your time on this beautiful planet we call home but also live smarter and more joyful, energetic lives—whatever your age you can choose to start.

In his book, *Lifespan*, David Sinclair explores the science of aging and the possibilities of extending human lifespan.[23] Sinclair, a professor of genetics at Harvard Medical School, is a leading figure in the field of aging research.

His book explains that aging is not an inevitable process, but rather a series of molecular changes that can be influenced by lifestyle choices and interventions. The author argues that by understanding the mechanisms of aging, we can develop interventions to delay or even reverse age-related diseases and extend a healthy lifespan.

---

[23] David Sinclair (2019), *Lifespan*.

One of the key concepts in the book is the idea of 'epigenetic changes', which are changes to the way genes are expressed without actually altering the underlying DNA code. Sinclair explains how these changes can be influenced by environmental factors like diet and exercise, and how they can contribute to aging and age-related diseases.

Another important concept in the book is the role of the 'sirtuin genes', which are a family of genes that help regulate metabolism and cellular function. Sinclair argues that activating these genes through interventions like calorie restriction and exercise can help delay aging and extend lifespan.

Sinclair also explores the potential of emerging technologies like gene editing to target cells that have stopped dividing and therefore contribute to aging and age-related diseases. He argues that these interventions could be used to treat age-related diseases such as Alzheimer's and cancer, and potentially even extend a healthy lifespan.

It is clear that the importance of taking a proactive approach to aging and investing in interventions can improve health span (the period of life during which a person is healthy and free from serious disease) as well as lifespan. *Lifespan* presents a compelling argument for the potential of science to extend the human lifespan and improve health in old age. It is a thought-provoking and informative read for anyone interested in the science of aging and the possibilities of longevity research. There are several ways that we can all assist our Earthly Suits in extending our 'health span', so giving us all more time to be *Unstoppable*.

Stay Social

Towards the end of our military career, we were invited to many (and I mean a few every week) social events. The usual format was that Liz and I would be welcomed at the door of whichever Officer's Mess or event centre we had been invited. Liz would then be guided one way and me the other. We might see one another across a crowded dining room, but really the next time would chat would always be the same.

At some point, late in the evening, I would feel Liz' arm wrap around my waist as she informed me that it was time to go; for her, at least. On a few occasions, I took that wise counsel, and we said our farewells and left. More often than not, I was well into the evening by then, so invented some reason to stay.

We obviously portrayed the perfect guests, but I was hiding a secret that even my best friend didn't know. In fact, as we attended our very last event, my best friend commented to Liz, "Stew's really going to miss this" and, "he's so good at it."

That was the lie: I actually struggled at these types of events. I always felt uncomfortable. Even when it was my own event. I'm convinced BBQs were invented to give the chef, like me, a place to hide.

Feeling uncomfortable is a problem, as it is proof that we are not living authentically. If we are not living authentically, we cannot be *Unstoppable*. Worse, we begin to minimise ourselves. I had no interest in fitting in and, if I'm being brutally honest, the alcohol was the crutch I needed to get through those evenings.

That discomfort was problematic—it stopped me from building relationships. I have a few close friends but have always struggled with small talk and networking. As herd animals we need those networks to grow and learn. Without them we become insular. This is affecting our collective health.

I remember walking into the Hard Rock Café Ballroom in San Diego—boy, was I excited—me receiving an invite to a 600-person event at such a cool location. As I stepped through the doors, I froze. My discomfort was in full attack mode. In that throng of 600; I knew one person. That meant I would have to make small talk.

Fortunately, as herd animals, we can learn to be social. We can unlearn the unhealthy habits that have caused us to become insular.

In this world, we are taught that it is wrong to be vulnerable. People will take advantage. Humility is scoffed at. We are divided into extroverts and introverts; party animals or wall-hugging weirdos! Our uniqueness is questioned so we attempt to fit in, and in doing so, we become boring automatons.

So how do we stay (or become) more social, especially if it has always been a struggle? How do we create more meaningful relationships where, in the past, it was all about being the loudest voice? My coach, Jeffery, shared advice that he received during a conversation with Tony Bennett—yes, that Tony Bennett, the *I Left My Heart in San Francisco* Tony Bennett—just be authentic. And that counts just as much for us introverts as it does for our extrovert chums. So how do we do it?

Use their name. That is apparently, the favourite sound of every human being—the sound of their name. Always use the name they give you—don't shorten it or add letters! My padre used to call me Stewie (aaaarghhh). Respect their name and make sure you remember it for next time.

Be interested. Humans are desperate to tell their story; so, let them. Use your body language and tone to show how interested you are. Don't worry, we are also nosey, so you'll get your chance. If you struggle with this concept, gamify it and challenge yourself to get a few facts about the person. This was one of the very first exercises that we set our 'spy' students when I was responsible for training in my military days; it was called intelligence gathering but the idea is the same.

Ask questions. Teach yourself to ask open questions, questions that elicit more than a yes/no answer. Their response provides you with intelligence to form your next questions. Of course, this is not an interrogation; you are attempting to build a friendly relationship here.

The word, about, is useful. Fortunately, as herd animals we love stories. We are desperate to tell stories, but we just don't like being told what stories to tell. So, use the word 'about' in your questions: tell me about the time, tell me about your day. The word, about, gives control of the conversation to the other person. This hands the responsibility over to your 'quarry'—they can choose where they want to take the conversation. This also works particularly well with teenagers who spend those years trying not to get caught. There is more about this in the chapters about, Communication and Collaboration.

Even a smile is a great tool.

When did a stranger smile at you in the street? When did you last smile at someone in the street? Try it. Recently, while out running, I decided to smile and wave at every runner I saw—sounds weird, I know—but every single runner smiled and waved back. What did I get from that simple act? So much more energy! I finished my run still feeling fresh rather than the usual tired mess.

What is the point of a name badge?

Ever wondered why employees wear name badges? I'd like to think it is to bring a level of personality to the environment. I think those name badges are more likely used when we want to complain about the level of service we have received. Name badges are a great place to start your journey to building your own social network. Next time you are at the grocery store, use your server's name. Even if it's only a, "Thank you (add name here)." This will give you the 'bravourism' to maybe ask a simple question.

As you become less uncomfortable 'loosening your tongue' with strangers, start speaking to 'strangers' at work. Practice speaking at the very start of meeting, you attend. With all these tiny shifts in building your network, your energy will begin to shift. You will feel more generous, and that generosity will be returned. As you now know, a more generous life is a healthier life, and this is why it is so important to become more social.

Eat Real Food

In the early 20th century, men masturbated too frequently!

I'm not making this up! In the late 1800s, a man named John Harvey Kellogg ran a health spa in Battle Creek, Michigan. He was a staunch advocate of a vegetarian diet and believed that spicy and flavourful food could lead to unhealthy sexual desires, which he thought were the root of many health problems.

Kellogg was a fervent supporter of abstinence, and he believed that bland and tasteless food could help control people's sexual impulses. He even advocated for a diet of plain water, nuts, and fruits as a way to promote chastity.

One day, Kellogg's brother, Will Keith Kellogg, who worked at the health spa with him, was cooking up a batch of boiled wheat for breakfast when he accidentally left the wheat on the stove for too long. When he returned to the pot, the wheat had become stale and hard. Rather than throw it away, Will decided to roll the wheat out and toast it in the oven, creating the first flakes.

John Harvey Kellogg was pleased with the new creation and started serving the flakes to his patients at the health spa. However, he was still concerned about the potential for the flakes to be too tasty, so he forbade his brother from adding any sugar to them.

Despite this setback, the flakes became popular with the spa's guests, who appreciated their convenience and ease of digestion. Will Kellogg saw a business opportunity and tried to patent the invention, but his brother claimed that he was the true creator and refused to allow Will to own the patent.

In the end, Will Kellogg struck out on his own and founded the Kellogg Company which became famous for its cornflakes and other cereal products. The company thrived, and eventually, Will was able to buy the rights to the cornflake patent from his brother.

So, in a strange twist of fate, the bland and tasteless cereal that was meant to suppress sexual urges ended up becoming a popular breakfast food enjoyed by people all over the world.

This example was one of the beginnings of convenience food which has only accelerated.

The industrialisation of the world made canning simpler to ensure food stayed edible for longer. The advent of large-scale expeditionary warfare required food that stayed edible for long periods, in different temperatures. At the time of writing, I have been out of uniform for nearly a decade, and I still have some leftover bits of 'ration packs' and I know they will be fine to eat for years to come.

Before this advance in food technology, we ate what we grew. We knew about pickling and salting to extend the 'shelf life' of food, but beyond a season or two, our food would 'go off'. Our cycle of farming led to where we lived—it had to be where crops and animals would thrive. This new science allowed humanity to push those boundaries, but it was also the beginning of humans ingesting 'unreal' food. To keep the food from putrefying, the food producers needed additives.

As humans, we like ease. The easier, the better, so from over-masturbating men at the beginning of the 20th century, we now have a multi-billion-dollar food industry that powerfully lobbies every government to shape their profits through how we eat. If you question this statement, count the number of fast-food outlets on your next journey (the higher the number, the lower the income of the residents in that neighbourhood) or count the number of additives in your next shop.

The food industry drives all of the food fads and diets you have ever tried—remember fat is bad or receiving a lollipop for being good at the dentists or doctors—receiving the polio vaccine on a sugar cube! As our reliance on convenience food grew, guess what, we started feeling more DIS-ease. How did deal with that DIS-ease? We welcomed the next biggest lobbying group in the world—big Pharma. We cured our DIS-eases (caused by not eating real food) by ingesting drugs. But not drugs that cured us in a holistic way. Modern drugs cure in a focused way; have you ever read about the 'side effects' of certain medicines?

To be clear for a moment, I am not decrying all food manufacturers, we need processed food. The salting for preservation, canning to extend a food shelf life, and pickling have not only allowed humanity to survive through the leaner months, but they have also allowed food to travel further from the source. It is ultra-processed food that is doing the harm.

Nor am I failing to respect the great advances in medicine, but we need to recognise the journey that humanity is on. To recognise that heavily processed food is causing DIS-ease and the drug industry feeds from that. Our medical services are so stretched that the 'easy' answer-to-hand over a 'pill' rather than having the time to explore and deliver a holistic diagnosis.

A Word on Diets

Diets don't work. Well, that's not strictly true. Diets will work for a period of time. New diets, like everything new, are exciting. That doze of dopamine, that intrinsic motivation, but once we hit that target weight, or let's be honest' we get close to that target weight, those old neural pathways start asserting their authority, and the new neural pathways are insufficiently established to survive the onslaught. I've also found that trying to repeat the same diet fails even more quickly—hence the multi-billion-dollar industry. It's all a marketing fad—we all know what we need to do, we're just looking for permission. But to change our behaviour doesn't work, changing our attitude to food is what is required. To do so, we must have an honest understanding of what our bodies need, versus what we want to put in it, how much we really require, and how it affects our Earthly Suit.

My first diet

The first diet I remember happened to me when I was about twelve years old. It was done to me, and my cousin, Garry. It was done to us for a good reason: we were fat! No consideration was given to why we were fat, or in fact, why the diet didn't work. The diet was based on an early version of Weight Watchers. I even remember the tiny set of kitchen scales I used to measure my food. The logic was sensible—put less calories in than I was burning; *et voila*, a thinner child. Three advantages of this diet:

- There was less ultra-processed food available back then in a small village in Scotland.
- I could not drive to find such food.
- I had little money to source such foods.

Where the diet failed, in the end, was a summer holiday to the seaside resort of Scarborough on the Yorkshire Coast of England. There was an ice cream shop that sold triple scoops in a waffle cone, topped with whipped cream, and strawberry sauce … and my cousin and I had holiday spending money. We walked for miles to get to that shop (most days) then went 'home' to the caravan and continued with our measly diet portions. The real reason this diet failed is that we just weren't into it!

Since that failed attempt at lasting weight loss, like most of us, I have created a love/hate relationship with dieting and food—even to the point of short stints of bulimia.

Diets that have worked:

- The Rosemary Connelly diet: the very first diet I completed as a married man. I was actually excited to engage in restricting my food intake with another; it worked for both of us. Based on portion control and interesting foods, this program worked, however, some of the dishes were questionable, I mean, blue cheese in spaghetti carbonara? I can imagine the stress in every Italian boiling now.

- Weight Watchers: the first time, not on the second attempt. I loved the points system; it was like gamifying food.

- The Low-GI diet: worked for a wee while but it became too 'samey' and it took effort to work out which foods, in which form, were really low GI. Nevertheless, I still look to low-GI foods to keep an eye on my food intake.

- Keto diet: I love this one. Removing all (most) carbohydrates from my diet. This one takes planning but, unlike GI, it's really simple. Even choosing your veggies is simple, green = good, less green = less good. As a real *Unstoppable* challenge, I took off into the wilderness for a week, with a full pack, and a tramp of over 100 km only carrying keto food. I term it the Waikaremoana experience. If you can get through the first few days and embrace the process, your body enters ketosis and autophagy. Studies are now showing that there are not only weight loss benefits but also long-term health benefits including remission from type-2 diabetes and less risk of developing old age-related diseases such as Parkinson's disease and cancer. [24, 25]

- If Keto is too extreme, maybe Intermittent Fasting (IF) is more your thing. This is now my standard practice, as it is simple. I don't ingest anything (except water) for between 8-12 hours every day. WHAT? That's like half a day with no food … what sort of devilry are you suggesting? Let's break that down. We should sleep for approximately 7-8 hours a night so by missing breakfast—the most hyped meal of the day—and not snacking before lunch, we easily hit the magic number. That magic number is a 16-hour fast. Studies are showing that it takes between 12-16 hours for our insulin to 'reset' after a meal. We are now snacking more than ever, and our snacks are getting bigger. The health

---

[24] Adrian Brown et al. (2021), *Dietary strategies for remission of type 2 diabetes: A narrative review.*

[25] Rafael de Cabo, Ph.D., and Mark P. Mattson, Ph.D *(2019), Effects of Intermittent Fasting on Health, Aging, and Disease.*

industry had its part to play suggesting we should eat smaller meals more often, and this might be the case for high-performing Olympians or top-level footballers and rugby players, but not the couch potatoes.

We now 'graze' from morning 'til night and when not eating, we are drinking liquids that do us no good: triple Frappuccino with caramel sauce topped with cream and a Mochaccino shooter … thanks, and please put this empty can of energy drink in the trash; I needed it to get to the coffee shop from the car. Our insulin system has no chance to reset, hence the uptick in type-2 diabetes sufferers. Even a few days of intermittent fasting is good. When did you last feel hungry, like proper hungry? Not, I'm bored so best I stuff my face. I'm talking about real hunger.

Every now and again, I amp 'IF' to a new level. I fast for a few days. Fasting has been a part of humanity since the beginning of our time. If we failed to hunt and kill the antelope on the savanna, we fasted. If our crops failed, we fasted. It is only in recent times, in the developed world that we have had constant access to food. Fasting has also been a part of the 'spiritual gig' to enable the yogi or hippy to reach higher levels of enlightenment. Fasting has been proven to be good for us. Up to seventy-two-hour water fasts are shown to help, through ketosis and autophagy, with weight loss. But not just any weight loss, fasting helps our bodies burn visceral fat—the unhealthy stuff—and also lowers cholesterol. Recent studies have even shown that extending the fast towards seventy-two hours causes the body to release stem cells that go hunting around our bodies for parts that need healing.[26] Please note, however, that all body types are different, and if you are on medication for any type of ill health, it is recommended that you check with your doctor first about any of the above.

---

[26] Joel Fuhrman (2020), *Fasting and Eating for Health*.

Whichever you choose, slavishly following the century-old path described above has led to an obese, pill-reliant society. Fortunately, for most of us, the solutions are in our own hands.

In his book, *Metabolical*, Robert H. Lustig explores the current state of health and wellness in our modern society.[27] As a paediatric endocrinologist and an expert in the field of obesity, metabolism, and nutrition, he delves into the causes and consequences of metabolic syndrome, a condition that affects millions of people worldwide and is associated with a range of health problems, including obesity, diabetes, heart disease, and cancer.

Lustig argues that our modern diet and lifestyle are the root causes of metabolic syndrome. He speculates that the consumption of processed foods and sugar, combined with a lack of exercise and chronic stress, are the primary culprits. He argues that the food industry has capitalized on our addiction to sugar, salt, and fat, creating highly palatable, calorie-dense, and nutrient-poor foods that are contributing to the epidemic of metabolic disease. He contends that chemicals disrupt our hormone systems, leading to a range of health problems, including obesity, diabetes, and infertility.

In addition to identifying the root causes of metabolic syndrome, Lustig also proposes solutions to address the problem. He advocates for a whole-food, plant-based diet that is low in added sugars, salt, and fat. He argues that this type of diet, combined with regular exercise and stress reduction techniques, can help prevent and reverse metabolic disease.

Metabolical really got me thinking about what I 'feed' on. Even the damage that diet drinks can do is confronting. I place this book high up on my 'must read' list for Unstoppable Force clients however, if you're not quite ready, the author puts the solution rather succinctly: 'Feed the gut, protect the liver'.

---

[27] Robert Lustig (2021), *Metabolical*.

If you choose not to read the book, and you really should, it completely changed my view of food and, I thought I was living healthily, here are ten ways to *feed the gut and protect the liver*:

- Eat real food—food that your grandparents would recognise.
- Eat fresh food (as fresh as possible).
- If fresh is too expensive, buy frozen.
- Read the ingredients: what are you actually buying?
- If you don't understand the ingredients: investigate.
- Shop around the edges of the grocery store (that where the 'realest' stuff is located).
- Grow your own.
- Make your own; at least you know what you're putting in it.
- Drink more water.
- Drink fewer fizzy drinks—even the no/low sugar options are bad.

I hear you! This approach is a shift to our eating habits; we have been eating poorly for such a long time that humanity has a habit: we are addicted to convenience foods, and as a result, our health is failing. Humans are becoming more sluggish; we are more easily controlled, and we are trapped in that cycle. Have a go at the ten steps above and see how life begins to shift towards the *Unstoppable*.

Making that shift can be fun, you will find different restaurants in which to eat, and you might even find a new hobby in cooking and preparing food. You will spend less time filling your empty time, you'll learn more and when you do choose the processed option—enjoy it but make it a treat. Over time, you will choose fewer of those 'treats' as you feel the repercussions of the additives.

While we are talking about nutrition, we should mention alcohol. From an individual who spent twenty-eight years on a 'drinking spree',

I now recognise the damage that 'overdoing it' can do. I also recognise the social aspect of enjoying a drink. I am not going to preach here, as I still enjoy wine and beer, although I haven't been able to stomach spirits since my 'year off'. But beer is nothing more than 'liquid bread' and our bodies convert all alcohol into sugar. Moderation is the key: make it a conscious choice and stop before you can't make a conscious choice.

Positive Material

The evening news is one of the few programs that wish you a good evening and then spends the next hour telling you why it's not. Current affairs channels have also recognised that our attention spans are now so short—around two minutes—and they can 'hit' us with so much more bad news within those sixty minutes. Within those soundbites, there isn't even time for any detail.

Social media algorithms are now so smart, they have trained us to waste hours scrolling and they are complicit in re-enforcing our bias. So, if we don't take time to research, we become more biased. Notice the rise in left- or right-wing extremism over recent years.

Feeding the gut and protecting the liver is only one part of being smarter about what we ingest. Have you ever taken stock of everything we are putting into our Earthly Suits? Try this exercise over the next few days (Unstoppable Force clients complete this exercise over ten days); make a note of everything you do over a 24-hour period. How much time do you spend on the following activities:

- Sleeping
- Eating
- Driving
- Exercise

- On social media
- In front of the TV/screen
- Learning
- Add any other activity you spend time on.

I specifically used the word 'spend' as this is exactly what we are doing. We might not know when our time in our Earthly Suit is coming to an end, but it is. How are you spending your time?

Recently, my wife and I completed our monthly finance and budget meeting. On analysing the results, I was shocked (and slightly amused) to note that we had visited the grocery store over forty-five times in the previous month. We had not particularly spent more money than usual, but how much time had we wasted? The exercise above will highlight areas where you are not only wasting time but also what you are ingesting.

The follow-up exercise is to get smarter with your time and with what you are putting into your Earthly Suit.

There is nothing wrong with spending time on social media but give yourself a time limit. We love watching shows on the various streaming services, but let's smart about how much time we spend doing so. Sometimes we will binge-watch a whole series in one day—nothing wrong with that, as long as it is planned.

If we are giving ourselves permission to spend some time on social media or streaming services and planning it; what else could we wisely ingest? When did you last pick up a book, listen to a podcast, or watch a fact-based series?

The 21st century has taught us that we must always be busy, we send our kids to clubs to fill their day. We are constantly surrounded by noise. We have forgotten how to be bored. Boredom is the gateway to our imagination. Give yourself permission to be bored. Just for a few minutes, ingest nothing. It will feel weird and uncomfortable, but do it anyway.

In these few moments of wonder—after the panic has subsided—choose how to spend the free time you have created by planning your social media and streaming time.

By being wiser about what we choose to ingest, we can lower our stress levels. Constantly watching 'bad news' stories or thinking about the 'perfect lives' we are seeing on social media (and grading our lives against them) increases our cortisol levels. The guilt we feel about wasting this time further increases the cortisol in our system.

Increased cortisol is linked to obesity, increased blood pressure, and heart disease. Time spent in study or out in nature causes our bodies to release different chemicals into our bloodstream that actually lower our stress levels. Next time you spend time outside or hold a loved one's hand be conscious and recognise the moment you sigh deeply. That sigh is the sign that your body is relaxing, flushing that cortisol and adrenaline. That sigh is your body thanking you for taking time away from the 'noise' of the 21st century and a sign that your earthly suit might last a wee bit longer in this *Unstoppable* life.

Negative Material

Our Earthly Suits are being bombarded from every side and ingesting negative material every day.

Mrs Darling (my wife) had never been to Hollywood, other than transiting through Los Angeles International Airport (LAX); she had never been to 'the City of Angels'. We changed that with a two-night break, staying in a hotel just up the road from Hollywood Boulevard near the Hollywood Bowl. It was only two nights, but it wasn't until we were on the drive back to the airport that we noticed.

I first experienced the vibrant green of New Zealand as our aircraft descended through the clouds when we emigrated to our new home. Over the next twelve months, we decided to ban the word, wow, from our vernacular. Even after nearly a decade, I remain in awe of the ridiculous beauty in which I am fortunate enough to live. Not only is the country beautiful, but it is also empty—just five million people squeezed into a land mass that would stretch from New York to Miami and nearly a third of them live in our capital city, Auckland. We have empty, quiet places. I can run on the beach every morning and not see or hear a soul. Due to this blissful existence, we were not ready for a stay in Hollywood, Los Angeles, and the full-frontal assault on all senses. It was constant noise and smog (and the smell of weed). The taste of traffic, the dirt and dust on our hands and faces … and the bright lights.

Even if I chose to take my twenty minutes 'out', my senses were still in 'panic mode' and operating in high-Beta. But I was usurped with the excitement of city living. The accessibility of everything.

I also noticed the irregularity of this sensory attack. In a city the size of Wales, the balance of wealth is on show. From the verdant streets and gardens of Beverly Hills to the concrete jungle of 'Downtown'. From the clean air of the Hollywood hills and golden beaches of Malibu and Santa Monica to the 'Skunk' filled air of parts of Sunset Boulevard. The mansions of Montecito and Santa Barbara to the tent cities amongst the high-rise of Downtown. The lower down the 'pecking order', the less opportunity to give our senses a 'rest'. The less opportunity to allow ourselves to recreate.

Our 're-creation' comes from those 'times out'. One of the purposes of National Parks and protected areas across our globe is to give us somewhere to go to reconnect with ourselves. Living under the constant barrage of inner city living with all the stress and strain, our energy is drained. We seek ways to dull that pain. To remove ourselves from our reality. Many in the tent cities cannot afford to escape their reality and fall deeper and deeper into 'control'.

Earlier in the book, we addressed the importance of bringing our brainwave activity back from high-level Beta to low Beta and Alpha frequencies to give our system a cortisol, adrenalin break. Our ancestors didn't have this problem, as they lived with and within nature. The socio-economic breakdown that we are experiencing across the developed world is, in part, due to the lack of access to 'wide open spaces', for the most needy elements of our society; and, this has become a generational problem. Kids that are brought up in inner cities associate with similar activities and habits; the circle of life begins again. Getting kids away from negative influences must become a priority. Removing them from the negative material to which they are bombarded from before birth would, I truly believe, see a fundamental change in humanity's future.

As we prepared to fly back to New Zealand, we took the opportunity to drive through the Santa Monica mountains. Without thinking, we removed ourselves from the battlefield of the inner city. After the 'attack' of downtown, it only took a few moments for us both to feel the reset that nature offered. That drive into the greenery of the mountains where the air was clearer began the reset. To extend our vision from the mountain to the clouds in the sky and onto the ocean's horizon exercised our eye muscles. The smell of the pine or eucalyptus trees cleared our noses of the constant 'fug' of weed.

Nature has a pace of its own and, as a part of nature, we need to 'go home' more often. Nature has very little negative material, and that which does exist normally gives us a warning before the attack. The negative material of the modern world is insipid, it attacks chronically. It finds its way through our weakness and once it gets hold, we are usurped. The obvious negative material, we can do something about. The underlying cause of our habitual need for those is a far greater challenge. But challenge it we must, to become *Unstoppable*.

Exercise

What is exercise? In our house, it is anything from walking the dog (Liz) to committing to physical activity until you throw up in a bucket (me).

Which is right? Neither/both? Is a quick run around with the vacuum cleaner enough?

We are fortunate to live near the ocean and, throughout the summer months, I am dragged, most afternoons, for a swim. The ever-attentive Mrs Darling will pop her head around the office door announcing the end of my working day, already adorned in her swimsuit. It is such an amazing way to relax, a bit of nature, a bit of exercise, and a debrief for the day. As I was swimming, one day, my foot caught on the sandy bottom—*a stone*, I thought—and dived down to look. I resurfaced with a tuatua in my hand. A tuatua is a clam endemic to New Zealand. One tuatua … I wondered if there might be more. It turned out there were, lots more. All I had to do was dive beneath the waves, dig with my hands into the sand, and gather.

Five minutes before, I was a recreational swimmer, now I was a forager and boy did I forage! After thirty minutes, I had two pockets full. Some garlic, herbs, and half a glass of white wine later, we were feasting on my catch. The problem was that, even after thirty minutes of my watery effort, I had gathered way too few clams to match the energy I had expended during the physical exertion.

This was the life of our ancestors. Life was a constant battle between energy (food) gathered and the energy exerted to gather it. Walking for water and carrying it back to camp was not exercise but a necessity. Running after a gazelle all day was not a fun run, it was shopping. Our Earthly Suit was built to exercise as a necessity to survive. Now we pop to the gym for sixty minutes or jog down the street and think it is sufficient. We celebrate with cake and coffee or eat a bar of chocolate despite knowing the calorific intake well exceeds the energy used. At the gym, we sit on machines built for comfort and watch TV. The mentality with which we approach exercise as a luxury rather than a necessity is killing us.

During my military years, there was an expected basic level of fitness. It was tested every six months. Every soldier was required to attain a certain number of push-ups, a certain number of sit-ups, a squadded run, and then the best possible time over a 2.4 km course, all based on age. Annually, we donned our assault vests, body armour, and helmets and signed our rifles from the armoury and the Physical training staff took us on a 12.8 km 'tab'; a pass was completing the route in under 2 hours. For some, that became the standard whilst for others, it was recognised as the basic level.

As I moved on to more arduous training, the exercise regime shifted as did the 'love' shown by our physical training instructors. Our fitness now required unarmed combat, longer and faster runs. We worked hard because we all understood the threats that we might face. Any combat unit preparing for military deployment underwent increased physical training to prepare them for the increased stress that combat operations in desert and high-altitude environments have on the human body. My training ensured that I would be capable of the toll that specialist operation missions take; mentally and physically.

Training for a marathon is no different. When we undertake an arduous endeavour, we must change the way we prepare. It is now time we recognised that, for most of us, our exercise regimes no longer prepare us for the lives we would love to truly live. And by committing to a new regime, not only will we live that life, but we can live it for longer.

When I was in Command, I had the responsibility for my team of 200 and also the thousands of recruits and trainees that passed through my gates. I no longer needed the same level of physical fitness as operations in Afghanistan and Iraq required, but I did have a standard. Whenever there was a fitness test scheduled for the staff or the trainees, I would take part to let them see the seriousness with which I took my personal exercise regime and hopefully instil something similar in them. You never know who you might be fighting alongside, and I personally prefer my fellow combatants to be fit enough to endure similar to me.

Skip forward a few years and I'm now a 'civvie'. What level of fitness do I require? What should my exercise regime look like? I struggled with this for years. I tried to keep up with the high standards of fitness but what was the point? I still love the intensity of exercising until I throw up in a bucket, but is it necessary? Try it sometime, at least once … but is it even good for me? The truth is, having a balance is the key. So maybe the answer to the question posed is, our personal exercise regime should probably lie somewhere between, walking the dog and vomiting up our breakfast.

What we can see, anywhere we look, is that the inhabitants of the developed world are not taking sufficient exercise. Our lives are becoming more and more sedentary. Many of the tasks that keep us fit in the past are no longer required. I can't remember the last time I hunted my supper. The march of technology has allowed us all to become lazy. We have also become far too comfortable, so when we feel uncomfortable, the 'voices in our heads' scream: UNFAIR, STOP! And we do. There is a whole industry based on our willingness to get started and our failure in consistency.

As an advocate of the tougher end of exercise regimes, I recognise that I am a part of the problem, just as someone who says that walking the dog is sufficient is equally a part of the problem. Exercise is a very personal decision where we must take all parts of our lives and our health into consideration. However, I believe we should all do more than we are and should do so a few times a week. Doing so should include:

- Perspiring (horses sweat)—you don't have to lose your body weight in sweat every time you exercise, and
- Getting out of breath, but only to the point that a full sentence takes more than one breath.

That is where we should all start and with commitment and consistency, we will feel the benefits.

And the benefits are so much more than we realise. It might not feel like it in the moment, but exercise will keep us well, and we will fall into DIS-case less often and our recovery from injury and illness will accelerate. More than that, not only will our clothes feel a bit looser the following will also happen:

A consistent exercise regime can extend our lives.

We will sleep better. (See below).

We will think with greater clarity. As we exercise, our brainwave activity decreases. The Beta 3 activity decreases to Beta 1 and can even drop to Alpha wavelength which is the level of brain activity where our ideas and daydreams run wild.

We will enjoy our food more and, over time, we will shift our calorie intake to foods that will fuel our new lifestyle. Cravings are how our brain tells our bodies what they need. After a five-day 100 km tramp, with limited carbohydrates in my diet—it was an experiment—the first thing I bought (and ate like a man possessed) was a large bag of sea-salt potato chips; my body knew it needed carbs and salt. When we exercise consistently, our body will tell us what it needs to refuel and recover … it's unlikely to be heavily processed.

Our confidence will grow, we will stand straighter, and our voices will boom. There are even studies that suggest people who exercise regularly are more likely to get promotions at work.

Oh, and the sex will be better. So even if you don't believe anything else I've written about exercise, it must be worth trying for this reason alone. And no, sex does not count as exercise—even the most vigorous bedroom gymnastics are too short-lived to make that much of a difference… Sorry.

Sleep

"Oh, no!" came the cry from our kitchen. "She's left her sunglasses." The 'she' in this proclamation was Lucy, a school friend of Liz. She and her daughter had, very Englishly, popped in for a cuppa on their way to the airport. Lucy lives in New York and was holidaying in New Zealand, so popping in was quite a big deal. The last time they had spent any time together was forty-two years previously, when they were still at boarding school. A random social media post had alerted the two that they would be in the same area, so why not catch up? It never fails to amaze me how, good friends can drop straight back into a conversation after years, even decades apart. Two old friends, catching up, so comfortably, so 'at home' that belongings are put down and forgotten in an, "I'll get it next time" sort of abandon.

Having enjoyed their 'cuppa', Lucy and her daughter headed off towards the airport, starting their long journey home, planning to refuel the rental car on the way. Knowing the route, and only gas station on that route, I jumped in the car with the aforementioned sunglasses thinking I could catch them before refuelling was complete. I headed to the garage and jumped into Raven.

Raven is a black Model 3 Tesla—owned and driven because she is cool and a fun ride, and she farts when I indicate left or right. I am not so naïve to believe that owning a Tesla saves the planet. Yes, the emissions are lower than the gas-guzzling utes (trucks) that all New Zealanders seem to aspire to own, but the natural resources required to build the batteries that enable the silent acceleration still rapes our planet. As I jumped into the driver's seat, I checked the battery charge: 15%. Hmm, I think I can make the round trip.

Range anxiety is a real thing driving battery-powered vehicles. It's not so simple as just pulling into the next gas station. Planning is required. On our very first trip in Raven, we nearly got it catastrophically wrong. We'd flown to Auckland to celebrate a belated twenty-fifth wedding anniversary and picked the car up to drive home to become accustomed to this new style of driving. We also wanted to download all the Apps we would need to stay charged throughout the country.

It started well, heading south from Auckland, we stopped for a coffee having identified a charging station. Coffee finished, and twenty minutes later, we were back on the road with more 'joules' in the tank. A stop in Hamilton for a business meeting gave another opportunity to 're-fuel'. The promise of an overnight charge in the famous Chateau Tongariro, at the base of Mt Ruapehu—an active volcano—gave us the confidence to continue the journey south. The onboard computer informed me that we would arrive with about 20% battery charge, however, there was a problem.

Raven had not yet 'learned' how heavy my foot was, or that, being new to the vehicle, how much my manual breaking would diminish the regenerative breaking process. We rolled into the hotel car park with only 11% charge to find a gas-guzzler parked in the EV-charging spot. But worse was to come: we needed a specific charging cable (which we didn't have). We had no choice but to roll down the hill to the local village campground that assured us of a charging station. Arriving with 8%, we were faced with the same issue: an incorrect charging cable. The final option was to find a normal plug and accept a slow charge to get us moving, but food was needed first. As we pulled up to the restaurant (6%) and parked up, Raven got involved and informed me: You have insufficient power to park up. ARGGGHH! Maybe just enough to limp up the hill to the hotel?

As we got to the road junction, I spied what looked like an EV parked up to something that looked a wee bit like a charger. It was, and the EV owner was just leaving. Crisis averted. We plugged Raven in and walked back to the restaurant. This was a salutary lesson about the life of an EV owner and the last time I had ever let the battery drift 'into the red'.

Returning to the sunglasses story, I arrived at the gas station just as Lucy was pulling out. I returned the sunglasses and set off for home. Reversing into the garage, Raven reminded me that, with 3% left in the 'tank', I had insufficient power to park up. I plugged her in, and by the following morning, she was satiated; back at 100%.

That same day, I was ending my first 72-hour fast of the year. During this process, I continued life as usual—alarm at 0500 hrs, meditation, 5-mile run, and a swim in the ocean—it's really amazing how much time you get back when food and eating are not a thing. The third day of the fast had felt particularly brutal but it was a Wednesday, and the same 'workday' routine was required. Reflecting on the precarious challenge (first world, I know) I had faced in getting the sunglasses back to their owner, I wondered how my body was responding to the fast. My pulse was the normal 45-52 beats per minute. My blood pressure was in the healthy zone, but I was 'off'. Was my 'tank' empty? Looking in the mirror it was obvious I had many kilojoules—stored as fat—in reserve before I could even claim to be running low. My potential and latent energy reserves were doing fine. I told myself, *Stop being a wimp*! A few days of fasting and this ….

But I had a problem, I didn't feel *Unstoppable*. In the developed world, we pride ourselves on 'drive'. The most successful are driven. Being *Unstoppable* requires deeper wisdom. Our Unstoppable Force comes from an ability to monitor our energy levels and respond before we receive the message: You have insufficient power to park up! That evening, I listened to my body. I turned my alarms off before retiring for the night and drifted off to sleep.

I awoke nearly eleven hours later; I was refreshed and *Unstoppable*, once again.

This lesson has been less than 150 years in the making, but it is one that we must all reflect on. Sleep is more important than the credit we give it. Sleep is now seen as wasting our time, but a lack of good sleep is killing us. In his book, *Why We Sleep*, Matthew Walker describes his lifetime fascination with slumber and how, as our world gets faster and faster and work has become a 24/7 activity, we are creating a population of zombies marching towards an earlier grave.[28]

---

[28] Matthew Walker (2018), *Why We Sleep*.

In 1888, the lights were turned on for the very first time in the Southern Hemisphere. For the first time, electrical lighting enabled the inhabitants of Reefton, a gold mining town in South Island, New Zealand to see in the dark! And at that moment, as with every other business owner in the world, Kiwi businesses could start on shift work. No longer was the sun the only source of 'bright' light. Prior to that, much like the rest of the world before the harnessing of electricity, workers and their families, got up with the sun and retired to bed not long after the sun set.

The advent of electricity has enabled the world to advance and electric lighting has been positive in so many ways—take a moment and think about how different your life would be if candles and the sun were your only source of light! However, as with all great advances in technology, there is a downside. For thousands of years, humanity had existed as a part of nature, her cycles and rhythms. The advent of electric lighting changed that. We could now get up before the sun and stay up long after she had dipped below the horizon.

Our extended days have, while increasing revenue for our employers and the tax man, corrupted our circadian rhythm and our sleep patterns. Over the last 150 years, this has compounded and, however much sleep you are getting each night, it is unlikely to be sufficient.

When our kids were little, they had routines. After their evening meal, they had time to play, then bath time, then into bed and stories. In the very early days, I would sit on the floor next to the cot and sing to them. That routine meant, not only did the kids get to know the relationship to timing and bed, it also meant that Liz and I could enjoy supper and the evening together. Even when we travelled between time zones—we lived in Germany and travelled to see family in the UK—breaking the routine didn't create issues because the kids always easily moved back to the routine once we returned home.

So, the answer is simple. Get more sleep! Here are five things you can start doing right now to improve your sleep.

1. Maybe you remember the unfairness of being sent to bed 'early'. We didn't only do that to get some peace before turning in ourselves. We did it because we knew the world of hurt that was awaiting if our little cherubs got insufficient sleep. So why not do the same for yourself? We all know we perform better with a good night's sleep. Set a bedtime and keep to it. Set an alarm and get up as soon as it rings—no snooze button! Hitting the snooze button is the first step to ruining your day and your life. Three things happened when you hit snooze:

   a. You committed to wasting the first part of your day.

   b. In the extra time in bed you are telling yourself you missed the alarm, you acted without the integrity you planned last night, and … flushed your body with Cortisol (stress).

   c. You reminded yourself how unimportant you are and that tasks don't need completing.

   So tomorrow … when those feet hit the floor when the alarm goes off act like your life depends on it. It does.

2. Remember how screen time increases your brainwave frequency—less of that in the hours before bed.

3. Make your bed in the morning—it makes bedtime more inviting, whatever sort of day you've had.

4. Take care about what you are eating and drinking in the hours before bed.

5. If you can't sleep, don't be afraid to get up and have a drink of water, read for a while, and then try again. Lying in bed when sleep won't come just increases the tension.

Don't Stop Believing

Why should we make the effort to understand what makes humanity 'tick'? Does it really matter if money is all we care about? We're all going to die anyway, so shouldn't we enjoy the food and drink and not 'overdo it' in the gym? Are the streaming services and social media not there to take away from the pain of this life?

Who are we to take, as Scott M Peck describes it, *The Road Less Travelled*?[29] We are the *Unstoppable* ones. The ones who have got to the end of ourselves and asked, "Is this it?" The ones who chose to live with the pain of uncertainty knowing that the prize was a certainty that endured.

When we understand ourselves, when we have removed our need for instant gratification through choosing what wealth really means to us, when we have taken the decision to prioritise all parts of our health; we will find balance.

As a small child, I was so excited when I was given my very first bicycle. The freedom of life on the open road. But first I had to learn to ride. Back then, stabilisers were fitted to the back of the bicycle—safety wheels to ensure I didn't fall over as I learned to balance. I could depend on them, no need for balance, I could get on with speed and freedom.

In time, the stabilisers were only really necessary at the beginning of the ride. Setting off, and at a slow speed, I was wobbly, all over the place. As I built up speed, my confidence grew as I maintained balance. There was, however, a flaw in this. A false security in my confidence. When it came time for the stabilisers to be removed, I still had not figured out the balance thing at all. That took an adult holding on to the seat and running behind me until I'd gathered sufficient speed to provide that balance.

Those safety wheels created a habit that I had to unlearn to truly learn to ride. For the freedom I sought, I had to give up everything I had learned.

---

[29] Scott M Peck (1990), *The Road Less Travelled*.

Life in the 21st century has created a similar effect; when we are truly able to see the opportunities that self-belief delivers, we must unlearn everything life has thrown at us, and that is why this new self-belief will very likely feel like an imbalance. This is the test that we have so often failed in the past. Maybe you began to ask the deep questions about 'where you came from' and the answer wasn't forthcoming. Maybe you chose to be the one to break the generational cycles, but it caused heartache and arguments; you gave up. Maybe you recognised that your world was deeper than monetary wealth but felt uncomfortable giving words to those feelings just in case you lost some friendships. Maybe that habit or addiction was just too hard to break. These were all the signs that you were on the path towards balance—true balance—but the 21st century developed world said no.

If you have taken the time to read this far, you will have become aware of the many of the challenges that have beaten you in the past. You should now have a deeper understanding of why they are so powerful. First up, feel no shame that there is still work to do; this is your life's work. Be proud that you are facing these challenges once again.

Do the exercises in this book. Read more deeply through the areas that challenge you most and 'lean in' to every one of them. Every day, move towards your new self with a deeper self-belief. Move towards the challenges, little by little you will overcome them. You are in the thermal; it is the whirlwind that removes all the 'baggage' that had you unbalanced. As you climb higher through the storm, you will begin to feel lighter. You will see with greater clarity, and you will sense that balance returning.

For some of us, we may never have felt 'balance' before. But for all of us, it will feel right. You will see the difference in the mirror. Your acquaintances will notice, and in some cases, your acquaintances will change. You will awaken with a sense of calm.

Nowadays, balance bikes are all the rage. Toddlers zooming around on bicycles with no pedals but learning the most important skill of riding—the skill of balance. We will return to this later as we learn how to share our Self-Belief and Belonging with the rest of humanity.

For now, congratulations, for through an exploration of what Being Unreasonable means (and what it is not) you have found the prize. You have found your balance through self-belief. With that balance, it is now time to find where you truly belong.

Belonging in the World

The coldest shower.

If you are ever invited on a Darling camping holiday, please, for your own sanity, politely decline. That your presence had been requested at the most sacred of events clearly means you are much loved but really: DECLINE! Don't get me wrong, Darling holidays are such fun with exciting adventures and many local delicacies to enjoy, not to mention the games nights and pretzel poker evenings. Unless of course, you are one of those who seek moist misery in your leisure time, despite all the frivolity that may entice you to join us, the reason for your polite 'no thanks' is the weather.

I had been watching the rock for the last six hours. I had said that should the river water envelope the rock, we would move the tent to higher ground. It had rained straight for three days. The flood defences built on the other side of the river were adding to my consternation. Of course, the concrete-protected youth hostel would survive, but what of those of us on the riparian campsite opposite?

Finally, there was no other option: it was time to move. The kids were sequestered at the café with snacks, being minded by four Kiwi extreme sportsmen who were equally pissed off with the inclement weather, and we began the task of moving. A few hours later, the banks broke, not only at the campsite but along the entire Lauterbrunnen valley, Switzerland. The flood, during that summer, wiped out the whole railway line from Interlaken up to the village, and power was out for three more days. The debris from the flood closed the main highway between Lucerne and Berne. And still, it rained. Gardens were washed out, and homes and restaurants were destroyed. At one interlude in the biblical deluge, we took a drive up the valley and watched, jaws agape, as what looked like the entire mountain collapse high above and destroy the road less than 200 metres ahead—we retreated to the campsite and our tent.

We had food and plenty of water, and we had books and games to play but as the days went on, we were beginning to get a bit stinky. No power meant no heated showers. The water from the campsite was drawn through a pipe fed by the Stubbach Waterfall, which in turn is fed by the glaciers and snow melt from high on the Schilthorn mountain. In short, the water leaving the showerhead had a temperature of approximately Absolute Zero! It was, however, time to introduce the Darling children to cold showers.

As a coach, I often take a cold shower and suggest Unstoppable Force clients might do the same. Cold showers are good for us for a variety of reasons, including their ability to improve our physical and mental health and they can increase our alertness and energy levels by stimulating the release of endorphins and boosting our circulation. This can help us feel more awake and focused throughout the day, improving our productivity and overall sense of wellbeing.

Cold showers can also have a positive impact on our immune system, as they help increase the production of white blood cells, which are responsible for fighting off infections and diseases. This can help reduce the risk of illness and improve our overall health.

In addition to their physical benefits, cold showers can also improve our mental health by reducing stress and anxiety. The shock of cold water can activate our parasympathetic nervous system, which helps promote relaxation and reduces feelings of stress and tension.

Finally, cold showers can also improve our skin and hair health by closing our pores and preventing the loss of natural oils, which can help keep our skin and hair moisturised and healthy. This is all well and good but—ever tried getting your kids to do it …

Standing in the shower cubicle, I made my first mistake: I put out my hand to test the water— immediate frost bite! I now had to convince myself that this was still a good idea. There was no escaping it; I had to take the plunge and, to the sound of every expletive in my extensive repertoire, probably heard as far away as Geneva—I did. Now, cleansed of days of grime and feeling quite pleased with myself—how 'nails' am I—I began to coerce my son to attempt the same.

Less than an hour after my expletive laden shower, and after nearly a week of rain, power was restored and my family, to this day, remind me of my sadistic nature and poor timing.

At the extremes, human beings will react. My response to the freezing shower water was to shout my head off and commit to washing as quickly as possible, knowing that the water may be uncomfortable, but it wasn't going to do me any harm. If I had stepped into a stream of boiling water, my natural response would be to jump straight back out—probably with a similar chain of expletives—knowing that boiling water would cause lasting pain and injury.

Have you ever stood in a shower, enjoying the feeling of that water cascading over your skin? I've heard it described as a warm hug, often we will go so far as to wrap our arms around our bodies to extend that feeling of love. After a while, the water feels less warm. As we are not quite ready to give up on that feeling, we turn the temperature up a notch. After a few minutes, we do it all again. Finally, we turn the water off, either because someone else is shouting to use the bathroom, we can no longer see due to all the steam, or simply because we have exhausted the hot water supply. We see our skin is bright red and we feel sweat run down our back. The temperature of the water, that felt so comforting as we left the shower, was actually doing us damage—we had injured ourselves.

We act in the extremes; we don't notice incremental changes.

Be Kind; Stay at Home

A lone figure pushed open the door of the Duomo di Milano. As the door opened, the thin beam of light revealed the unsettled dust of a near-empty cathedral. The construction of this mighty edifice started in the year 1386, although it was only (finally) declared complete in 1965. It is larger than the Basilica of San Pietro in the Vatican City with a capacity for 40,000 worshippers, in April 2020, it was empty. The lone figure of Andrea Bocelli walked across the deserted Piazza del Duomo towards a single microphone.[30] As the haunting words and melody of *Amazing Grace* echoed around the piazza, the visual backdrop displayed cities across Earth—and all were empty. No one was in sight; all were at home due to the global lockdown caused by COVID-19. The world was conforming.

It is likely we need to return to the period 1939-1944 to find another period of global conformity. On this occasion, the Second World War engulfed Earth and everyone was engaged in the 'Total War'.

Total war is a military strategy that involves using all available resources and tactics to defeat an enemy. This type of warfare is characterised by a complete mobilisation of a country's economy, society, and military to achieve victory, with no restrictions on the use of force or targeting of civilians. It is a brutal and devastating strategy that aims to destroy an enemy completely. While it can be effective in achieving military victory, it comes at a high cost in terms of human lives and societal devastation.

In 1914, thousands of young men queued outside recruitment offices across the UK, some even willing to lie about their age, in order to become a part of the great adventure of World War One. Even when it became clear that the 'War to end all Wars' was getting bogged down in the trenches and attrition of Northern France, still they queued. Desperate to conform, and the same happened across the British Commonwealth and the United States.

Don't get me wrong, in these three examples, the reason for conformity was the collective good. We were keeping one another safe from a threat we didn't fully understand whether it was a virus, a tyrant bent on world domination, or the aftermath of a drive-by shooting in downtown Sarajevo that resulted in the end of some of the great European Empires of the 1800s.

---

[30] Andreas Bocelli (2020), *Amazing Grace*, https://www.youtube.com/watch?v=bpXwOSHTwsY

There is, however, a challenge with conformity—human beings don't like it for any length of time. As the threat, real or otherwise, diminishes or as understanding grows, we feel the need to stand up for our rights. In our rights, we find belonging. How else might we find conservative Christians, far-right groups, nurses and midwives, and environmentalists join forces to condemn government decisions?

At times of mass uncertainty, humanity will conform due to fear or for 'the greater good', and some will then claim rights over responsibility. This results in that conformity beginning to break down and, as the last example shows, often in a heated, illogical, and aggressive manner.

However, there is another type of conformity that, on a daily basis, saps our very uniqueness. It's called 'fitting in'—an acceptance of incremental change.

We spend our lives 'fitting in' and that is often the seat of our anxieties—not being who we actually are because we are herded by society. This is why one of the first exercises that any Unstoppable Force student completes is 'The 16 Personalities Quiz'. You can complete it by going to this link: **https://www.16personalities.com/free-personality-test.**

Based on the Myers-Briggs Personality Type Indicator, this quiz is a great starting point to get to know new members of the *Unstoppable* community. It is often the first time that people have either completed a personality quiz or had a conversation about the results. For the most part, students are surprised at how accurate the result is, and where they first disagree, a wee bit of introspection causes a realisation that 'fitting in' had caused them to forget that part of themselves.

During one of his visits home, I suggested to our son that he complete the personality quiz. At the time, he was going through a tough time in the restaurant industry. Not only was there extreme undermanning across the country, but he was working in one of New Zealand's top luxury lodges which brings pressure all of its own. On completing the quiz, and brain-storming the results (Logicians do that), he found a new sense of calm that has remained with him. He realised that many of his strengths were the very things that 'fitting in' has caused him to ignore. He, along with many Unstoppable Force students, are able to find others to 'belong with' and, in many cases realise that a deeper understanding of ourselves removes much of the need to fit in. By knowing who we are, we become comfortable in our own skin.

How else can we find that comfort? We can look back into our individual past and realise we have always belonged to something greater.

A Path to Belonging

A few years ago, I had been reflecting on the loss of my father in 1982. It was a result of a question I was asked on the publication of my first book, *Lead through Life*. Why did I write it? There were, and remain, many answers to that question, but one of them was to ensure that my children had a record of a part of me. This response had resulted in a realisation that I knew very little about my ancestors—especially on my father's side of the family. And time was potentially running out as there only remained one member of that generation of my family. Fortunately, my aunt was very gracious with her time and knowledge and was able to share some stories.

My father was born into a loving, warm family and was brought up with good Christian ethics, though they only went to church for christenings, weddings, and funerals. My grandmother was the 'boss' of the family and in post-war Britain, she did most things around the house, gardening, decorating, you name it she did it. To make ends meet, she also worked part-time as a debt collector for a loan company, collecting money from her customers (that was how they did it before credit cards came along).

My grandfather had various jobs, he started as a cinema manager but as cinemas started closing down, he went through many different occupations, driving a baker's van, a chauffeur, working in a garage. In the end, he landed a role as a cinema manager, the career he truly loved. He was due to start on the next Monday, but he died on that Sunday night.

In the generation before my grandparents, only three generations ago, the memories have become clouded. My great-grandfather was one of three brothers. When their parents died, one inherited the house, one got the money, and my great-grandfather inherited the furniture removal business. In a sad twist of fate, he did not upgrade his tools of trade from horses to an internal combustion engine quickly enough and the business went bankrupt. The brother who inherited the money went on to start Vernon's Pools—an early version of the football pools, based on predicting the outcome of football matches taking place in the coming week.

In three paragraphs, I have summed up the collective knowledge of my paternal ancestry but even these discoveries have provided me with a 'grounding', a belonging that removes many of the fears of loneliness that I endured in my younger days.

Imagine a world where we are taught about the importance of ancestry, where the first question is not, What do you do but, Where are you from? I was first introduced to this idea when we arrived in New Zealand. Actually, it is more than an idea, as Whakapapa, as it is named, is a central concept in Māori culture and refers to the genealogy or ancestral lineage of an individual or a community. For Māori, Whakapapa is more than just a record of one's ancestors; it is a living connection to the past, present, and future, a source of identity, and a guide to behaviour and social norms.

One reason why Whakapapa and ancestry are so important to Māori is that they provide a sense of belonging and connection to one's roots. For Māori, the concept of Whanaungatanga (kinship) is paramount, and knowing one's Whakapapa helps individuals understand their place in the wider community and the world. Whakapapa is seen as a sacred link between the physical and spiritual worlds, and it is believed that one's ancestors continue to guide and protect one throughout their life. The knowledge of one's ancestors and their actions provide a blueprint for how to live a good and meaningful life, and it helps individuals understand their roles and responsibilities within their Whanau (extended family) and Hapu (sub-tribe). For example, if a person knows that their ancestors were renowned for their hospitality, they may feel a greater sense of obligation to welcome and care for visitors in their own home.

Whakapapa is crucial to the maintenance and transmission of the Māori language and culture. Many Māori words and phrases are rooted in the names of ancestors or places, and understanding one's Whakapapa is essential to fully grasp the meaning of many Māori traditions and customs. By passing on Whakapapa and genealogical knowledge to future generations, Māori ensure that their cultural identity and values are preserved and celebrated.

Under New Zealand law, Māori have specific rights and privileges based on their status as indigenous peoples, and knowledge of one's Whakapapa is often used to determine eligibility for these rights. For example, to claim ancestral land or fishing rights, individuals must be able to demonstrate a direct link to the land or resource through their Whakapapa. Through the knowledge of their Whakapapa, Māori connect with their past, present, and future, and maintain a strong sense of cultural identity and tradition.

In researching this question on my radio show—*The Resilient Show* which aired in New Zealand from 2020-2022—I was fortunate to interview two amazing human beings who have embraced this culture. In both cases, despite being born into the Māori culture of New Zealand, it took them many years to embark on that journey of discovery, partly because, throughout their childhood, the very idea of indigenous beliefs and concepts having any place in a modern society was silenced, often with physical violence.

Here are both of their stories.

Dane Robertson (in his words)

I've got nine brothers and sisters. They're all half brothers and sisters; when my mother and father met, they already had children. My dad had had four children before me, three sons and a daughter, and then he had me when he met my mum. My mom had two sons before she met my dad, and then two daughters, and two daughters and a son after me to different fathers. My mother and father remained married until he died when I was sixteen.

Theirs was a very tumultuous relationship, very turbulent, very violent, very angry. And so, I grew up with the knowledge that I had a lot of siblings even though I connected with some of my father's children, two of them died before I was born and the other two were never really in my life. I became closer to my mother's side of the family, as they were always around with the exception of one brother who was adopted out. It was a very, very, complicated environment.

Up until my awakening or personal reflection journey, I was pretty unconscious—just drifting through life. I was a person who was not really living up to the potential of what I innately believed was possible. I was the type of person who always sought validation in some way, whether it be through external validation from another person or validation through friendship groups. Really, I was looking outside of myself and not really taking accountability for myself. Not really having a deep desire to grow as an individual. But also, pretty unaware of who I actually was and how I arrived at this place in my life. Those thoughts have only come about over the last few years.

The type of person that I am now is a person who is always trying to understand more about who I am. How my thoughts create perspectives and knowledge, and I try to question a lot more. I don't think the Dane

Robertson, who is part of the past, really questioned anything, because he didn't really have any aspirations to do more. Whereas now there are so many aspirations and so many dreams and visions of what Dane Robertson now wants in his life. I actively question the types of things that are around me, within me and outside of me and I try to look for the answers. So much more than the old me just drifting through without anything.

The Māori part of me is always knocking on the door, it's always kind of there. I remember a conversation that I had about seven years ago, with my auntie and uncle, while we were sitting around a table. Uncle was a part of the group who took the Māori language petition to the steps of the New Zealand Parliament at Wellington fifty years ago, and he's been a big influence in my life; he's been a figurehead. Anyway, I was sitting at a table with my then girlfriend, now wife, Libby, and my uncle was talking to his grandchildren … in Māori. I remember sitting there, because I didn't speak any Māori at that stage, thinking to myself, *Man, I feel so dumb. I feel as though I should know this, but I just haven't taken the opportunity to learn.* In that moment, I felt that opportunity knocking on the door. It's always there. It's always inviting you in but it's our responsibility to really walk in and take that invite.

I felt that was one of the moments where I was at a beginning, ready to accept that invite. I'm going to take that first step and just really try and better myself. From then on, I started to learn the language. But with learning the language, also comes learning the history; it's part and parcel. It's just the way that it works in order to understand the depth of what words actually mean. It's important to understand where those words came from, how they were used, why they were used, and in what context. And so that initial journey helped me to understand, more deeply, the world that it was a part of.

This searching also led me to question my relationship with alcohol as I really got going into a real self-development journey without the social crux of alcohol in my life. There was a real moment in time that was influential. That moment was influential in my new existence.

The next step was to understand my lineage. On my Māori side, I've been able to trace back to the experiences of particular people that have helped influence the way that I am now. My grandparents, my grandfather in particular, he was someone who spoke Māori, but he was encouraged by our society, at that time, that we shouldn't be speaking Māori at all, we should only be speaking English. English was the way forward—only speak English. And so, he encouraged that in his children—my mother and her siblings. That same indoctrination was ingrained in them growing up, which flowed onto me. It is interesting to reflect upon the decisions made by our grandparents, and our great grandparents on the back of colonialisation and how society has changed perspectives; it forced a particular belief or ideal and they capitulated. That was one thing that I had to come to terms with. I don't want to say I've ever arrived at a particular philosophy but my philosophy, at the moment, is that they were influenced; not forcefully, but they were influenced to consider that English was going to be the way forward.

On my Scottish and Australian side, I was able to find just bits and pieces of fragments of stories about how my great-grandparents or grandparents were married off to one another. I'm fascinated by the way people lived in the 1900s and the late 1800s. The way things were different helps us to gain a bit more understanding and knowledge of the ways that they thought back in those times. I haven't done too much journeying into my Scottish and Australian side, but I know that that's coming in the future, and is something I look forward to.

I have a philosophy that it's important to know where you come from in order to know where you want to go. I believe that having a solid understanding in that—and it doesn't even have to be in depth; it can just be learning and knowing about your parents, grandparents, great grandparents—can give you a greater sense of grounding, and a greater sense of personal stability. Then you understand what people have gone through in order for you to be here.

From that, I think your perspective changes that it's not just about you anymore. It becomes about a greater purpose; you've got all of these people in your life who were actually a part of your life… and their DNA runs through you. It's such a powerful thing to really understand that you're greater than just your mother, father, brother, and sister. I think it's important to know you've got cousins, you've got aunties, uncles, you've got great uncles, you've got a whole story of how your grandparents came to this land through all these different stories. Having those stories can really bring a powerful sense of identity. That's what a lot of people are lacking; is the sense of individuality, identity, and security in themselves. For me, that's been a huge awakening.

I enjoy being alone, I'm comfortable being in my own energy and my own space. And I've only been able to do that by working through everything that I believe that I needed to work through in order to get to that space. A lot of people can't be alone with their thoughts as it brings up too much that they don't want to deal with. Yet, I enjoy being alone and I enjoy solitude even though I have more family members, more connection now.

I believe 100% that I'm a very spiritual person and that I'm not alone in the sense that I have ancestors who are watching over me. From an indigenous cultural outlook, it's a shared perspective. I have the belief that it's not just me walking through this life, it is the journeys, the thoughts, the perspectives, the feelings, and the emotions of my ancestors, which flow through me, and I can connect with them. I can still ask them for guidance and help and I am a lot more comfortable with that now. I think understanding where you come from and allowing that to ground you is one of the aspects of not feeling alone. We never have been and never will be. That's a very powerful thing to help bring stability and groundedness to people.

I was always the type of person to try and fit in. I didn't feel like I ever belonged anywhere. I've always felt I've been a multifaceted and different type of person. I've never really just fitted into the mould of being a man who only likes cars or only likes hunting and fishing; I've never been that type of person. I never associated myself with groups. I always felt on the outside. Being half-Māori/half Pakeha (white European). I had a friend group that was Pakeha, and I felt on the outside—felt like the brown boy in the mix. In the Māori group, I felt like I was the white dude in the group. I never really felt a part of either. Going through this journey, I've become comfortable with the fact that I don't have to fit into any groups. I feel a lot more comfortable knowing that I can have friends from any background, and that's okay.

It also means I've never had a 'best friend'. I've never had a core group of friends who have shared my life. A part of that makes me a little bit sad. But I think one thing that's helped me to overcome that, is that knowledge that I actually like, a lot of different things. And being okay with that has allowed me to realise that I don't need a group. All I need is one or two people with whom I can really connect. Fortunately, one of them is Libby, my wife. We get along extremely well, and I am so thankful and fortunate for that. I could share every single moment of every single day with her and not feel as if I was missing out.

The biggest way that my journey to belonging has changed my relationship with Libby is by allowing me to know who and what I stand for. It has developed a sense of stability between us, and I believe that in a relationship, a male or masculine energy typically provides the stability for the female or the feminine energy to flow in the yin-yang energy style. By going through this journey and understanding who I am with all my strengths and my weaknesses, all the hidden quirks of my personality traits, and understanding them with greater efficiency and greater awareness, has allowed me to have that stability of knowing what I bring to the table. Libby is the flag and I am the flagpole. Individually, we can both exist and be successful. Belonging together, we become truly *Unstoppable*.

Nick Manarangi (in his words)

I have an admiration for the 'old me' in some respects because 'he' didn't really think too much, which was his downfall. He was 'flying by the seat of his pants' you could drop him anywhere: jungles, cities, other places, and he would be fine because he didn't know what he didn't know. He hadn't been tainted by the experience. That's a double-edged sword, right? The older we get, the wiser we get, and the older we become, the more we overthink. When I was younger, I just 'smashed the door down', I was a go-get-it, type of person.

That was me when I left New Zealand. To understand why I left along with 1000s more like me, and I believe to understand what's playing out at the moment with the young ones fleeing overseas, we need to return to the 1990s. I had no idea what was going on politically, but the vibe around me and my friends at my age was, Let's get the hell out! The brand name for us was, the Brain Drain. I was part of that whole, "Let's get out of here. Last one out, turn the lights off. This country is going nowhere." It was all doom and gloom.

I didn't actually get away till the early 2000s, until I saved up some money to get out of New Zealand and to go to Sydney. I had a lot of friends over there and the whole idea was to save up that money to eventually get to London. We all imagined London as a paradise where the roads were paved with gold, the land of milk and honey. What my little stint in Sydney showed me was there's a lot more going on over in Sydney than there is in Auckland.

In Auckland, I was in a job that I hated, my friends were in jobs that they hated. Our hourly rates were low. I can't even remember how much it was, but there was never enough money. There was never enough money in the week for me to get by and have the life I wanted. At that stage, there was nowhere near enough money to go partying, buy a nicer car, and have disposable income. That was what Australia afforded us when we landed there, we were, like: "Oh, my God, we've got all this money!" And that set me up to be in a bigger city and be around other people. Live at a faster pace with a lot more disposable income, and kind of prepared me for when I got into London. Then, when I got into London, that was like, "Holy hell!"

I lived in Sydney for two years. I was at the point of thinking I could actually live there forever. My thoughts: *The weather's good, the money's good and I've got some friends*. But I stuck to my guns as I convinced myself, *If I don't go now, I'll probably end up staying*. I was even thinking about buying furniture and a TV and settling down. I remember seeing a couch in the window of a furniture store and thinking, *That's a really nice couch*. My next thought, *Oh, no! I'm turning middle-aged*. So, I got on an aeroplane and headed off to 'The Big Smoke'.

I spent one month around Thailand and sometime in Dubai, and then, I ended up in London after that. When I arrived in England, it was freezing cold; I had come from Thailand and Dubai, both of which had been absolutely boiling at 45 degrees, every day. When I got into London, it probably was only about 10 degrees, but it felt negative 30 degrees. And it was grey.

At my age, arriving from Thailand and drinking every day; to Dubai, not drinking at all. And then being dropped into London and getting back onto that partying vibe, the socialising, and being introduced to a huge network of friends, finally, it felt like I was a part of something. I was part of the crew. A crew. I belonged in the crew.

My first job was selling; my whole career was in advertising sales. I was contract publishing to an advertising media company in London. Thinking back now, the differences between our office culture in Sydney, and in the UK, it was such a contrast. Sydney was a positive kind of vibe with people chatting with each other; at lunch we'd all go to the curry house and bring back our curries and sit around in the office. But that just wasn't a thing in the London office. In London, I sat next to somebody, I said hello to them in the morning and that was pretty much all I'd get all day. It was the same for the duration that I was there. I didn't last long at this company, maybe two and a half months. I thought it was just that first office but apparently, 'chatting' just wasn't the 'London' thing to do. That lasted for about ten years, and in that time, I met my wife, and we had kids.

We'd been living a certain lifestyle, but when the kids came along, obviously, that life changed. The little boxy one-bedroom place where we lived wasn't cutting it. So, we paid a little bit more for a two-bedroom place with a little garden at the back, which was actually quite rare for a lot of my friends. After my wife had been together for eight years, we decided it might be time to change it up and head out to New Zealand.

We got back to New Zealand in the summer and our lifestyle was similar to our London experience but then, as everybody who's come back from a long stint overseas will probably agree, there are many differences. I soon realised, within the first year, that I wasn't being myself. I'd lived overseas, and as chameleons, some people adapt and change the way they think and even change the way they speak. Being in sales, using my voice to convince someone to buy something is my number one weapon, the number one asset I've got. So, the mannerisms I had developed over ten years overseas—now that I was back in NZ—had to all change. I had to bury everything in the way I communicated with people. I had to really find out who I was, to be my true self.

And that was the beginning of my real Māori journey.

When you embark upon a Te Reo—a Māori—journey, it doesn't matter what nationality you are from, one of the first things we do when meeting someone is that we introduce ourselves and this is not like the Western world does, for instance, a simple, my name is Nick. A Māori greeting is along the lines:

Nō Hokianga ahau, i te taha o toku mama, he uri no Hokianga, ko Ngāpuhi, Te Rarawa, Ngāti Kahu me Ngāti Whatua.

I am a descendant of my mother's side from the town of Hokianga. I'm a descendant of the tribe of Ngāpuhi; one of the largest Māori tribal groups in New Zealand, located in the northern part of the North Island. It has a significant historical and cultural presence in the region, particularly in the area around the Bay of Islands. I am also a descendant of Te Rarawa another Māori tribal group based in the far north of the North Island, primarily in the region known as Te Hiku o te Ika (the tail of the fish). Te Rarawa has ancestral connections to the land, and their tribal territory extends from the Hokianga Harbour to Cape Reinga. They have a rich cultural heritage and continue to play an important role in the region. To finish my lineage, I am also from Ngāti Kahu and Ngāti Whatua.

On my father's side, I'm a descendant of Rarotonga, as well as China, as well as Ireland. I also discovered some fascinating ancestors. William Horde was from a wealthy family in Virginia, USA. He was a whaler that came down to New Zealand and he decided not to jump back on the boat home. He married a very high-ranking chief's daughter in Northland.

By going on this journey, I've actually gained a lot more confidence. Because I now know where I'm from. I always tell people if it's good enough for royalty to understand 1,000 years of genealogy—and Princes William or Harry could probably recite all their bloodline back—it's good enough for everybody else. It's just given me so much confidence, and now, I'm standing on the shoulders of those guys who went to war, started a family, and created my past. It's a humbling experience to know where I've come from. I hope that, as more people undertake these journeys of discovery, it will make us all more humble. If more of us went on this journey, there is an opportunity for New Zealand to grow and heal as a nation.

Our ability to know ourselves gives us the confidence to be our true selves. There can't be anything better than all of us understanding our true uniqueness in the world. Of course, there is likely to be trauma as we begin to understand what our history actually was, rather than the narrative of the victor. But if we lean into that trauma, then we come through the other side of it as stronger individuals, stronger communities, and stronger as a nation. Everyone across the country celebrates their heritage but recognises that we must grow together.

*

These are three very different journeys of three men seeking to find belonging. My drive to take my journey was due to the threat of losing access to my family history. For Dane, it was a recognition that his smorgasbord of bloodlines had created so much uncertainty in his own understanding of who he was that he needed to begin to unpack his history. And it took Nick a decade-long road trip to realise that everything he was seeking was deep within his DNA and himself.

In all three cases, the answer we were all seeking, lay deep within us. It is the same for all of us. However, we must commit to the journey so that we can truly find ourselves. Our greatest treasure lies where we all fear to look; deep within. Our uniqueness is the result of the confluence of our bloodlines. We no longer need to fit in, we already belong. When we realise that, we release the confidence to become our true selves. The confidence to release our Unreasonableness; to become *Unstoppable*.

Part 2: Raise the Standard

Turn and Face 'the BUT'

It's Not Big Enough is an unpublished poem by *Unstoppable* student, Nora Kavi.

> *One day you may ask*
>
> *It's impossible to fly*
>
> *If your why doesn't make you cry*
>
> *How can we strive*
>
> *Or feel alive if we*
>
> *Don't ask why*
>
> *It's a high when*
>
> *We know why*
>
> *We thrive and fly.*

That Deep Dive

Nora Kavi was attending one of my Unstoppable Force workshops. Nora is a senior charge nurse who attended the workshop to learn new strategies to support her in leading highly skilled medical professionals in an under-resourced healthcare system. She had heard me quote a friend of mine who once said to me, "If your WHY doesn't make you cry, it's not big enough." I've long gotten used to workshop attendees taking notes or doodling, but I could see that Nora was deeply focused on her workbook. What resulted in her focused work was the poem above. Take time to re-read the words, this is what it takes to become truly *Unstoppable*. Our WHY is so big that nothing will stand in its way.

For most of us, we set goals that we know are achievable and, quite often we don't quite achieve the goal because we, really deep down, didn't care about it. We never really bought into the WHY. Even completing the goal is anti-climactic, as we are already looking for the next thing. What we are actually doing in setting and achieving these goals is doing a disservice to ourselves, our families, and our communities. We are playing with small goals in an attempt to silence our 'still small voice' that is constantly reminding us of the Unstoppableness we were born with. So, we can say, "Look at me, look at all these things I am achieving." Yet, in the silence of the night, as we drift off to sleep, we are still faced with a 'BUT'. That feeling that there is more inside, there is something bigger.

Most of us are frightened to face 'the BUT', however, when we do, we begin to see that path towards *Unstoppable*. We dream of changing the world for the better, of making life for our family and community 'better'. What 'better' actually means will be different for every one of us, and so it should be. It is that uniqueness that makes life exciting. That uniqueness is also why most of us wake up the following morning and live another day, fitting in, hiding our uniqueness the way we have always been taught. To be embarrassed by how *Unstoppable* we could become; if only.

When my mum was diagnosed with breast cancer, I decided to run the Edinburgh Marathon and raise money for a cancer charity. I set a challenge of running a sub-3-hour 40-minute marathon—and smashed the goal.

I had never been a great fan of running, unfortunately, as an Army physical training instructor once informed me—we can't very well waltz into combat. So, I 'embraced the suck' and learned to love running. But that marathon distance? Those training miles? Could it be done? This was more than just running; this would be a mind and body experience. Could I do it?

A few years later, I chose to run the Edinburgh marathon again—to lose weight, on this occasion. My time was slower because the interest wasn't there, the answer could only be to 'go large'. That internal drive to always seek more to prove to myself to know there is always more 'in the tank'. To prove that I still had the Unstoppable Force, even if the motivation was from within. To build that determination and show the world that we are all so much more than we give ourselves credit for. So, the following year, I entered the Jungfrau marathon in Switzerland. It is described as 'the most beautiful marathon in the world'. I cannot confirm that definition however, Liz who supported my efforts—drinking hot chocolate and eating cherry streusel, basking in the warmth of the late alpine summers— agreed with the organisers that it was indeed.

The start line for the Jungfrau marathon is in the centre of Interlaken, outside the historic Hotel Interlaken. Nestled in the breathtaking Swiss Alps, the hotel has a rich history dating back to its founding in the late 19th century. Established in 1868, this majestic hotel initially catered to affluent travellers seeking solace amidst the stunning alpine landscapes. Over the years, it became renowned for its unparalleled hospitality and luxurious amenities, attracting visitors from all corners of the world. Despite enduring the challenges of two World Wars and evolving travel trends, Hotel Interlaken maintains its commitment to providing a guest-centric experience, blending timeless elegance with modern comforts. Today, it stands as a cherished symbol of Swiss hospitality, offering a gateway to the enchanting beauty of Interlaken and its surroundings. A very different experience to the challenge the 800 racers had ahead of them. Over the standard marathon distance of 42.2 kms, the marathon climbs gently through the fields and farms of the Lauterbrunnen Valley to the alpine hamlet that gives the valley its name.

After passing the crowds of cake-eating, coffee-swilling spectators, the runners embark on the arduous journey from Lauterbrunnen to Kleine Scheidegg. This is an endeavour that demands both physical and mental fortitude. Setting foot on the path, every runner prepares to be tested by the unforgiving terrain that lies ahead. The initial ascent from Lauterbrunnen, with its steep and winding trails up the side of the glacier sculpted, U-shaped valley, leaves muscles burning and lungs gasping for precious oxygen. Pushing yourself further, the trail from Wengen offers little respite, presenting a relentless series of uphill climbs and treacherous rocky stretches. The weight of exhaustion bears down on weary legs, each step requiring a herculean effort.

Just when you think you've conquered the worst, the final stretch to Kleine Scheidegg awaits; it is a gruelling ascent that seems to defy gravity itself. Every muscle screams in protest as you trudge through the challenging, near vertical, terrain, your spirit pushed to its limits. This is now a purely mental struggle. When I am engaged in this level of challenge, it is the simple things that push me forward. I had seen images of this part of the marathon, a single file of tormented souls, struggling up this steep arete. I was now one of them. I was a part of something so much bigger than me. Humour is also an important aspect. Finding a man in full Scottish highland regalia, playing the bagpipes to keep us all moving, or a group of Alpine horn players keeping our morale upbeat. What right did I have to give up? I had no weight to carry, and these lunatics had hefted their 3.5 metre horns, up a mountain—get moving Darling!

The sense of accomplishment that awaits at the end of this wearisome odyssey, as runners gaze upon the majestic beauty of Kleine Scheidegg, nestled beneath the mighty Eigerwand, the North Wall of the Eiger, makes every ounce of fatigue fade away, replaced by a triumphant exhilaration … and a pint of beer as we cross the finish line (abruptly vomited up a few minutes later, in my case).

I ran that marathon two years in a row, treating the first attempt as a recce for the second year. In the second year, I knocked a whole hour of my time but … I was still left with … but. We enjoyed the rest of that weekend in the Swiss Alps, but my celebrations never lasted long. For me, it is always, *What is next?* Even this wasn't enough. I know I can push my body and mind to, and beyond, the edge, and these marathons proved this each time … BUT.

There is a risk here when we constantly push and succeed that we question what more is there. Why should I bother ... but this is a drift back to conformity. For me, I am always testing myself in different ways to see where I can challenge myself. It may not be physical extremes, it could be a new language, a complex recipe in the kitchen, or the next level of Sudoku! I once learned to play the trumpet in a month, when I say learned ... I could play the first six notes of the Imperial March from *Star Wars, The Empire Strikes Back*. (Four of those notes are the same). When we reach a plateau of success, try something new.

In our early years, our bodies taught us to do things incrementally; we crawl, we walk, we run. We read simple books before moving on to more complex texts. Society teaches us that goal setting should be incremental, school and county sporting events before the Olympics. Why not just 'go big' from the start? At the age of nine, my coach's son stated that he was going to be the first American to play in the NFL (American Football) and NBL (Basketball). The percentage chance of this actually happening is so low it might as well be zero—it's never been done before.

Setting so big a goal makes life really simple to achieve, when such a huge goal directs every activity you choose to do. If the activity is not on the path, a conscious choice is required. We grow into the person that the goal requires, and that growth is the rebirth of our Unstoppable Force.

I prefer to think of my Unstoppable Force as driving me towards a mission that is so big it might not be achieved in my lifetime. Of course, there will be milestones along the way, but each of those will be on the path to the success of the mission. In military terms, we can think of this using the following three words: Tactics, Operations, and Strategy.

Tactics are the small tasks and goals that we habitualise to move us towards our mission. For me, they might include early starts, daily exercise, journalling, meditation, monthly fasting, and time blocking for work.

Operations are the activities that shape the 3-month and 12-month periods. Right now, they include writing daily, building the brand of Unstoppable Force, and building the Unstoppable Force community.

Strategy is the multi-year activity that will ensure I remain on the path. I already know the subject of my next book, the plans beyond Unstoppable Force Mastermind are already forming but need the foundation of the current tactics and operations to come to fruition.

Every tactic, operation, and strategy begin with me and my mission. This means knowing who I am and what I stand for. We are all taught to fit in, and this stops us from investigating who and what we are. Fitting in stops us from asking 'why' we are and as such, we play small.

To be *Unstoppable* we must know what we stand for. If we stand for nothing, we'll fall for anything. How we are motivated? What is our purpose? Ever thought about your values? With clarity in values, purpose, and motivation, relationships will shift, and your 'tribe' will see you growing. You will feel the different energies of where you are trying to 'fit in' and where you truly belong.

Being *Unstoppable*, and living the Unstoppable life, might not feel right for you, right now, but please keep reading. If you read on and are still not convinced, that's okay, please go and live your life in peace and acceptance but be conscious when the moment arrives. For those who are looking for ways to experience giving your all … Keep reading.

Just Sign Here

And with that signature, my life was no longer my own.

A group of us stood on the hallowed carpet beneath the dome of the Royal Air Force (RAF) College at Cranwell in Lincolnshire. We were given one last chance to change our minds and hop back on the transport to the railway station. All of us declined. And so, we all solemnly voiced our oath of allegiance to Her Majesty Queen Elizabeth II and signed a document that entered us into military service. We would not step back on that carpet until the day we marched up the College steps as Commissioned Officers.

We were all so excited. Some of us had only recently finished school, and even shaving daily was a new experience. Others had been through university and met the experience with a level of false confidence. Yet more already had years of service behind them and were challenging themselves to the Commissioning course. Whatever our backgrounds, we stood smartly awaiting our turn. The sunlight shone through the cupola hundreds of feet above our heads, highlighting the dust particles in the air. There was a hint of warmth and familiarity in the air. The blue carpet emanated a subtle, comforting scent, reminiscent of a blend of freshly dried linen and a touch of aged wood. A gentle earthiness to it, like a faint whiff of a meadow after a light rain. The scent was unobtrusive, not overpowering, but simply hinted at the passage of time, the number of times this ceremony had taken place since the formation of the Royal Air Force in 1918. There was a cosy history of the space and the camaraderie. I don't remember the gravity of that moment or that signature, but I had signed up to a life of values and standards—a life of service. The values and standards of the Royal Air Force (RAF) were and remain:

- Respect: Promoting mutual respect and tolerance among all personnel, recognising and valuing the contribution of each individual, regardless of rank, background, or gender.
- Integrity: The foundation of the RAF's ethical behaviour. Personnel are expected to be honest, and trustworthy, and maintain the highest standards of professional and personal conduct.
- Service: The RAF is committed to serving the United Kingdom and its allies. All members dedicate themselves to the defence and security of the nation, showing loyalty, selflessness, and a willingness to put the needs of others before their own.

- Excellence: The RAF strives for excellence in everything it does, including maintenance of high operational standards, pursuing continuous improvement, and delivering outstanding performance in all aspects of its mission.

In addition to these core values, the RAF also maintains a set of standards and codes of conduct that cover areas such as discipline, appearance, fitness, and professionalism. These standards ensured consistency and discipline and made discipline very simple. We all had a standard, the same standard, to keep. Whether trainee officers, commissioned officers of any rank, or all the non-commissioned officers, we all knew where we stood. Failure to uphold those values and standards meant punishment and on occasion, time in jail. We all failed at times and the punishment reflected the 'crime'.

On transferring to the British Army, my values changed. Not out of choice! The RAF and the British Army fulfil different roles, and the values, while similar, are different. The values of the British Army are:

- Courage: Including both physical and moral courage. Soldiers are expected to have the bravery to face and overcome challenges, as well as the moral courage to do what is right even in difficult situations.

- Discipline: Soldiers are expected to maintain self-discipline and adhere to the regulations and orders given by their superiors. Discipline ensures the effective functioning of the military organisation.

- Respect for Others: Soldiers are expected to treat all individuals with dignity and respect, regardless of their rank, background, or gender. This value promotes teamwork, cohesion, and a positive working environment.

- Integrity: Soldiers are expected to demonstrate honesty, trustworthiness, and ethical behaviour, at all times. Maintaining the highest standards of personal and professional conduct is essential to uphold the integrity of the Army.

- Loyalty: Loyalty to the British Army, the Crown, and fellow soldiers is a crucial value. Soldiers are expected to be loyal to their unit, colleagues, and the mission, demonstrating commitment and dedication to the Army's objectives.
- Selfless Commitment: Selfless commitment refers to the willingness to put the needs of the Army and others before one's own. Soldiers are expected to show dedication, sacrifice, and a sense of duty in serving the nation and protecting its interests.

For over two decades, my life was simple. Uphold these values or face the consequences. As a senior officer, my role was not only to uphold the values but also to deal with those who failed. Our values created a community in which we all knew we could rely on one another. We lived in a world of clarity and direction, where people were authentic. Our collective values provided resilience and allowed us to build strong long-lasting relationships that supported lifelong emotional wellbeing. Those who stepped outside those boundaries too often were not welcomed back. Most of the time, the values and standards are self-policing, and only when the 'crime' is very severe does it make it up the Chain of Command. It is the power of the Mess system and military rank structure that keeps soldiers safe on the Battlefield. We stand shoulder to shoulder with our comrades, knowing we are fighting for the man or woman on our left and right and, just as importantly, they are fighting for us.

While both of our kids loved most aspects of being a part of the military community, at times, they really struggled with the rigidity of the values system. As I became more and more senior, and my roles provided greater responsibilities; these hung heavy for two teenagers discovering themselves under the glow and intensity of my work. I think the positives outweighed the negatives and they both now have high standards.

But all things come to an end and the day arrived when it was time to move on from my military life. I realised this while attending a Commissioning Parade at the Royal Military Academy, Sandhurst

(RMAS), and I turned my back on the steps of Old College, those same steps that I marched up as I transferred my commission to the Intelligence Corps. It was then that I set forth on my next adventure. I still look back fondly on my military career, but it was now time to look forward into the future, a future in which I could build my own values atop my military values and standards: What did I stand for? What were my values now? Were they different?

It took me over two years to establish my personal values. It has taken until the writing of this book, nearly ten years, to understand my standard. This has been deep and, sometimes, painful work, which is most people and businesses don't bother. When you engage in this work, be kind to yourself, and accept that it is not an overnight experience. Nor is it easy. Nor is this work ever completed; you will be tweaking it every day for the rest of your life. Even for those of us who have experienced a lifetime of the highest values; this is not easy stuff.

We all have some type of values and standards that guide our lives whether we are conscious of it or not. It is those values and standards that enable us to find out where we belong and those same values that allow us to recognise when we are fitting in. Our values and standards help us create friendships and fall in love, and they are the reason friendships and relationships end. It was values and standards that created the very first tribes and it is values and standards that cause war and conflict. This is why it is so important to establish what you stand for, and in knowing what you stand for you become *Unstoppable*.

What Do You Stand For?

How do you find out what you stand for?

Most of us drift through life unconscious of our values. We adhere to the values of our families, our communities, countries, and faith or belief system. There is nothing wrong with this except that we will never grow into our true *Unstoppable* futures. We should question those values; frequently.

In his book, *The Code of an Extraordinary Mind*, Vishen Lakhani uses the word, Brules (he invented it), to describe values and standards that we keep, 'just because', rather than actually taking time to see whether those Brules are really helping our growth and development or tying us to our past outdated selves.[31]

The definition of a Brule is—a Bullshit Rule. The first step to establishing our values is to review the values we have been living by up to now. We can all achieve this by asking one simple question: **Am I living my fullest, best life**?

If the answer is 'not yet' then it is time to review your values. When I was attempting to establish my values, I found it inspiring to read novels, watch movies, and listen to music. When I related to the character or song, I noted what values I was relating to. For my 40th birthday, Liz gave me tickets to see the musical, *Wicked*, in the West End in London. She had secured the best seats in the house, front row in the centre of the Dress Circle. I have always enjoyed a good musical but this one blew my mind. Based on the book by Frank L Baum, it is the pre-story of *The Witches of Oz* that makes Dorothy's journey to meet the Wizard so challenging. The last scene of the first half of the stage show involved the hero, Elphaba, lifting off the stage on her broomstick.

As she rose into the sky, singing the song, *Defying Gravity*, she stopped at exactly the level where we were sitting. The words of the song, *Defying Gravity*, are all about choosing not to accept the status quo. Through a life of bravery, tenacity, and enthusiasm, we can be whatever and whoever we choose to be. It took a few more years for me to establish bravery, tenacity, and enthusiasm, as three of my values, but as the emotion coursed through my body watching that green-skinned witch rise into the theatre, I knew what it would take to become *Unstoppable*.

My first three values are a vision of who I chose to be—they are future-focused. Do I achieve them every day? Sadly no, but I recite them

---

[31] Vishen Lakhani (2019), *The Code of an Extraordinary Mind*.

and journal on them every day and review each day, every evening, as I brush my teeth. I can say I move towards them every day.

Likewise, my other three values, to be an inspiration, to be honest, and to be present towards everyone I meet, require that I review my journey towards them, every day. I choose to have six values, the first three are more about how I choose to be and the second three how I choose to be perceived in the world. All six keep me future-focused and ensure that I am accountable, not just to me but also to everyone I meet.

The values of Unstoppable Force are different but closely aligned with my personal values as Unstoppable Force is more than just me.

Having values makes life simpler. Choosing friends and choosing where to work can all be based on the person you are growing into. In the workplace, just as in families, our values will reinforce all activity. We all remember the times, where we fell short of family values and spent time on the 'naughty step', equally some of us will have been to visit the HR department! Values make us accountable; people know what they get. Personally, we know when we are aligned with our future self and when we are not playing our *Unstoppable* self. Just like my coach's son, we can then choose to get back on the path towards our mission; or not.

To start, or review, your own values complete the Unstoppable Force Values Exercise. Use this link to receive downloads of worksheets mentioned throughout this book:

https://unstoppableforce.co.nz/worksheets/

Complete the exercise and take your new values out to play. It is unlikely that this first attempt will result in your final values, but you have started —most folks don't even get that far.

To Love and Be Loved

The day had started early, it was still dark as we left the house. It was now the other end of the day and, alone, it was dark again. I sat on the second stair, just behind our front door, in tears, having just informed my family of the news. On the drive home, I had stopped for fish and chips and washed that down with a couple of glasses of claret that had been oxidising in the kitchen. But it could be put off no longer; I had to tell the world the news. As I waited for the phone to be answered, I took a deep breath before announcing to the world for the very first time: I was a dad.

On that late July morning in 1997, our beautiful daughter, Rachel, was born, and in that moment life changed. I had a new purpose. Less than seventy-two hours previously, I had been commanding covert operations in Northern Bosnia Herzegovina. That was a purpose I had been trained and prepared for, but this one?!

We waste years of our lives asking, *What is my purpose?* Whether we disappear into a cave in the mountains, fasting and meditating, or use our lack of 'purpose' as an excuse for our drifting through life … I now have a view that it is all rubbish. We have purposes throughout our lives, and they are plain to see if we get out of our own way.

I am a son, husband, brother, and father. I have been a boy scout, a soldier, a spy, an officer, a businessman, and an entrepreneur. All those titles should convey a purpose. My 'job' in every one of those roles is to be the best I can be. As new purposes arrive, it is our responsibility to grow into those roles.

We all need to worry less about a lifelong purpose and instead lead a long life of purpose. Through a purposeful life, we will grow and discover a deeper purpose. In this way, whatever our role, we can have purpose, and live to the best of that purpose. We are an Unstoppable Force.

I have long held a view that humanity has but one purpose: to love and be loved. I know that sounds very bohemian, but what is wrong with that? Imagine a humanity where we all loved and felt loved. A world where that love started with the man (or woman) in the mirror. An exercise I often use with Unstoppable Force clients, and one I do every morning, is to look in the mirror and say, out loud, "I love you" to the reflection. Loving and being loved requires us to live our best life, to live to our values.

Some clients really struggle with this, at first; a life of trying to fit in can do that as they have been told, or feel, that they're not good enough. Unconsciously, they have drifted through life without taking responsibility for what they see as they brush their teeth or shave, and this breeds self-loathing. With repetition comes comfort, and sometimes, they begin to believe it. By believing that simple statement (of love), we grow into our purpose. By loving that reflection, we go that step further to be a better parent, lover, employee, or boss, and our purpose for that moment is further revealed; we are *Unstoppable*.

As I reflect on the days after Rachel's birth, and the birth of her wee brother, Andrew, two years later, this new purpose of being 'daddy' was revealed in every new task, and every task was done with love … How could it not be? I was Daddy. Over the last twenty-five years, I would love to report that every task of being a 'dad' has been done with love, but over time, those tasks became processes. I've always loved both our children, but it has only been in recent years that I have started to invest in every task with purpose.

Life in the 21st century has become very easy, very process-driven. The 'rat race' has become the norm. People drift, feeling hollow. We have been hoodwinked into believing that this is our lot. We watch as the media tells us 'the world is burning', we question our politicians and leaders as they tell us 'they (the politicians) are the only source of truth' and we wonder what is our point. Suicide rates are on the rise, mental health issues are on the rise, and we look with futility at humanity. Access to information is greater than it has ever been and that increase in available knowledge has only raised more and more questions. Uncertainty reigns, reinforced by a world screaming: WHAT IS YOUR PURPOSE? We look outwards for that purpose and retreat believing we are too small to make a difference.

But what a difference each of us can make if we are purposeful in every task we undertake. No longer do we see the most mundane task as a chore but an opportunity to 'be'. Every task becomes an opportunity to be a little bit more *Unstoppable*.

To be the best you can be in everything you do by loving every person, including yourself, and allowing yourself the vulnerability to be loved is a simple statement so why do so many struggle with purpose? It is because you are disengaged, whether through the process or numbing yourself to your sense of inadequacy, you have made life tedious. The certainty you seek to cover your uncertainty has caused you to forget that humans thrive on variety. The uncertainty in the world is causing you to play small—you have stopped!

Renewing our sense of purpose, in every task, even the smallest can be the start of finding variety again. To reignite our purpose all we must do is change things up a bit. Cook something different or start a new hobby. Return to the Wealth Matrix and have a go at increasing one pillar of wealth—you will feel purposeful again. You will feel more energy. You will begin to look forward again. You will start seeking ways to be more purposeful in other parts of life, and the next step along your path shall be revealed. As your energy increases you will see further along your unique path and through living purposefully every day, we all become *Unstoppable*.

As your energy grows, others will see you in your new light. Opportunities will be revealed. You will meet new people; those whose energy reflects your own. Other relationships will be left by the wayside as they prefer to remain. You will feel a sense of belonging in this new tribe you are creating. This is your tribe, a place where you truly and unapologetically belong. No longer is it only you that is *Unstoppable*—your whole tribe is on the move.

A Word on Motivation

When you set out to become *Unstoppable*, even with the most audacious mission, there will be those days. Those days when the motivation is just not there. It is trite to say that those are the days when we must take massive action towards the mission—and that is true—but why do you have those days? In the early days, you are adjusting to a new standard, and you are simply resisting change. Hence the importance of that mission being truly aligned to your values and why you must be purposeful in all you do. But there are still those days. In his book, *Atomic Habits*, James Clear suggests that even making tiny moves is better than none at all.[32] Even if you don't want to do that gym session, complete some of the exercises, that will often lead you to completing the whole activity … you were sweaty already.

When I got back into running after a long break, my tiny action was to put on my sports gear and running shoes as soon as I got out of bed. After my meditation and journalling, I was all ready to run, so why not just get on with it? These hacks work, but becoming an Unstoppable Force requires us to understand motivation at a deeper level. Fortunately, there are only two sorts of motivation and once we know which one we are dealing with, we can act appropriately.

Short-term motivation comes from the excitement of a new activity, the first week of a gym membership, and a new relationship. As the word 'exciting' suggests, this motivation comes from without ourselves. It is extrinsic in nature—we need something or someone to make the activity feel worthwhile. Here are a few examples of extrinsic motivations:

---

[32] James Clear (2018), *Atomic Habits*.

Your job: the business owner provides you a salary to work a certain number of hours. You might remember how excited you were to land that new job and the gratitude you felt as you saw the first 'paycheck' arrive in your bank account. How long did that excitement and gratitude last?

Your gym membership: in that first 'free' month, you attended the gym diligently, soaked up the advice of the gym staff, and even felt a part of the community as you were welcomed every time you arrived. You were excited by the classes, the gym equipment, and even the smell of the body wash in the showers … but then the excitement wore off.

The new eating regime: a break from the monotony of the same meals every week. New flavours, and at the end of the first few weeks, you might even have dropped a few grams. But then those old flavours started calling, the excitement wore off, and you returned to the old habits.

One of the great things about extrinsic, short-term motivation is that our brains and bodies respond. Even the simple act of 'ticking off' an item on your 'to-do' list gives you a kick of dopamine—the feel-good chemical. Therefore, completing even the smallest of tasks feels good and often leads to doing even more. I'm not a great fan of short-term 'hacks' but as this is directly related to being an Unstoppable Force, I thought I'd let it through.

This extrinsic motivation sounds fairly damning but now we know that a motivation that comes from without ourselves is short-lived, we understand why our mission needs to be bigger than ourselves. We can also now use extrinsic motivation as a tool for those days when we are struggling.

Working with businesses and clients, I always ensure that they celebrate success—however small that success may feel—we must celebrate them. On those tougher days, use extrinsic motivations to get you through. Do something to celebrate completing that activity. During that celebration don't just celebrate surviving the day, also celebrate that you are *Unstoppable*, that you are moving towards your mission.

Celebrate that you opened your eyes this morning and that you have been gifted another day. That you were purposefully moving in the right direction. Remember, as an Unstoppable Force, you are playing big, and any move, however small, is still making a move in the right direction.

Our long-term motivation is what will achieve our mission. We have such enthusiasm for that mission that we will shape our lives to achieve it. The base of the word 'enthusiasm' is en thos—of God. It means that the drive we have for this activity comes from deep within us. This is intrinsic motivation. We don't need anyone or anything to drive this activity. We are doing it for ourselves or for something we deeply believe in.

My first Edinburgh marathon was completed with intrinsic motivation. I was running in that event to; prove to myself I could, and, to raise money for a charity. While the training was tough, the motivation was easy. My second time on the Edinburgh marathon was not as successful, I had already proven to myself I could, and there was no charity involvement.

Conversely, the first time I completed the Jungfrau marathon was really a reconnaissance mission for the following year. My intrinsic reason for my first attempt actually had nothing to do with the run; that week in the Swiss mountains was an opportunity to holistically prepare for my military command. The following year was a mix of intrinsic and extrinsic motivation. I still needed to prove to myself that I could improve my finish time, but the second time I was also running with a friend. We had trained together and held one another accountable for those months of training and during the event. Not only did I want to succeed, but I also wanted to see my running partner succeed.

Where is your accountability? It is that accountability that will see you achieve your mission and become truly *Unstoppable*. There will be times when you are the only person who will hold you accountable—this is your life, and we cannot expect even our loudest fans to always be there. But we can be smart and find help. I have an accountability group with whom I meet every week. We hold each other to a higher standard.

The Unstoppable Force Mastermind is a group of twelve high achievers who hold one another accountable throughout the year.

The concept of the Unstoppable Force Mastermind is based on my military career. Training and working in small teams, we lived shoulder-to-shoulder. Fighting for the man (or woman) on my left and right meant I was less concerned about my life—they had 'my back' just as I had theirs. We also problem solved together, a few brains rather than just one. My early experience in business showed me how powerful a similar experience could help business leaders.

You can easily start an accountability group of your own knowing that, as herd animals, we would rather let ourselves down than let our tribe down. Find other high performers and get together every week. We keep our group to four as it ensures that everyone gets appropriate attention during our call. Find people from different backgrounds with different skills as they will see your challenges through a different lens. For my Unstoppable Force Mastermind, I invite twelve individuals and businesses with different experiences and backgrounds. This is essential so that not only is there accountability, but there is also an acceleration as we learn at 12x the pace of an individual. You can find details of the Unstoppable Force Mastermind at the end of this book.

A mixture of short-term and long-term motivation will see you right. The bigger your mission, the more you will access your intrinsic, enthusiastic motivations. Extrinsic motivations will see you through the days when you lack momentum. An accountability group or mastermind will level the peaks and troughs of your journey but, in the end, it still lies with your enthusiasm.

Discipline

There will be days, we've all had them, when even the tiniest amount of motivation fails us. Maybe that extra glass of wine the night before, maybe the days, months, or years, where we feel we are getting nowhere.

There will be times when even your accountability group will be insufficient to haul your ass to the gym or your desk.

Worry not, there is still a solution to maintaining your new standard and living to your values. For most of humanity's history, it was thought that our brains were 'fixed' from birth; born stupid—too bad. Born a genius—the world is yours. Science is now showing that to be wrong. Our brains are malleable. Neural plasticity means that our brains create new neural pathways, and the great news is it only takes 30- 60 days.

This is exciting, as science is proving that we can be whatever we choose! All it takes is work. Once we have chosen our mission, all we need to do is work in that direction. If you want to be a writer, all you must do is write. If you want to be the best alpine skier in the world all you must do is practice. If we practice every day for 30-60 days, we create that habit. A new neural pathway is formed and the old one begins to break up. To accelerate the process, do the activity at the same time every day and raise your vibrations by bringing some fun to the process. You only have to be disciplined for that 1- 2 months period and before you know it you will want to do the activity more than you don't. This is the tool I used to get back into running; I ran every day for over fifty days. Now running is just one of those things I do.

There are now no excuses for achieving your big mission. If this is a confronting statement for you, just start. Just get started and the path will reveal itself. Our definition of work changes based on our thoughts, needs, and perspectives. Like running, conscious choices are needed to start, but the rewards are great when continued. Even for those struggling to get started.

Do Ethics Matter Anymore?

Even ethical issues disappear as we focus on our values and achieving that big mission. Whether it be called ANZAC Day, Memorial Day, or Remembrance Sunday, people from around the world set aside special days every year to commemorate our fallen. This may be very personal for families who have lost loved ones or for old soldiers; taking a few moments to sit in remembrance of a comrade who didn't come home.

But there should always be another side to our commemoration. It's an opportunity to reflect on what our values are, what our own personal 'rules of engagement' might be, and what rules of engagement we tolerate from those who lead us.

War is messy. It causes our young men and women to do what we are all told is wrong—to take another life. Some might say that, for this reason, warfare is unethical, however, the counter to that argument is armed conflict is nothing more than the extension of any country's foreign policy.

To go to war most countries will first attempt some form of diplomacy or form a coalition (in an attempt to prove they are the ones in the right). Having served in every major conflict over the last thirty years, I can attest that while messy, armed conflict passes a very high ethical bar. Following the bloody confrontations of the European wars in the 18th century, and aware of just how bloody they were, the Geneva Conventions were written. Having been updated on three occasions since, the Conventions are signed by most countries of the world and clearly set out the standard of what is, and what is not acceptable on the field of battle.

At the operational and tactical levels, these are written as Rules of Engagement (RoE) so every combatant and fighting unit knows how to fight. In the modern era, these RoE are rehearsed and trained so that all personnel know this before they arrive in-country. At the more specialist end of combat, we would rehearse every operation before leaving our operating base. Every operation is carefully considered by legal advisors at the International, national, and in-theatre levels to ensure that wars are fought ethically.

It all starts with a clear set of values and standards that are lived every single day from the moment we take the oath of allegiance until long after our last day of service. To not live these values and standards is where unethical activity begins.

Unlike the Armed Forces where such lived values and standards are clear, we can observe something of a 'values' vacuum in other areas of our social and political landscape. This is because we are constantly living in a reactionary way rather than taking time to think about what is right and correct. We make the soundbites without actually thinking about what we're saying.

Without clear Rules of Engagement, we are going to get things spectacularly wrong. We're seeing that in business, in government, and as a country. Recent allegations of bullying and clear examples of conflicts of interest within our political leadership in New Zealand seem to me to illustrate a values vacuum.

The leadership we see in any parliament is the leadership that will flow through our country, just as the leadership culture evident in any organisation is the leadership shown by the Chief Executive. The behaviour we tolerate in our political leaders is the behaviour we tolerate in wider society.

Too often, poor behaviour on the part of our elected representatives is minimised and tolerated. We see this again and again and it moves people away from believing in our democracy. Senior Members of Parliament claiming they were too busy to reflect on conflicts of interests seems to be a flavour of the month in New Zealand while 'Party-gate' in the UK and withholding classified documents in the US all point to elected representatives who are not being representative of the standards they speak of upholding. It also moves them away from thinking they too should be held to account if they act in a way that is not values-based.

Ethics are only an issue if you don't live up to your values. If you've done the values work and you've created a value-based business or organisation that lives by those values every day, then you aren't unlikely to have an ethics problem.

As a country, we need to ensure that those who represent us and create our culture of leadership at a national level are adequately prepared for the task. It's not enough to say I do personal development or, that you have a leadership coach. You need to have actually done the work to identify the value statements you can make about your business or organisation that everyone understands so that when you turn up for work, you and everyone else around you are conscious of those shared values all of the time. Then, when an ethical issue comes up, if there's any doubt, there's no doubt.

So, what is the leadership culture that we are tolerating as a nation? Does it honour those who have made the ultimate sacrifice on our behalf?

Shedding Our Old Skin

In our quest to becoming an Unstoppable Force, we are going to find that things and people drop away. My son mentioned to me, as he was embarking on one of his periods of growth, "This is going to get lonely, again, for a while."

He was bang-on. We had been in the United States for a few days, and we had both had the opportunity to be reminded, post-lockdowns, that there is a whole world out there. During that week, we had been exploring outside as well as inside. I don't think he quite realised what was actually beginning to manifest deep inside but, as you will read, he had begun to shape his 'why'. He was beginning to realise that, as his 'why' was so much bigger than him, as he changed, his environment was either going to change with him, or he would start looking for a new space.

Whether we realise it or not, living as an Unstoppable Force is an anathema to most. Drifting along with the crowd is the status quo. It provides a false certainty. When viewed this way, it seems obvious that those of us who have realised, or learned, that certainty is hidden deep within us and as such we can freely cast off the bowlines and set sail on a life of variety; very few will be able to join us on the journey.

As we look to manifest our long-term, massive mission, we will be questioned. Friends and family (especially) will cause us to doubt ourselves and, as they don't (can't) understand, they are likely to withdraw. Since I became an author, on the release of *Lead through Life*, to date, my family has bought two copies. At first, I was devastated that there was such little interest, but now I understand—they can't comprehend what I'm up to, and that is okay. But, just as my son said, "We've got to be prepared for it." This is the stepping-stone from 'fitting in' to finding where we are free to belong.

As we establish our values and start playing with the 'version one' we create, we will be faced with more choices. If our values are different from the current tribe; what shall we do? There have been three occasions in my life, that I can remember, when my values had shifted so much that I made life-changing decisions: leaving the Royal Air Force, leaving the British Army, and setting out on my own, which resulted in Unstoppable Force.

All of these actions have been documented elsewhere, and suffice to say, the tribes, at the time, thought I was insane in every instance, and I lost some close associates in the process. When we start truly living to our values, or we realise the values of our current tribe no longer reflect us, we either choose to remain fitting in or break free and belong in our new space. When we break free, we will start meeting our 'new' tribe. The new tribe that develops, or we are welcomed into, replaces the old one. We will feel more engagement, and more interest. We will feel we are participating in our life and the life of the tribe.

Aligned with living our true values, when we start living with purpose and being the best that we can be in every task we complete, we, and our tribe, are likely to drift apart. When we move beyond the 'norm' our current tribe might feel embarrassed that we are making the effort that deep down they know the whole team should be making. Your purposefulness has set a new level of accountability that they have chosen not to rise to. For the purposes of this book, there is nothing wrong with them making this choice—they have decided where they chose to belong. Just as we are choosing to become *Unstoppable* and seeking our belonging, their easier route to mediocrity is their choice and we must respect this.

The three stories of discovery you read (before) all had a part of 'shedding'. Whether it was the global travels that it took for Nick to investigate where he belonged, or Dane's, or my journey into our ancestry; we all came to a point where we realised that parts of our past had to become exactly that; our past. The good news is that in shedding our old skin, there is already a new one forming beneath. There are people out there who are waiting to join you on your quest to become *Unstoppable*. You will also find that many of your current tribe will come along for the ride.

When my son and I returned from the United States, and he began to live into his mission, he got a pleasant surprise. Most of the team with whom he worked, of which, prior to our trip, he had been a junior member, were up for greater levels of accountability and higher standards of purpose. He shared some of his ideas with the Head Chef, who liked what she heard, and from the junior player, he became the 'first amongst equals' in the kitchen.

Like my son's transformation, many of your current tribe, once the initial shock has worn off, will see you in a new light and think, *I'll have some of that.* They will align with your values, raise their game purposefully, and become accountable to your mission. Through this process, you have not been unkind, or 'dropped' any friends. You are still likely to see many of them socially. They have chosen a different path. Being the 'average of the five people in your circle' does not mean cancelling them from your life. It means meeting new people to hold you accountable to your higher mission, values, and purpose.

Those that have joined you are now a part of your tribe and your role as an Unstoppable Force has taken a new turn. You are now a tribal leader. You have a team to captain.

Captaincy—The Confluence of Self, System, and Situation

Leadership is an act of love with service at its centre. Unfortunately, and to the detriment of us all, leadership is often mistakenly thought of as being about the exercise of power and control.

We've all seen how damaging that kind of leadership can be. Most disturbingly, it's the kind of leadership we sometimes see when people are faced with a situation that overwhelms their usual sense of self and their core values.

By thinking leadership in terms of self, situation, and system we can help ourselves stay on track as leaders and lead teams and organisations that thrive.

Cycles of negative behaviour often stem from the social environment, the system, in which individuals grew up. Recognising the influence of family dynamics, cultural norms, and socioeconomic conditions on our core self can help us prevent negative behaviour and promote responsible and effective leadership.

In familial cycles of negative behaviour (abuse), individual traits and experiences contribute to harmful patterns. Recognising and addressing these underlying factors can break the cycle and foster more effective leadership.

This means that when we are under pressure as a leader we don't default to the emotional deficits of our past or act from a place of psychological damage. Rather, we stand firmly on the bedrock of our values and remember that leadership is about service to others, not control of others.

The Stanford Prison Experiment conducted by Philip Zimbardo in 1971, is a well-known example of a system creating a situation that overwhelmed the self. The situation in which the volunteer participants found themselves played a pivotal role in their behaviour during the experiment. Immersed in a simulated prison environment, the participants' attitudes and actions were influenced as the participants assumed roles as prisoners or guards, and this led to the emergence of negative behaviours among some of the guards (previously volunteers on an equal footing).

In the Abu Ghraib prison atrocity of 2003, the situational factors of the Iraq War and the hostile environment fostered abusive behaviours among some American soldiers. The shocking photographs from Abu Ghraib reveal disturbing parallels to the behaviours observed in Zimbardo's experiment, providing real-life proof of how the situation can override individual moral compasses and lead to extreme mistreatment of others.

Understanding situational factors, such as the stressors and power dynamics in CEO and governance settings, is crucial to avoiding situational overwhelm.

So how do we instil those positive leadership traits in our muscle memory so that we can remain true to the right kind of leadership under pressure? This is when we can help to create a system around us that supports healthy leadership qualities in everyone.

The first step is fostering a positive leadership culture within the workplace from the bottom up. Empowering employees at all levels to contribute ideas and participate in decision-making enhances engagement and motivation. It fosters open communication, trust, and respect, allowing diverse perspectives to be considered. This leads to better problem-solving, collaboration, and psychological safety.

Bottom-up leadership also encourages a sense of ownership and accountability among employees. When given autonomy and responsibility, individuals take ownership of their work, fostering a positive feedback loop. This shared accountability strengthens teamwork, support, and the overall work culture. It also assists the executive in identifying succession plans and future leaders.

If you're a new leader, read about historical leaders to gain a comprehensive understanding of different perspectives and approaches to leadership. None of us are inventing leadership. When we read about other leaders what we are doing is putting ourselves in the presence, even on the page, of the leaders who do, or did, it well (or badly) so we can 'catch' good leadership approaches from them and avoid bad leadership approaches. We also expand our references away from the current system in which we find ourselves.

By studying the experiences of leaders from various times and contexts, new leaders can learn from their successes, failures, and the consequences of their actions. This broadens their perspective and enables them to adapt and integrate lessons from diverse leaders into their own leadership style. It fosters critical thinking, empathy, and a nuanced understanding of the complexities of leadership.

This is particularly important when leaders don't have the prior first-hand experience of the situations, and they're being expected to lead others through. And, as every situation is different from the last, prior experience may not create the answer for the new experience; it can only point to a solution.

Let's face it, that's more and more the case for all of us as we're encountering events for the first time, such as the impact of human-induced climate change and the rapid evolution of AI. We're also encountering these new situations at pace. We simply don't have the luxury of decades to acquire leadership experience, however, it is no excuse to placate your ego by finding a 'Leadership Coach' who also lacks any level of 'real' experience.

The good news is you are not alone as a leader. You can create a strong sense of self, gain insight into the situations you face and how others have handled those situations well or not well, and work to create a system that supports healthy leadership.

We can develop the skills, insights, and an ethical compass necessary to navigate the complexities of our position and governance roles and lead our organisations to success while fostering a positive and inclusive work culture.

Cocoa Pops, Sir!

Good choice makes the milk 'chocolatey'.

During one of my monthly inspection parades, on a parade square of over 200 troops, I had taken a moment with one of my most junior soldiers and asked, "What did you have for breakfast?" Months later, in a cookhouse at Kandahar Airbase in Afghanistan, I met that same soldier. Looking slightly dustier, he stopped me and asked, "Hey, Colonel, what are you having for breakfast?"

That moment on the parade square, I had created a relationship with that individual. No one else was a part of the conversation, and so, he still remembered many months later. This is leadership. Whatever and whoever you are leading, it all comes back to the individual relationship that you have with every member of your team. Good leaders understand this and take time to get to know every single person on their team. In doing so, we realise where our gaps are, where our future leaders are, and what each individual requires for them to grow.

Leadership has, for the most part, had a bit of a bad name—something done to us by arrogant 'shouty' people. We often shy away from the word leader because we've heard that 'leadership is lonely'. In my experience, it's only lonely if you are doing it wrong.

Of course, the big decisions we sometimes have to make can only be made by 'the leader' but leadership can be inclusive and while we will lose some people along the way, we will 'find' the right people for our tribe. The biggest challenge I see with leadership is that we are only given access to leadership courses once we have proven that we have leadership ability. How daft is that? In a world where science is, at last, proving our brains are plasticky, that we can create new neural pathways and therefore harness new skills, any skill is ours for learning, including leadership.

The next obvious step is to pick up a book, a biography potentially, of a leader you respect. Even after taking that step, how do we discern what made him such an amazing leader, or what made her stand out from the crowd? We should also consider that leaders 'dark side'. We could watch a movie in which a great lead character shows off leadership skills, however, we will also likely be introduced to the darker side of his character and watch them shy away from the challenge of leadership.

Society often does not want us to become too accomplished in leadership as we then begin to ask the difficult questions that those in leadership positions don't want to be asked. We begin to call out the BS! Leaders by definition are not conformists—we should always be seeking a new path. This is why humanity is no longer licking water off the walls of caves in a barren wilderness—leaders in all walks of life have, and are, making life better for all, every day.

So, how do we simplify the art of leadership to make it accessible to all and accelerate the improvement of life for all? This is the subject of my first book, *Lead Through Life*. This chapter is a synopsis of that book, potentially with a few updates in my thinking.

To start our journey into leadership, we must first realise that we are all leaders! Whether a mother, brother, father, sister, friend, colleague, boss, or peer, we will all have experiences that enable us to help others or, to jump right to the capstone of the Lead through Life Framework, to serve one another.

The Lead through Life Framework

Take some time to reflect on that statement and recognise the area in your life, or times in your life, when you have done something to serve a fellow human being and now shift your narrative to a realisation that, in that moment, in that part of your life, you were a leader. Congratulations!

Going Boldly

Now we need to go a level deeper. What did you do on those occasions that enabled you to lead? There would have been a 'way' in which you do things. There would have been a style in which you led. If you look on any search engine or book about leadership, you are likely to find trillions of ways to describe leadership. So, let's keep this really simple. Leaders can be described as; nice, strong, kind, weak, poor, aggressive, domineering, influential, and as a leader, there are times that you might be many of these—hopefully, not all of them. In my experience of leadership, leadership is an act of Service and to serve we must be of use and be kind. If this is our starting position, we can be all of the definitions above, and even at the times we feel we have been a poor leader, we can kindly reflect on our actions and learn.

Having so many words to justify how we lead is a challenge in itself and you might ask, *Which one should I be right now*? As we are busy working out which word describes how we think we should act, the moment will pass, and a new word will be needed to describe how we will deal with the situation. Let's get back to simplicity—there is only one word you need to describe how you lead. We must be *bold* leaders.

Boldness frees us from the lexicon of leadership types, and that freedom allows us to become whatever sort of leader the situation requires. How can we be bold leaders all of the time? Do the work in the previous chapter on values. Once you have created a strong set of values—and live towards them every day—you can be bold every day. No longer shall you shy away from difficult and challenging situations, you have your values to fall back on. Using those values not only allows you to be bold, but it also empowers you to take the next step in your leadership journey; your leadership style.

In every bold choice we make, there are only three considerations, and all effective leaders understand that each choice they make impacts not only themselves but also the individuals, tasks, and teams they oversee.

The individual represents a vital component of any organisation. Their skills, motivations, and personal development contribute to the overall success of the team. Leaders who prioritise the individual understand the importance of nurturing talent and fostering an environment that encourages growth and innovation. By recognising and addressing the unique needs and aspirations of each team member, bold leaders empower individuals to unlock their full potential. However, focusing solely on the individual may result in a fragmented team or hinder the accomplishment of collective goals. Thus, while the individual's growth is crucial, bold leaders must strike a delicate balance with other considerations.

The Task is the raison d'être of any organisation. It represents the goals, objectives, and milestones that drive progress. Leaders who prioritise the task demonstrate a strong commitment to achieving tangible results. They possess the vision and strategic acumen to align individual efforts with the overall mission. By setting clear expectations and establishing a sense of purpose, bold leaders can rally their teams around common objectives. However, hyperfocus on the task may lead to burnout, neglecting the human element necessary for sustained success. Therefore, while the task is undeniably important, it must be carefully balanced with other considerations to ensure the wellbeing and cohesion of the team.

The Team embodies the collective strength and synergy of individuals working together. Leaders who prioritise the team recognise the power of collaboration and effective communication. They foster a supportive environment where trust, respect, and open dialogue flourish. By nurturing a cohesive team, bold leaders can harness the diverse perspectives and skills of individuals to overcome challenges and drive innovation. However, prioritising the team at the expense of individuals' needs or task accomplishment risks compromising performance and inhibiting growth. Therefore, while team dynamics are paramount, they must be harmonised with the other considerations to optimise overall outcomes.

As a bold leader, it is crucial to recognise that the individual, the task, and the team are interconnected and equally important. Effective leaders strike a delicate balance, understanding when and how to prioritise each consideration to achieve sustainable success and create an environment that fosters growth, innovation, and collaboration.

Leading with Style

Once again, there is a sizeable lexicon to describe leadership styles; my experience and the experience of thousands of users of the Lead through Life Framework is that the whole lexicon can be simplified into three words: autocratic, democratic, and laissez-faire (delegative).

- Autocratic: think dictator, my way or the highway! Often thought of as a very military style (not true) but very useful to ensure a team knows exactly who has the lead, what is required, and that there is little room for discussion. The leader gains few friends, may lose some in the short term, but through strong communication can prevail and, if successful, will generally gain respect, thus making future requirements for change more acceptable.

- Democratic: the leader shares the decision-making role and provides guidance and assurance so for the most part the ship is heading in the same (correct) direction. A very useful style for creating higher productivity, achieving better group contributions, and improving group morale. Democratic leadership can lead to better ideas and more creative solutions. Sometimes the leader will require to be autocratic but that is generally with individual members of the team. Democratic leadership requires that there is still a leader and can be very time-consuming.

- Laissez-faire (Delegative): a hands-off approach where decision-making is devolved to the team members. The leader does not get involved in decision-making unless asked by the team member. This style works with a highly experienced and trustworthy team but requires regular, honest feedback from the leadership. It is not useful during times of high pressure and change. Great examples of this style of leadership can be seen in hospital operating theatres and busy kitchens with brigades of chefs. In my Special Operations background, laissez-faire leadership was a proven battle-winning style but look at the environments I've mentioned; they all had highly skilled, passionate people doing complex and complicated tasks. Often, leaders who claim to be deploying this leadership style are nothing more than inexperienced managers.

The truth is that any leader will use all three of these leadership styles at different times and in different circumstances. The key to your leadership maturity is to know when to use each style, and that only comes with experience. How do we get that experience—by trying and learning? This can be uncomfortable for all involved but stick at it as the world is crying out for more 'real' leaders.

Leadership success ultimately returns to the need for leaders to be capable of recognising every opportunity as a leadership opportunity for growing themselves and their team through the use of the correct leadership style.

Once we know the only leadership type, you need and are practicing the three styles of leadership, you will be *Unstoppable*. However, there is more to leadership than just Type and Style. There are principles by which you will live and lead.

The Eight Principles of Leadership

As explained in my book, *Lead through Life*, the eight principles of leadership are summarised as follows:

Courage

The next time you are out with nature, perhaps walking a trail, take a close look at the edge of that trail, where the path meets the undergrowth. Look at where the forest ends and the grass begins, or in that space where the waves crash on the beach. In these margins you will find the highest number of species, fighting for survival. These places are the places of struggle where only the courageous, tenacious, and enthusiastic survive.

Life begins in these edges and your life as a leader will grow at the edge of yourself—beyond your comfort zone. Figuratively, these are the places we must go to find our courage, we must step into the zone of the unknown as this is where real growth happens.

In the UK, the greatest range of species are found along the sides of motorways or on military firing ranges. This is because most people don't go there; it's too dangerous and a path that is untrodden; allowing for freedom and new growth. To become courageous, we must put ourselves into dangerous places and experiences—where most folks won't go—as we seek out our courage.

We do not become courageous; we grow in courage through the experiences we undertake. The smarter among us will seek out 'growth opportunities' to flex our courage. My son describes these experiences as Type 2 Fun: you realise it was fun afterwards, not when you are in it!

On a recent occasion, I was sitting in the middle of the Buller River in South Island, New Zealand. We had just run, and survived, the last white-water rapid of the day and I was not having fun. The other members of the trip had paddled around the corner to the take-out point and were out of sight. I sat in my kayak, in the deep of the canyon that had been carved out over thousands of years by the fast-flowing water as it made its way off the high peaks of the southern Alps, into Lake Rotoiti and onto the Tasman Sea near the town of Westport. As I sat there, I reflected on the beauty of the moment, the wonder of nature, and to my surprise, how shit I had become at white-water kayaking. At that moment, it hit me—I hadn't paddled water like this for nearly twenty-five years and I was scared.

I was 'out of my depth'. This wasn't even Type 2 Fun. I had, as usual, taken a massive leap into the Zone of the Unknown and, on this occasion, I had leapt too far. Fortunately, I had instructors keeping me right and assuring my safety.

The importance of 'testing' our courage before it is really required is the key to leadership. There is a reason why courage is the first of the Eight Principles of Leadership in the Lead through Life Framework: all other principles flow from our understanding and ability to conquer our fears. How much Type 2 Fun can we handle? That just takes practice and having the right team around us.

The answer to growing our courage 'muscle' is to start small. Tiptoe into the Zone of the Unknown, if it's too much, you can always step back. Try something different to test yourself. Get used to living with discomfort and the more comfortable you will become. Over time, my white-water confidence and ability have returned, and I once again love my time on the river.

Oh, and don't overthink it. Too often, the sound of our ego, whose job it is to protect us from 'the scary stuff' will get too loud and we will step away from a growth opportunity. When this happens, be kind to your ego, remember, it's only doing its job. Thank your ego for being concerned, explain why you're trying something different, and get on with it. The ego is a quick learner, when it realises it/you survived it quietens down ... until the next time.

Of course, your willingness to step into the Zone of the Unknown is based on your motivation.

Motivation

Parts of this book took months not to write! I knew there was at least one other book after *Lead Through Life* and even once Unstoppable Force was registered, and delivering massive results at Unstoppable Force events, workshops and with my 1:1 clients, still the words wouldn't come. I could sit and look at the screen and ... nothing ... then, I'd sit down and smash out the best part of a chapter in a day! Inspiration would take hold and for a few days, I would conscientiously write. Then the resistance would return. In his book, *The War of Art*, Steven Pressfield describes 'resistance' as our inability to identify, defeat, and unlock the inner barriers to creativity.[33] Even after reading it cover-to-cover, probably in some lame excuse to save me from having to write, the inspiration would once again dwindle. Where was my motivation?

I wrote about motivation earlier. In the case of this book, my motivation, or the resistance, was actually a place. Trying to write in my study at home was failing. There were too many distractions, a needy Golden Retriever to fuss over, a wife to talk to, social media to scroll. Frankly, you name it, and I used every one of them to impede my writing. I then chose to start writing; I looked to my mission and purposefulness and realised, in this part of life, at least, I was not being an Unstoppable Force.

One of the greatest excuses—because it was true—was the battery life on my laptop didn't hold sufficient charge for even an hour of writing. I was stuck in my home office, obviously. However, when I made the choice to write, solutions began to appear. Maybe I could approach a local café and ask if I could, for the price of a coffee, sit at one of their (lesser used) tables and use their power—and drink that coffee. The first place I visited said no; they had no power points in the restaurant, but they pointed me to their other restaurant, next door.

Since then, I have visited The Appleshed in Mapua, New Zealand, four days a week and the results are this book.

Motivation is indeed a short-term and a long-term thing, but we must ensure that we are not being hoodwinked, by ourselves, to find excuses that stop us from becoming *Unstoppable*.

When it comes to motivating our team, the same two types of motivation exist but as the 'captain of our ship', our pursuit of excellence and success can trigger various resistances that impede our progress and hinder our ability to reach our full potential. It is essential to identify

---

[33] Steven Pressfield (2002), *The War of Art*.

and address these barriers head-on. By understanding the detrimental impact of these resistances and adopting strategies to overcome them, we can unlock our Unstoppable Force.

- Self-criticism, although often seen as a tool for improvement, can become a significant barrier to success. Constantly berating ourselves for perceived flaws erodes self-confidence and stifles creativity. To overcome self-criticism, it is vital to cultivate self-compassion and adopt a growth mind. By embracing failures as learning opportunities and nurturing a positive inner dialogue, we can channel self-criticism into self-improvement and build resilience in the face of challenges.

- Negative thinking breeds self-doubt and limits our ability to see opportunities amidst adversity. It traps us in a cycle of pessimism and undermines our decision-making capabilities. To combat negative thinking, we must consciously reframe our thoughts and focus on the positive aspects of any situation. Practicing gratitude, surrounding ourselves with positive influences, and challenging negative beliefs are powerful tools for breaking free from the grip of negativity.

- FOMO (Fear of Missing Out), fuelled by the digital age and social media, can lead to a constant sense of discontentment and distraction. It diverts our attention from our own goals and saps our energy by comparing ourselves to others. To overcome FOMO, it is crucial to define our own priorities and values. By embracing the concept of JOMO (Joy of Missing Out) and cultivating mindfulness, we can focus our energy on what truly matters and find fulfilment in our own journey.

- Self-doubt undermines confidence and prevents us from taking risks necessary for growth. It is vital to recognise that self-doubt is a normal part of the human experience. To overcome it, we must challenge our negative self-perceptions, acknowledge our accomplishments, and seek support from mentors and peers. Developing self-empowering affirmations, setting achievable goals, and embracing discomfort as a catalyst for growth can help us transcend self-doubt and realise our full potential.

- Perfectionism, often disguised as a pursuit of excellence, can be paralysing. It breeds unrealistic expectations and inhibits progress. To overcome perfectionism, we must redefine success and embrace the notion of iterative improvement. By setting realistic goals, learning from failures, and fostering a culture that values effort and resilience over flawless outcomes, we can break free from the shackles of perfectionism and unleash our true potential.

- Obsessions, whether with work, success, or control, can lead to burnout and prevent us from achieving a well-rounded life. It is important to establish healthy boundaries and practice self-care. Creating a balance between professional and personal spheres, setting aside time for relaxation and hobbies, and delegating tasks, when necessary, can help alleviate obsessions and promote overall wellbeing.

- Magical thinking involves relying on luck or external forces rather than taking proactive steps towards our goals. To overcome this resistance, we must embrace a growth-oriented mindset and recognise that success is a result of effort, dedication, and strategic decision-making. By taking ownership of our actions, setting realistic plans, and cultivating a sense of personal responsibility, we can break free from the limitations of magical thinking and achieve sustainable success.

- Procrastination, born out of fear, perfectionism, or overwhelm, hinders productivity and delays progress. Overcoming procrastination requires adopting effective time management strategies, breaking tasks into smaller, manageable parts, and utilising tools for accountability. By fostering discipline, creating a conducive work environment, and focusing on the intrinsic rewards of completing tasks, we can conquer procrastination and enhance our productivity.

As captains of our ship, it is crucial to recognise and address the resistances that impede our progress and limit our potential. By actively working to overcome self-criticism, negative thinking, FOMO, self-doubt, perfectionism, obsessions, magical thinking, and procrastination, we can unlock our *unstoppable* potential. Through self-awareness, intentional mindset shifts, and adopting effective strategies, we can pave the way for personal growth, leadership excellence, and enduring success.

However, we also have a responsibility to recognise those same resistances within each member of our team. Captains hold a vital role in guiding and supporting our teams and effectively addressing these resistances by implementing strategies that foster a supportive and growth-oriented environment.

To help teams combat self-criticism and negative thinking, we can create a culture of open communication and constructive feedback. By encouraging team members to embrace self-compassion and a growth mind, leaders empower individuals to focus on continuous improvement rather than dwelling on perceived failures. Addressing FOMO by setting clear goals, effectively communicating the organisation's mission, and aligning individual aspirations with team objectives can help team members find fulfilment in their work, reducing distractions caused by comparing themselves to others.

Supporting individuals in overcoming self-doubt and perfectionism requires leaders to provide mentorship and create a psychologically safe environment. Recognising and celebrating individual accomplishments, setting realistic goals, and encouraging calculated risk-taking help team members develop confidence and strive for excellence without being paralysed by the fear of failure.

Obsessions can be managed by promoting work-life balance and emphasising the importance of wellbeing. By encouraging breaks, supporting personal interests, and delegating tasks, organisations can foster a culture that values holistic growth and prevents burnout.

To combat procrastination, implement effective time management strategies and provide tools for accountability. Setting clear deadlines, breaking down tasks into manageable steps, and encouraging intrinsic motivation help individuals overcome procrastination and enhance productivity.

Our role is to support our teams in overcoming resistance. Through mentorship, a supportive environment, and a focus on holistic wellbeing, we can create a foundation for teams to unlock their full potential.

All these resistances will manifest slightly differently in every member of your community. Our role is to know how to motivate that team member through those challenges. Relationships are the key to unlocking our team's resistance.

Above all, celebrate success.

Call out individual members of the team when they go above and beyond. Not only will they 'feel the love', but the high performers in your team will also all respond. Why, because they want the next call out. On occasion, I have included gifts like nights out or weekends away to reinforce the value of the tasks that were completed. While you might argue that this is short-term motivation, because it is unexpected and a 'surprise', they have the same effect as long-term motivation. Just watch the motivations of your whole team shift.

Intellect

Common sense is not common practice, as one of my mentors says. When we talk about intellect in leadership terms, we are not talking about a PhD, or a 1st Class honours student. We can all think of some very 'clever' people who are not smart. The intellect of a leader is shaped through learning and experience, personal or vicarious. My geography teacher once told my mother at a parent-teacher interview that I could learn all I needed to know about geography from the textbooks that the school provided.

That may be the case, but I could not experience geography, that can only be achieved in the great outdoors. The intellect of a leader is similar, you can read all the leadership books out there—and you should—but then you need to experience leading. This is how you grow in intellect, not through being an intellectual. To simplify this, the Lead through Life framework further breaks intellect into three areas: judgement, imagination, and flexibility.

Judgment

Using our judgment requires us to give up control. The opposite of using our judgment is to be judgemental. Being judgemental is easy, we use our experience and knowledge along with all our biases and decide what we are seeing. When being judgemental, we take no time to consider other viewpoints. This is what happens when we react. Often, being judgemental occurs when we are experiencing the four Fs that we discussed earlier in the book—we are in survival mode, the reptilian brain. Remember the 4F's: fight, flight, fright and 'procreate'!

To use our judgement, we are taking 'others' situation, and points of view into consideration. We have taken a moment to ask the question: I wonder why. This is the simplest tool to train ourselves to move from being judgemental to using our judgement. As leaders, we are expected to see the bigger picture which will often come with more experience and maturity, but that might not always be the case. Asking, I wonder why, provides an insight that most will fail to achieve—too desperate to get to the answer. The moment that it takes to ask this simple, yet profound question raises the thinker beyond the standard 'Beta 3' reaction.

Imagination

Around the age of 5-8 years old, it is likely that someone said to you one of the following:

Just grow up, or

You're too old to be playing with that, or

Don't be stupid.

The first time it was said, you probably ignored it, maybe even the second time. But you began to listen as the attack continued. That attack probably came from a parent, a teacher; certainly, from someone you respected. Then the voices started in your head: *What if I am stupid? Maybe I am too old to play? Maybe I should grow up?* Once those questions start coming from within you, it is a huge challenge to quiet them down again. At that moment, your imagination begins to die. You stop dreaming!

Then, one day, years later, your boss asks you to be innovative! What is innovation? It is the focused use of our imagination. So, we go full circle, but we are so out of practice that it takes time to be imaginative again. Those voices return and we give up before we get the 'muscle memory' back. As leaders, we must always think outside of the box (what box?). It is our imagination that will move our businesses, and our ideas forward. Our teams look to us for our imagination. Whether we call it, entrepreneurship, innovation, and design thinking; it's all imagination and it is our job to re-acquaint ourselves with this skill and to look for others in our team who still have it.

Once we have truly got that imagination muscle firing, our team will look to us and say, we are intuitive, that is the prize of working on our imagination. To get started, read some novels, take up a paintbrush, see shapes in the clouds. Daydream!

To build imagination in your team, tell them what you require, don't tell them how to deliver it. Remember, in the British Army, this is called Mission Command; you'll be surprised by your team's ingenuity, and you might just learn something.

Flexibility

What is the point in removing bias by asking, I wonder why, and re-training our imagination? It gives us choice. There is a standing joke in our family; it's Wednesday, must be sausages for supper. It's easy. Writing that shopping list, figuring out the menu for the week. Sausages on a Wednesday keeps it simple. Imagine the uproar when another dish is suggested! Too often, we get stuck in a rut. We do the same thing because it is easy.

In combat, as in espionage operations, this is one sure way of getting your team killed, the enemy will see your patterns. In business, your competitors will see how you are making money and copy you. In these examples, the only way to stay alive is to always find ways to do things differently; keep them guessing. As a leader, our role is to use our judgement and imagination to stay flexible. Always be thinking differently to stay ahead.

You might find that constantly being flexible makes you feel uncomfortable. What happens if it doesn't work? You learned a valuable lesson and every time you use your flexibility, you will get better and better at it. Your imagination will grow, and your bias will shrink. And your presence as a leader will increase.

Presence

Ever been walking down an unfamiliar street after dark and felt that someone was watching or following you? Ever been thinking about a close friend and then a message from them drops in?

At a quantum level, there is much to unpack here, however, in the simplest of terms—you felt a presence, that person's presence.

As the captain, this is what we are looking to achieve. Presence is easy when you are with the team—they can see and hear you. Or they know you are in the building.

What about when you are not there? On these occasions, your presence is what ensures that the standard you set, the accountability you expect, and the values of the organisations are upheld.

Being an inspiration when you are physically present instils in the team a standard. When you are 'there' your behaviour and standard must be unquestionable. When the team's standard drops below 'the' standard it is your responsibility to them and that community to deploy your autocratic leadership style and stamp it out. The team will quickly learn that breaking the standard is unacceptable and, with practice, your autocratic leadership style will become so impressive that no one wants to be on the receiving end.

You can relax back into the democratic you—the person everyone, including you, prefers to be around.

A word of warning: with time, your presence can weaken. Unintentionally, the team will normalise the abnormal. As human beings, we seek the easy route, and if you're not sure about that statement, think about every invention since the beginning of humanity—was it invented to make life easier or more difficult? Over time, tiny little shifts will show that standards are dropping. This does not mean you can never take time off, quite the reverse. Taking time off enables you to conduct some succession planning. The team members who uphold the standard for the longest are your 'go-to' guys. They are more likely to be the members who know you best.

On taking command of the Defence School of Intelligence, in my Army days, I went without an Adjutant (think Chief of Staff) while I waited for the 'right' man to be released. My Regimental Sergeant Major (Senior Soldier) was never meant to have even been promoted (that year) or offered one of the British Army's most coveted positions. I did not care; I knew they were the two men who understood my standard. This is how important it is to have a team who can cope with living purposefully to the highest of standards. It is your presence, when err, present or not, that empowers this.

Rally

I was walking the length of *The Ovation of the Seas* cruise ship berthed in Circular Quay in Sydney, Australia. The thousands of passengers were being disgorged towards a gaggle of taxis and buses. Some passengers were struggling with outsized baggage whilst making their way towards the train station. Through the middle of this, a teacher was ably herding a class of over thirty children toward the Museum of Modern Art (MOMA). In this diaspora of humanity, the schoolteacher shouted, "Go!", and every single child shot off at top speed. Being ex-military, frankly, I was shocked to my core! Within a few seconds, my beating heart was stilled. Every child was sprinting towards another teacher who had been pre-positioned under a shade-providing tree. This is the sort of inspired planning and leadership that brings me to the second part of presence. That second teacher was the Rally Point for the students. A place that they all knew to go to when they arrived at MOMA.

As captains, it is our responsibility to always be that rallying point. Most of the time this is no big deal, as our Unstoppable Force is moving in the right direction with little guidance, but we can drop our standard and pretend, for a while, that "this laissez-faire leadership style is easy." It is in those challenging times that our ability to rally the team is important. This might be due to an issue that affects the whole team such as a recession, illness, pandemic, but more often a member, or a few, of the team are 'out of sorts' and you need to be there for them.

The second part of being the rally point for the team harks back to the English medieval use of the word. The call 'to rally' ordered all knights to move at speed towards the King. On the medieval battlefield, the King could always be seen as his flag (standard) bearer rode beside him. The call 'to rally' often meant that the King's life was in danger. If the King was killed his standard would fall and the battle lost. Your role is to assure your team that the 'standard' never falls.

When it comes to our inspirational presence or our ability to rally the team, our priority is to manage our energy. Our lasting energy will be our presence in our absence and our certainty will be our rallying energy.

Energy

Earlier, you learned about the importance of energy, and that everything, including us, comprises of energy. The frequency of our vibrations (the energy waves we manifest) are the moods and emotions that other people feel. Remember arriving at the party you weren't looking forward to, as the door opened you felt the energy of the room and in a very short time, your vibrations shifted from low (misery) to high (party animal).

In our captaincy, not only are we responsible for manifesting our own energy in line with the occasion, but we are also, in part, responsible for the energy of the team. We must be ready and practice for this because raising the team's energy takes ... energy. But it is always worth it.

Once again, this is an activity that is different for every individual. Sometimes we find our energies align easily. Mostly, they will be the people you refer to as friends or our closest work colleagues. The folks with whom the energies don't so easily align are less likely to get invited to join you for coffee or drinks. As the captain, it does not matter the energy—it is our job to raise it.

A highly energised team is *Unstoppable*. That high energy comes from the love and gratitude they share. These are the teams who stand shoulder-to-shoulder and hold themselves accountable to the person on their left or right. These displays of energy are based in long-term motivations.

The answer to heightening the energy within the team is therefore similar to improving the motivation of the team; be gracious and celebrate success.

A truly exceptional leader understands the fundamental role of energy and vibration in driving their team towards greatness. By harnessing the quantum concepts of energy and vibration, we can inspire and empower our teams to become an Unstoppable Force, propelling their organisations to new heights of success.

At its core, energy is the life force that permeates everything in the universe. In the quantum realm, energy is not simply a static entity but a dynamic force, constantly in motion. As a leader, it is crucial to recognise that our own energy has a profound impact on the collective energy of our team. By exuding high levels of positive energy, enthusiasm, and passion, we set the tone for a motivated and inspired workforce.

Energy is contagious, and when leaders embody a vibrant energy, it creates a ripple effect throughout the organisation. Employees feel uplifted, motivated, and driven to give their best. They become more engaged, creative, and willing to take risks. By infusing your leadership with energy, you create an environment that nurtures innovation and empowers team members to unleash their full potential.

In addition to energy, vibration plays a crucial role in shaping our reality. Quantum physics reveals that everything in the universe, including thoughts, emotions, and actions, carries its own unique vibrational frequency. Our thoughts and intentions emit vibrations that impact not only our own mind but also resonate with our team.

By cultivating a positive and optimistic mind, we create a powerful vibration that permeates the organisation. This vibration acts as a catalyst for growth, attracting opportunities, and fostering a culture of success. Conversely, a negative or fear-based mind can create discord, hinder productivity, and stifle innovation. To empower teams and cultivate an Unstoppable Force, it is crucial to lead by example.

Our leadership responsibility has the power to shape the energy and vibration within our organisation. By understanding and harnessing the quantum concepts of energy and vibration, we can empower our team to become an Unstoppable Force. Lead with high levels of energy, inspire through purpose, and foster a positive and growth-oriented environment. In doing so, you will create a vibrant and dynamic organisation that thrives in the face of challenges, driving innovation, and achieving unparalleled success.

I say responsibility as, in part, every member of our team has chosen to be a part of that team. They bought into the higher standard when they remained during that 'growth sprint' or when they joined the team. But everyone has a bad day—and there is nothing wrong with one bad day. When that day turns into a week and that week drifts towards thirty days, if you don't deal with it, you are facing major team issues.

Having a personal relationship with every member of your team will improve your ability to see those shifts and help them raise their vibrations.

Humility and Vulnerability

When 'Captain' Richard Branson's first attempt to win the Blue Ribband Trophy and become the fastest man across the Atlantic came to a watery end, one of the last shouts from Chay Blyth before he left the sinking Virgin Atlantic Challenger was aimed at the captain: "You know you are meant to go down with the ship!" All crew members were winched to safety, and some went on the continue the challenge aboard Virgin Atlantic Challenger II, a few years later.

As Branson freely admits, his part in the Blue Ribband Challenge began as a relatively cheap marketing stunt to launch Virgin Airways. There was a whole team behind the attempt including Chay Blyth, the Scottish yachtsman and rower, who along with many other feats of daring, was the first person to sail single-handed non-stop westwards around the world, in 1971, on a 59-foot boat called *British Steel*. Branson has also said of both attempts that, at times, he felt no more than a passenger.

However, the responsibility for the crew and the vessel, ultimately, lay with one person, him—The Captain. With this responsibility comes a bucketload of vulnerability. Anything that goes wrong is on his shoulders. Any decision that must be made is his.

This is sometimes referred to as 'the loneliness of command'. I don't align with this but recognise that sometimes the vulnerability we feel when unprepared for the big decisions might feel lonely. As 'captains', we must get comfortable with vulnerability. It was only recently that I reflected on the vulnerability required to live a covert life. I was vulnerable all the time. Whether it was physically vulnerable on the battlefield or morally and emotionally; it became a way of life. One that I had forgotten for a few years.

We don't talk enough about vulnerability, especially us men. Vulnerability is considered a weakness, so we just don't go there. We must learn to lean into our vulnerability as this will support us when the 'metal meets the meat'.

I was talking with one of the members of my accountability group about some of the challenges he was facing, and I suggested he take a walk in the woods. He looked at me incredulously when I added that he had to go with no music, phone, or devices. Like many of us, he was challenged by this simplest level of vulnerability—being alone with our thoughts. This doesn't have to start with a multi-day, 'into the wild', style of adventure, just get out, silently, into nature. Build up to multi-day tramps and you will be surprised how 'lightly' vulnerability will sit with you then. You will also feel that your decisions come more easily.

That's quite a load for us captains as responsibility and vulnerability when it all goes 'tilt', doesn't stop there. We are also faced with humility when we get it wrong, or the team gets it right.

When we get it wrong, we must have the humility to admit it and ask for advice and forgiveness. The more experienced of us might seek advice before we make the leap—this is how we counter the 'loneliness of being in command'. It doesn't mean we are abrogated from making the decision, but at least some of the team might agree (and feel a bit shit if it all goes wrong).

Our humility will serve us well when all our victories are the victories of the team or individuals. Of course, you will be celebrated as the captain, but pass that win to the team. It will stand you in good stead when you need the team to dig you out of your next mistake—there will be one (many).

It has been shown that we need to build our 'emotional bank account' with our team. It only takes one mistake, to undo four successes. By celebrating successes and ensuring the team is rewarded is a simple way of building credit for the occasions it all goes wrong.

The concept of the emotional bank account was popularised by Stephen Covey in his book, *The 7 Habits of Highly Effective People*.[34] It refers to the metaphorical idea that we all have emotional bank accounts with others, and every interaction or communication we have with them can either make deposits or withdrawals from these accounts. The emotional bank account can be understood as the emotional connection and trust that the team has with the leader or the company. Every interaction, message, or communication can either contribute to building a positive emotional balance or depleting it.

Making emotional deposits in the bank account involves actions and communication that enhance trust, respect, understanding, and empathy. This can include acknowledging and valuing team members' opinions, addressing their concerns, being transparent, showing appreciation, providing support, and fostering a positive and inclusive work environment. On the other hand, emotional withdrawals occur when actions or communications create negativity, misunderstandings, mistrust, or disregard for the reader's needs and emotions. This can include making decisions without considering

---

[34] Stephen Covey (1989), *The 7 Habits of Highly Effective People*.

the impact on employees, using insensitive or dismissive language, being inconsistent, or failing to address important issues.

When the emotional bank account is in a positive balance, your team are more likely to trust and engage, feel valued and understood, and have a higher level of commitment to the organisation. However, if the emotional account is constantly depleted, we become disengaged, sceptical, and less receptive.

Our ability to live with vulnerability and humility can have a transformational effect on our team and how we are viewed in our Captaincy. It is why introverts often make better leaders than extroverts although this is seldom recognised. Introverts take time to create individual relationships. Introverts are often happy to listen. Introverts are comfortable with the silence and calm required to make good decisions. They also listen to their gut. These skills might be tougher for a naturally extroverted leader.

To be fair, extroverted leaders are valuable too, they just bring a different skill set to the team. Either an introverted or extroverted captain can be successful if they have the humility and vulnerability to be open to learning. Our integrity will help us identify how much learning we have ahead.

Integrity

In truth, I've not been living my true self for a long time. When I left the military and emigrated, little by little, Stew Darling diminished. No one trains you to be a civilian, I've not found a training course; and military resettlement didn't do it for me. As I tried to find my way in this new country and life, I could find myself fitting in. Towards the end of 2022, I started hanging out with a new tribe. These high performers hold me to a higher standard. I began to feel more like the Special Operations Lieutenant Colonel of my past. I began to feel more like him too. During the years in between, I had been living a lie. I had been in a toxic relationship with myself. Ouch!

Because this happened so gradually, I didn't really notice. I knew something was off but just assumed that this was the way of life post-military. I have since discovered that living true to myself is more comfortable. Living with integrity might not be easy but it is simple. I've concluded that it's better to be someone's shot of whisky rather than everyone's cup of coffee.

I once heard Rachel Hollis speak; she is the thought leader and author of *Girl, Wash Your Face*.[35] During her presentation, she said, "It's okay to polarise your audience."

I didn't understand. Should we all not get along? As we look at the world today, are many of the issues not caused by polarising beliefs? Surely, it would be easier if we all got along. I have now become aware that this is not what Ms Hollis meant. We must stand for what we believe in but, we must also be willing to learn through research and listening. Our first thought must be kindness and usefulness. We must look to the bigger picture without losing our identity in the process.

The loss of our identity is exactly what the negative side of fitting in is. The loss of our identity is what makes it so easy for us to be controlled. Living with integrity stops the negative 'fitting-in' and requires us to break away from conformity. This works when we live with responsibility rather than defending our rights. This in itself is a choice, but every choice comes with a responsibility, and in this space, lies our integrity.

When we reflect on our values and live purposefully, we can bring it all back to our integrity. This is why I am so intentional with regard to 'checking in' on my values every morning and every evening. Living our true life requires us all to raise the standard through which we review our values and our lives.

Our integrity towards the members of our tribe is so important that it must become implicit. Our integrity becomes a part of who we are.

---

[35] Rachel Hollis (2018), *Girl, Wash Your Face*.

When the world looks at us, they feel that we are trustworthy and that we will always act with integrity.

Whether you choose to use the principles of captaincy or align with other leadership models, your integrity is all. It takes all these principles to live with integrity and you will need to love with integrity to uphold all of these principles throughout your life and for your team. They will look to you for that integrity and at times you will be required to 'educate' them about their integrity. Being an Unstoppable Force means you are the standard bearer, and your standard must be brighter and fly higher in everything you do. As an Unstoppable Force, your standard will define where you truly belong. It will define your tribe and, as you serve that tribe with integrity, your Values, purpose, and mission will become even more defined. Your tribe will come to love you just as you love them.

All You Need Is Love

The motto of the Royal Military Academy, Sandhurst, the gates through which every Commissioned Officer must pass, is Serve to Lead. This motto declares the pinnacle of leadership and captaincy. This is why Service is also the capstone of the Lead Through Life Framework. There can be no higher example of captaincy than the person who devotes their life to the Service of others.

Do you remember the first time you fell in love? Not the 'way hey, I'm in here' sort! The real feeling of love. I still 'feel' the first time I met Liz. It was at a pub in Cambridgeshire, England. We had each gone out that evening with a group of friends, and as someone in each group knew each other, we ended up joining our tables. Liz sat opposite me, and that was it. I was smitten. Fortunately, so was she, maybe not quite as quickly—I'm a fast mover—but I'm sure she was. I nearly proposed six weeks later; that's how sure I was of my love for this amazing woman.

When we are in love, we serve one another. Early on, it's likely to be fairly simple as we enjoy the merry dance of getting to know each other; buying a coffee, opening a door if we are chivalrous. Dressing nicely … washing. As a relationship matures, those acts of service will deepen as we learn more about each other. A healthy, lasting relationship is all about the give and take of that service. We have now been married for nearly three decades and there have been many opportunities for us to 'serve one another', and frankly, service each other. Even now, I make Liz a cup of tea every morning, and I love doing it.

When we fall in love, we will do anything for that person, we will bend our whole lives out of shape to make sure they remain a part of us. When we meet someone and our lives are already aligned, we move more quickly from that honeymoon period to building a lasting relationship. But those early heady days of falling in love are like some sort of drug—we become chemically fuelled as our bodies are flooded with the 'love drugs'; oxytocin and dopamine. This is why we do all manner of daft stuff; we are on a high.

In captaincy, these feelings of love should be similar to those we feel for every member of our team. Tough call, which is why so many fail to achieve true captaincy.

Remember the first time you saw your baby son or daughter? That rush of love that you felt. As you looked at that helpless bundle, you committed to being the best parent ever and loving them more than anything else. Remember when that bundle had their first tantrum on the supermarket floor, or when they turned teenager?

This example is more likely to be similar to our experience of captaincy, whether we are the captain, or being captained! The initial excitement wears off and we fall into process. Life becomes mundane and so does the relationship. We begin to see faults in our team and individuals in the team but refuse to take responsibility for them. We begin to focus more on what's wrong than what is right. We blame rather than seek solutions. We stop serving and fail in our captaincy.

The highest form of service, is love. Hence, my view that humanity's purpose is to love and be loved. As a captain, we must learn to love every aspect of our team. This must be our standard. When we see our team, and that includes ourselves, fall short of that standard, it is our responsibility to call it out and do what is necessary to raise the bar.

*

In the simplest, but most challenging form, captaincy is little more than being a good citizen of the world. Living with the highest standard of helping those around us achieve a life where they live towards their highest standard. When I talk of a life of generosity, this is what I mean. For captains, this is our responsibility.

If this chapter has left you wanting more, go to:
www.unstoppableforce.co.nz
to get a copy of *Lead Through Life*.

Communication: Perspective, % Rule, and Team Building Tools

What is the right perspective?

A distinguished art critic was studying an exquisite painting by Filipino Lippi. Lippi was the son of the early Renaissance, Italian painter, Fra Filippo Lippi who was born around 1406 in Florence. He was considered one of the most important and influential painters of his time. As a young Carmelite monk, he struggled to conform to the monastic life but due to his artistic talent, he was allowed to pursue painting.

Lippi's innovative techniques and humanistic approach to art paved the way for future generations of Renaissance painters and bridged the gap from the Gothic style to the Renaissance. He developed a distinctive style characterised by naturalistic and emotionally expressive figures, vibrant colours, and an innovative use of light and shadow. His subjects often included religious themes, and he excelled in depicting intimate and tender scenes. Lippi's influence extended beyond his lifetime, including to his own son, Filippino Lippi.

The art critic was troubled by the painting in front of him at London's National Gallery. It was Filipino Lippi's 15th century depiction of Mary holding the infant, Jesus, on her lap with Saints Dominic and Jerome kneeling nearby. The proportion of the entire picture seemed slightly wrong. The hills in the background seemed exaggerated as if they might topple out of the frame at any minute onto the gallery's polished floor. The two kneeling saints looked awkward and uncomfortable.

Robert Cumming, the art critic, was not the first to criticise Lippi's work for its poor perspective. But he may well be the last to do so because, at that moment, he had a revelation. It suddenly occurred to him that the problem might be his! Maybe the painting had never been intended to come anywhere near a gallery, Lippi had been commissioned to create the painting to hang in a place of prayer. The critic dropped to his knees in the public gallery before the painting and suddenly saw what generations of art critics had missed. From his new vantage point, Robert Cumming found himself gazing up at a perfectly proportioned piece. The foreground had moved naturally to the background, while the saints seemed settled in their awkwardness like the painting itself, having turned to grace. Mary now looked intently and kindly, directly at him, as he knelt at her feet between the Saints Dominic and Jerome.

It was not the perspective of the painting that had been wrong all these years. It was the perspective of the people coming to look at it. Robert Cumming, the humbled man on a bent knee, found a beauty that Robert Cumming, the proud art critic, could not. The painting only came alive to those on their knees in prayer. They had to see the painting from the correct perspective.

But which perspective? Whose perspective? In the example above, the source of truth was the artist. This is one of the greatest challenges we face in the 21st century when information is everywhere. The information might be everywhere but from whose perspective. This is summed up perfectly in the image below.

Who is correct? From one perspective, the number six is the 'right' answer, from the other, nine is 'right'. The excuse we use is that both are right, the freedom to choose is all that is important. However, both perspectives could be wrong for the same reason—if neither participant asked the originator what they had drawn. Without doing the research, and gathering the intelligence, we embark on the wrong path. This is the basis of 'fake news' and the pace of the news cycle often causes mainstream media to respond to the 'echo chamber' without time, or recourse to establish an objective narrative.

The evening news is one of the few programs that will wish you a 'good evening' and then spend the next hour telling you why it's not. I advise most clients not to bother with the media as it has become nothing more than negative 2-minute sound bites. Why two minutes—because that is the audience's attention span. How can the journalist hope to get to the meat of the issue in two minutes … they can't. The mainstream media has become nothing more than a perspective, an opinion piece.

Once we accept this, we find ourselves in an unenviable position; we can choose what to do next. We could ignore all media, dream up our own version—and create a false narrative or, we could do some research, this is the path of Unstoppable Force. There is only one truth, whether believed or otherwise. We just need to do the work to uncover it. This is the history of science—and why 'older' science is wrong—it has been overtaken by more research and more discovery.

Once upon a time, the world was believed to be flat and that the sun orbited the Planet Earth. Scientists observed, experimented, and disproved the old theories.

Our values and captaincy are the same, yet people will disagree with our style and our standards. Of course, they should, as our style and standards are subjective; it is our perspective on how 'it' should be done. This is why we are ostracised from groups, and it becomes lonely for a while. We believe we are right but still have not gained the words to explain our perspective. Once we are clear, our new tribe will begin to emerge as our truth begins to emerge.

Becoming more vocal about our standards is how we develop our leadership skills. As we live out our standards, our ability to communicate happens without us even opening our mouths. As people begin to listen, we will find ourselves speaking to bigger and bigger groups. We will also face people with differing views who might twist our narrative. We must, therefore, learn to communicate clearly and keep a record of what we are saying.

These communication skills are the next tools we must master to become *Unstoppable*.

There is little point in having high standards, living by your values, and aligning with new leadership skills, if you don't know how to get your point across. The self-belief you will gain knowing you can shape the outcomes of conversations without even opening your mouth is the outcome all Unstoppable Forces use to hold themselves and their tribes accountable.

The Words Hardly Matter

Many years ago, we were invited to a friend's wedding. We were so excited, for a couple of reasons. Firstly, two of our friends were getting married, so it would be an opportunity to get dressed up and have some fun. Secondly, it was the first time we had left our baby with the grandparents; we were going to be free from parenthood duties for the weekend.

Military weddings are a spectacle, it's an opportunity for us all to dress in our ceremonial uniforms, wear swords, drink champagne, and CELEBRATE! The wedding ceremony is an important part of the day; however, let's not get carried away. Unfortunately, on this occasion, the priest did. I am sure that he felt the captive audience needed a damn good 'talking at' before the debauchery began. Too quickly, we all zoned out, the man of the cloth was … boring!

An old boss of mine used to take pages and pages of notes at Army briefing meetings that he attended. I questioned him about this, considering he had 'minions' (me) present to do that for him. His response: "These meetings and presentations are so dull that, if I didn't take notes, I fall asleep."

In both examples, the length of the sermon or military briefings could be blamed for our boredom but, think about your favourite Podcast—you would happily listen to episode after episode. I'm a great fan of audiobooks when I'm driving. I listen to whole books during a journey and seldom 'zone out'. So, what is causing our tedium? It's the monotony and that has little to do with the words.

Our communication is so much more than the words we use. Words only count for 7% of our ability to communicate.[36] A baby communicates very well, months before a 'word' passes their lips. Our pets are most 'vocal' without words. We can understand a 'foreigner' even if we don't know the words they are using. So, what else are we using to communicate?

A parent will know if their baby is crying because it is tired, hungry, or in pain, and they will respond accordingly. I remember when our two children were very young; Liz had a physical response to the 'I'm hungry' cry—our kids were breastfed, and seldom left wanting. It was the 'tone' of the cry that caused the physical response. Throughout our lives, our response to 'tone' counts for 38% of how we communicate. Hence the ease by which we can understand people's emotions. Happiness, sadness, and anger are all communicated through the tone we use.

The remaining 55% of our ability to communicate is through our body language. This is why first impressions are so important. What we often fail to realise is that the first impression doesn't wait for us to open our mouths. If we wait that long, the moment is lost.

---

[36] Albert Mehrabian (1967), *Decoding of Inconsistent Communications and Inference of Attitudes from Nonverbal Communication in Two Channels*.

All of this is deeply embedded in our subconscious, so much so that we have forgotten how important these three percentages are. As an Unstoppable Force, we use these skills every moment; we don't wait for the next job interview to think about first impressions or wait to be offended before we puff our chests out. We use our body language, our tone, and our words constantly to shape our environment. But this is more subtle than always walking around in the 'Superman' pose (shoulders back, chest out, distant gaze). How would it be if we considered how we could achieve our desired outcome, whatever it might be, through our body language first, then the tone we might use and lastly think about the words.

Many years ago, before we moved to Canada, we had to transfer some money from our bank, in England, to Canada. Our visit to the bank was fraught, to say the least. I entered the premises, like Superman, and was rather direct in my body language and tone. I knew exactly what I wanted to happen and had made a judgement that the bank teller needed a 'stiff' education. No one enjoyed the experience.

God and the universe obviously saw an opportunity for my education and, a few weeks later, I found myself in the same situation. This time, I was more considerate. I reflected on the previous visit and chose to be more humble the second time around. On this occasion, I entered the bank with a slightly less confident pose, I quietly waited my turn. On meeting the bank teller, a different one, my tone was quieter and more conversational. Within a few minutes, the transaction was complete, and everyone was happy—except the employee from my first visit who had watched on, jaw agape, as the totally different experience unfolded. The words I used during both visits were virtually the same, but words only accounted for 7% of the conversation.

These percentages are often attributed to Albert Mehrabian, a psychologist and professor emeritus of psychology at the University of California, Los Angeles (UCLA). In the 1960s, he conducted several studies on nonverbal communication, particularly in the context of conveying emotions. His research aimed to understand the relative importance of different communication channels in conveying feelings and attitudes.

Mehrabian's experiments involved participants receiving messages with inconsistent verbal, vocal (tone of voice), and facial expression cues. The participants then had to determine the true feelings or attitudes of the person delivering the message. From his studies, Mehrabian concluded that in situations where there is a discrepancy between verbal and nonverbal cues, the nonverbal cues have a greater impact on the interpretation of emotions. His research specifically focused on the communication of feelings and attitudes in a limited experimental setting. We use the percentages of 7%, 38%, and 55%, however, in reality, the significance of verbal, tonal, and nonverbal cues can vary greatly depending on the context, culture, and individuals involved.

Communication is a complex process, and multiple factors influence its effectiveness. While nonverbal cues such as body language, facial expressions, and tone of voice can play a vital role in conveying emotions, words remain essential for conveying precise information, expressing complex thoughts, and engaging in meaningful conversations. Therefore, it is important to remember that communication involves a combination of verbal and nonverbal elements, and the relative importance of each can vary depending on the specific situation and individuals involved. The 'weighting' of each of the three 'ways' we communicate, whether exactly 7%, 38%, and 55% seem to reflect my experiences and the experience of Unstoppable Force students.

Shaping the Battle Space

A word of warning, in this chapter and the next, you might get the feeling that this is manipulation. That is exactly the case. If that sits uncomfortably, read the next few pages anyway and see if your view changes. But let's be very clear, as an Unstoppable Force we manipulate the environment, not the individual. Maybe we use the word 'shape' rather than manipulate … It's still manipulation!

We use our understanding of communication to 'shape our battle space'. Being conscious of the power of our body language and our tone and practising every day we gain a superpower that most of society has forgotten. We become more engaging and a more interesting conversationalist. If we find ourselves talking to larger groups, it is our body language and tone that will keep our tribe or audience engaged. When we get this right, they will not only remember what we shared, they are more likely to believe it.

Psychopaths and Anyone Who Reads Your Emails

Please phone McNanny. As it is for most children, they have two grandmothers. Over the years, to differentiate, ours were given nicknames: Blue Nanny and Brown Nanny for a while after my sister's wedding, due to the colour of the outfits they wore. This one lost favour when people started asking how our kids could have a 'brown' nanny, and so, Liz's mum became Nana. The one that lasted was the nickname for my mum, Blue Nanny, became McNanny, as she is from Scotland.

Just give McNanny a call!

I'll message her.

No, phone her!

What does it matter?!

This was the ongoing argument in our house after every birthday and Christmas. What I hadn't realised was that it was the same for our kids when they communicated with friends —SMS, Messenger, WhatsApp, etc. This had become the means of communication. It wasn't that they didn't want to speak to McNanny, it was just that the means to do so was changing.

Another group who communicates differently are psychopaths. Psychopaths live amongst us, and 1 in 25 of the population has psychopathic tendencies.[37] That most likely means you've worked with one; or many. If you are one of the few who believes they have never, ever worked with a psychopath, maybe a side-ways glance in the mirror is necessary. For the most part, psychos are okay. Not the axe-wielding, stab-you-in-your-sleep sort—as this type is quite dangerous. The 'everyday' psychopath is different, that's all. A psychopath's brain analyses the world differently from the rest of us. The psychopath's brain does not compute empathy in the same way. All this means is that they respond less empathetically to the world around them until they react to the world … very emotionally.

Now think about how we communicate. For thousands of years, humanity has communicated through stories; face-to-face. Our brains are wired to use 100% of our communication skills to deepen familial relationships and create tribes and communities. In the last few centuries, technology has removed the need to communicate face-to-face and in doing so, it has caused us stress. Fortunately, this is being recognised, and remedied by the big tech companies; emoji anyone?

Created by Shigetaka Kurita, a Japanese designer, in the late 1990s, emojis enhance and express emotions, ideas, and concepts in digital communication. Before emojis, text-based communication lacked visual cues and nonverbal expressions that are commonly used in face-to-face conversations. Emojis were created to fill this gap and add a layer of emotional context to written messages. The visual representation of facial expressions, gestures, objects, and symbols allowed for a more nuanced and expressive form of communication. Although it didn't take long for users to abuse even that new way of displaying emotions; eggplant!

We now communicate with ever-shortening phrases GSOH, LMFAO, LOL, and expect others to understand. At least in 'the olden days' when

---

[37] Dr Martha Stout (2005), *The Sociopath Next Door*.

we wrote a letter, by hand, with quill and ink, we had time to reflect on the words, and as necessary, rip it up and start again. We had every chance to change our minds on the content right up to popping the enveloped letter in the mailbox. The recipient, on opening the letter, had time to reflect on your words before penning their considered response.

Nowadays, we fire off emails, and text messages, left, right, and centre, with little thought. We read emails, create the most light-hearted funny response, and hit send without even really thinking about how it might be received. Much like our psychopath acquaintances, we are operating in an empathetic hole. Why? Because we are only using 7% of our communication abilities. I am not for a moment suggesting we stop with technology—email is a very powerful tool, if we use it smartly. As an Unstoppable Force, the question we should all be asking is how I can communicate to a higher standard. The answer is simple: use more of our communication abilities.

How do we do that?

Bring 'tone' into the conversation. Pick up the phone. We are now using 45% of our ability. Our recipient is receiving almost half of 'us'.

What more could we do?

We could use technology to our advantage and get on a screen. At least now we can see one another, we can watch eye movements and see some body language. Best of all, we could go and see the other person.

While this may not always be possible, this is the highest standard of communication.

Technology has its place but too often we allow it to run the show rather than harnessing it to make us better. With the simple steps laid out above, we can change workplaces and communities. We can bring emotion back to communication and allow vulnerability a place to foster deeper relationships.

When to use emails?

Emails are a great tool as an objective record of a meeting or to set the boundaries for a meeting. Remove subjectivity from emails and we will remove most family and workplace arguments. We remove the opportunity for individual perspectives to shape the environment. The biggest problem with perspective is that, once written down, it very quickly becomes believed, and once repeated, it becomes fact. If you question that statement; take a look at organised religion. I rest my case.

Dealing with psychopaths is similar; remain completely objective.

Words Come Too Easy

In spite of what's written above about the importance of body language and tone and that only a small percentage of our communication is through our words, words are important. To be *Unstoppable* we must be smarter with our word use. Richard Branson tells a great story about the 'establishment' taking Virgin records to court over the use of the word, bollocks.

In the early days of Virgin Records, the business was struggling to entice recognised bands to sign up for the record label. After Mike Oldfield's, *Tubular Bells*, they had missed several opportunities. Then, along came *The Sex Pistols*. Both EMI and A&M records had attempted to manage Jonny Rotten, Sid Vicious, and the rest of the band, but struggled with their controversial behaviour. After the A&M offices were trashed by the band, Branson offered to take The Sex Pistols 'off their books' and the record label jumped at the chance.

The establishment was desperate to hold the band to account and got their chance when the album, *Never Mind the Bollocks, We're the Sex Pistols*, was launched. Posters advertising the album—including the word, bollocks—were displayed in high-street windows. Imagine, a swear word, on public display, in 1977! By the time the case got to court, Branson's lawyers had found the perfect witness; a professor of etymology, who gave evidence that the original meaning of the word, bollocks, was … a man of the cloth—a priest. As (some) priests were known for lengthy, turgid sermons, the word became synonymous with 'talking rubbish'. Hence, our use of the word today.

As a final attempt to convince the court, the prosecution lawyer asked the etymologist whether the clergy might be offended by the album title. At this point, the witness removed his jumper to show his dog collar. Not only was he an expert etymologist, but he was also a priest. Case dismissed; the album title and advertising remained.

While this is an amusing anecdote that shows the worst of 'the establishment', it also serves as a warning to all of us to consider the words we use. Are you excited or enthusiastic? Did you decide or choose to read this book? Are you brave or courageous?

The media are leading the charge on the denigration of language and seem to prefer to normalise Hollywoodisms rather than take the time to use correct language. So much so, that the evening news has become more of an entertainment program than actual news. Phrases like, 'take them out' have replaced 'destroy' in articles about conflict and war. The media are normalising the abnormal; take someone out for a pizza or a glass of wine. Destroy the enemy.

Further, suicide is now phrased as, 'died suddenly', just in case anyone is offended or upset. With the number of people taking their own lives on the increase should we not be talking about this more rather than, yet again, allowing the media to normalise the abnormal?

Our standards are tested every day in ways we do not realise. As Unstoppable Forces, it is our responsibility to raise our voices every time we hear, see, or feel the abnormal being normalised. It is a race to mediocrity and below.

I married a witch, a hag, if you will. She won't mind me revealing this fact, honest. Historically, 'witches' were wise women who understood the power of nature and used herbs for healing. Often, these 'crones' had green hands or fingers as they spent much of their time making remedies from nature—remember the wicked witch in *Wizard of Oz*. As these wise women were so handy with their remedies and understanding of the natural world, they became the 'go-to' to assist with childbirth. Witches were the original midwives.

At the time, these crones were much revered, even the word 'crone' comes from the same base as 'crown'. But then, in religious circles; these same women became vilified; outcast, and even tortured for their troubles. The words they used, to calm and help their 'patients' came to be called 'spells' a further opportunity to ostracise. This is the power of words.

Every word we use can 'cast a spell' on our audience. If we choose to understand what we are saying.

The actual meaning of the word, enthusiastic, is Of God. To be enthusiastic therefore means, motivation comes from within. To be 'excited', requires an external stimulant. To decide means to cut off. Think of other words ending in 'cide': suicide, fratricide, regicide. The word, decide, literally means to kill something. Maybe it is better to choose. And finally, to be courageous, means to do something from the heart; from the French 'coeur'.

When you speak, be more considerate of your words. Cast your spells wisely and become *Unstoppable*.

Throwing Stones in a Millpond

In the end, we were over an hour late at our destination. Skimming stones can do that. We had taken a break from driving along the shores of Lake Wakatipu towards Glenorchy, in New Zealand, and walked down to a stony cove near where the big 'Orc versus hobbit, elf, dwarf, and man' battle was filmed for the *Lord of the Rings Trilogy*. The water on the lake was so still, and there was a perfect reflection of the Hector Mountain range in the lake. That was until the first stone was thrown and a beautiful single ripple was sent out from the epicentre. The water of the pristine bay very quickly became a maelstrom as we all joined in. Tiny pebbles were thrown as far as we could. Our son, Andrew, finding the most massive rocks, created the biggest of splashes—all over his clothes—right on the shoreline. Our daughter, Rachel, skimming flat stones across the water created multiple tiny ripples with each bounce. In the end, we couldn't tell one wave from the next, and even the skimmers were struggling to make more than one 'bounce' before being engulfed by the waves.

Our ability to communicate has become similar to this image. In a world that is so noisy, how can we be heard? How do we ensure our message is understood? A failure to communicate is often the beginning of the end for businesses and relationships. To be *Unstoppable*, we must ensure our words successfully get through the clamour.

The most basic fighting unit in the British Army is a 'fire-team'. A fire team consists of four soldiers. By putting two fire-teams together and adding a leadership element, a 'section' is created. Three sections, with leadership, are called a platoon which by now numbers around thirty personnel. By adding several sections and capabilities together a company is formed. A company, commanded by a Major, numbers approximately 150 soldiers. Throughout my military career, I was aware of these numbers but was never aware that there is a psychology at work here.

Proposed by anthropologist, Robin Dunbar, Dunbar's Number refers to a theoretical cognitive limit on the number of stable social relationships that an individual can maintain. The most commonly cited Dunbar's Number is around 150. In the context of team sizes, Dunbar's number suggests that there is a limit to the number of interpersonal relationships and social connections that can be effectively managed within a group. Beyond a certain threshold, just like the lake water disturbed by our stone-throwing, it becomes increasingly challenging for individuals to maintain meaningful and close relationships with every team member.

This cognitive limit is likely rooted in the size of the neocortex, the part of the brain responsible for social cognition. The neocortex has a finite capacity to process and maintain information about social relationships. As team size increases, individuals have more difficulty keeping track of social dynamics, remembering details about others, and building deep interpersonal connections.

In his experiments, Dunbar showed that two factories of 150 workers are far more productive, and less stressed, than one factory of 300 personnel. The British Army got it right. As the teams decrease in size, we optimise our cognitive tools of community. The optimum size for a team is between 5-9 people. Larger than that, the fighting starts. Why? Communication begins to break down.

The best organisations recognise this early and build a solution into their growth plans.

A Team of Teams

Strong communication happens because, in the smallest of organisations, everyone knows everything. Whether the team is formally briefed or simply overhears conversation, everyone feels comfortable knowing everything they feel they need to know to operate. Much of what they are hearing is unnecessary for their role but it's human nature to be nosey—we like to know what's going on, as it gives us certainty. Beyond that magical number of nine, our brains struggle to process all that information—but our egos still want to know what's going on.

To keep calm and carry on, *Unstoppable* organisations get ahead by creating teams of teams early. As the team grows beyond five people, and before it reaches nine, start creating your 'fire-teams'; smaller teams of three (ish) people with specific responsibilities; think sales, marketing, or production. Give a member of that 'fire-team' responsibility for 'reporting' to you—the Section Commander. As the organisation grows, those original fire-teams will grow into sections each with a few fire-teams. You are now the Platoon Commander and, while your lines of communication have extended, because the foundations were set when the organisation was small you have survived the next stage of your organisation's growth.

Before growing beyond 'section size' make it clear to the team the four roles through which communication will occur. Who has responsibility; who is accountable; who should be consulted, and who should be informed? RACI is a project management and organisational tool used to define and clarify roles and responsibilities within a team or across different stakeholders involved in a project or process.[38]

- Responsible (R): The person or people who are responsible for completing a specific task or activity. They are directly involved in executing the work and are held accountable for its completion. There can be multiple individuals assigned as 'Responsible' for different tasks.

- Accountable (A): The person who has ultimate ownership and authority over a task or activity. This individual is ultimately answerable for the successful completion of the task and is responsible for ensuring that it is done properly. There should be only one person assigned as 'Accountable' for each task.

- Consulted (C): The individuals or groups who provide input, expertise, or guidance on a particular task or activity. They are consulted for their knowledge or perspective before decisions are made or actions are taken. They may offer suggestions, advice, or feedback. Their input is taken into consideration during the decision-making process.

---

[38] Project Management Institute California Inland Empire Chapter (2022), Smith, Michael L., and Erwin, James. *Role & Responsibility Charting (RACI)* (PDF).

- Informed (I): The individuals or groups who need to be kept informed about the progress, decisions, or outcomes of a task or activity. They are not directly involved in executing or making decisions but need to be aware of the status and results. They are typically kept updated through communication channels, such as meetings, reports, or emails.

And practice. As an organisation grows some of your team will need/want more information, and others will be happy with the communication plan. Remembering our Captaincy responsibilities, every member of the team has different needs—we must meet them.

Looking to the Future

There is a powerful side effect of growing a team in this manner, one which I used throughout my military career. It identifies future leaders. Many organisations look outwards for their next leaders, but what could better than growing your own? Some of your 'fire-team' commanders will become your Section Commanders, if you give them a chance. Others won't, and that's okay. Some members of the fire-team will show skills and abilities that might be better suited to other parts of the business. As the captain, it is our job to delegate until we are uncomfortable; and then delegate some more to stress test the team and business. A strong structure, set early, will provide you with that freedom of manoeuvre. If you are keen to dabble with the laissez-faire style of leadership, set your organisation up like this first.

This structure might sound like it flies against current thinking. Some of the most successful businesses such as Apple and Google have a far flatter structure that works well for ideation and cross-pollination of ideas. More traditional businesses (and militaries) prefer the model above. However, if you scratch deep enough you will find the most successful organisations run a mixture of the two.

Remember Mission Command—tell me what to do, not how to do it. Not only does Mission Command build trust with our team, but it also lets them try new things. Mission Command gives room for failure and learning. As the captain, you must be comfortable with your team failing as their failure is how they grow into your next generation of leaders.

Mastering this skill is the key to succession planning and a contented workforce with a caveat; this is called the feedback loop. Your feedback loop can be as informal as spending time with each of your team leaders however, far better to use formal debriefs and reporting to move the business forward. It's far better to use your time with the team to get to know the team.

Simple Words

Who knew that communication was such an important part of the business? Frankly, I wish I had considered it more deeply as I transitioned from the British Army. Our ability to communicate clearly with our team, as with our families, unlocks a freedom that many of us miss because we are so desperate to offer … freedom. Large organisations all have a robust structure, communications tools, and strong leadership; this enables them to look like they operate with a flat structure.

Communication is the tool that all Unstoppable Forces use to seamlessly move between the three leadership styles. Using our words deliberately, being diligent in our body language, and how we use tone in every conversation will ensure that we rightly belong and fully participate in our families, communities, and workplaces. Strong communication is the keystone of every successful business.

Businesses in the Unstoppable Force programmes have access to this system and reporting tools to accelerate towards becoming a high-performing organisation.

Participation

Congratulations, not only for making it this far in the book but also for becoming a participant in your life. With a deeper understanding of what you stand for, your captaincy, and how you communicate this to your tribe, not only are you participating but you are now participating at a new higher level. You are holding yourself and those around you to a new level of accountability.

And it might feel a wee bit weird. You might not even recognise yourself! That's okay.

Remember the Hans Christian Anderson story, *The Ugly Duckling*. The story is about a duckling who looked like every other quacking member of the family until one day. On that day, the duckling began to grow, to look different. So much so that the other ducklings ostracised our hero. Our hero was left thinking he was, indeed, ugly; a misfit. Until he saw his reflection in the lake and realised, he was beautiful; he wasn't a duck after all. He had outgrown all that family; he was a swan, resplendent in his opalescent white feathers.

History is replete with similar stories, as far back as the first book of the Old Testament of the Bible, we hear of Joseph, who, being the favourite son, was sold by his brothers into Egyptian slavery only to rise through the ranks to become the most senior adviser to the Pharoah. Whichever the story, it is always from the struggle that the hero emerges. But to emerge the hero, we must lay down the old self, and all that baggage, and be born anew.

As you practice your values and hold yourself to a higher account, lead and communicate by example you will, possibly for the first time, be truly participating in life. Life will be happening for you rather than to you.

As you look out from this new vantage point, you will see more clearly the mediocrity through which you previously struggled. You will see friends and family caught up in the conformity of the world and want to scream. At work, you will begin to see why your colleagues and even the business is stuck. You will be desperate to help. Your new self-belief and accountability have fostered something new in you—a wish to share your experiences.

You now have the confidence to use your voice. You are no longer embarrassed about … you. You are beginning to see how valuable that uniqueness is and are now thinking of ways to share your genius with the world. You will also be less inclined to involve yourself with the petty silliness of the world.

Your responsibility is now to find ways to bring your unique genius to life while maintaining your new standard. As you are finding out, the world won't make it easy. You are now a part of the 2% and much like our duckling friend, you will be pushed, shoved and even abused as society tries to get you 'back in your box'. Do not let them win!

You will face conflict, have to deal with stress (yours and theirs), and face people who are afraid of the change you are offering. In the next part of the book, we will address each of these in turn, and all you need to do is remain disciplined in your new practice. Create that new habit and look forward to building new relationships with people who are sufficiently conscious to hold you to your new standard. Even in this task, the 'old' you is likely to growl and fight. This is uncomfortable work—which is why most people quit. This is totally natural. Remember, this is only your ego protecting you from the change you are instigating.

Every time I sign up with a new coach, in the following days I waste hours trying to talk myself out of getting started. About a month into working with a new accountability group, I'll start finding excuses or blaming them for being more successful than me. DUH, that's why you are a part of this group. The higher standard.

We have a fir tree in our garden. When we moved houses, I dug it out of the ground and replanted it in the new garden. The tree had been in the ground for approximately a year and was still less than 30 centimetres in height. A bit rubbish considering I planned to adorn the tree in lights every December. When that little tree was planted in the new soil, in less than a year it had sprouted to nearly double the height, and at Christmas, it was just strong enough to support some lights. Just by moving it into better conditions that tree began to grow into its potential. I fully expect that, in the next few years, that little tree will be adorned with brighter and brighter lights, so spreading joy further and further afield.

Create for yourself a better environment, one that will challenge, support, and sustain your growth, and you too will see your light spreading. As this growth occurs, your self-belief and standards will continue to grow. Your participation will give you greater and greater amounts of joy and your generosity will increase. You will choose to be and do more and more and to share your genius and experiences. As you do so, the conflict and stress will melt away. Those who are ready for change will embrace the person you have become.

It is now time to lean in again. To learn how our generosity will continue our upward spiral to create a truly fulfilling life. A life where we are free to be our best selves and to build a better environment to welcome all those who are ready to start their awakening. It is time to determine our sacrifice.

Part 3: Determine Your Sacrifice

The Ultimate Sacrifice

Coaxing the Black Bear from Hibernation

I've mentioned our 24-year-old son, and I'm now going to reveal that we've had a few challenges with Andrew. He was born with severe developmental dyspraxia, and he didn't start to speak until after his third birthday. He also has severe dyslexia. At times, in his college years, he experimented …

But as I watched him, he always found a way out of whatever hole he found himself. In his way, he is an Unstoppable Force. But he is also very, very, stubborn; he finds his way and seldom seeks help.

Recently, I was fortunate enough to be in California with my coaching group and mentors. And, because it was a larger public event rather than the more intimate Mastermind programme that I normally attend, I had the opportunity to take Andrew with me. To give him his due, he parked that stubbornness and agreed to come.

We had an amazing flight across the Pacific and spent our first night in San Diego, reminiscing about our visit there during his childhood. In those days, we had attended cocktail parties aboard an aircraft carrier and raced under the harbour bridge with two US Navy SEAL fast attack craft, they won. It was awesome to see Andrew relax, and we shared some intimate father/son moments that had been missing over recent years. After a quick visit to San Diego Old Town and a lunch of tacos and iced tea, it was time to head to the event.

On day one of the event, Andrew was physically ill with the stress of what he thought was coming. Having never really been on the receiving end of coaching and mentoring, and potentially being aware of some of the issues that might come up, his nerves were getting the better of him.

The successful outcome of Bo Eason's Personal Story Power Event is that attendees leave with a deeper understanding of 'their story' and a concept of their uniqueness. Both outcomes empower attendees to go back into the world better prepared to face the mediocrity of the modern world. Our son is establishing himself as a luxury chef and his successful outcome from the event was to tell his story and other people's story through food.

My coach is Bo Eason, an ex-American Football player, who played for the Houston Oilers and San Francisco 49ers, and went on to write and appear in a one-man off-Broadway show called *Runt of the Litter*. He also wrote the foreword to this book. During these events, Bo welcomes other world-class mentors and teachers to assist with the storytelling process. One of those coaches is Jean Louis Rodrigue; I know, right?

Jean Louis is a Hollywood legend and world-renowned movement coach who helps actors bring their roles to life through movement. You've heard of Margot Robbie, the actress; Margot Robbie of *Babylon* and *Barbie*, or Leonardo DiCaprio: 'I'm the king of the world'. Well, Jean Louis is their coach. He coaches them in their movement in these huge films, and here he was teaching us how to move like animals. Pick an animal and move like them. His book, *Back to the Body: Infusing Physical Life into Characters in Theatre and Film*, is an inspiring read.[39]

All 150+ attendees removed their shoes and got ready to move animal-like. We had wolves, brown bears, elephants, and even a couple of snakes moving around the theatre. In doing so, we were removing our inhibitions to speak and act in front of a crowd. Andrew hid at the back of the stage and quietly went through the motions of a black bear.

At the end of that day, we all gathered for dinner. The whole idea of the dinner was that we, the attendees, would sit at our tables and throughout the evening, all of the coaches would make their way around

---

[39] Jean-Louis Rodrigue (2023), *Back to the Body: Infusing Physical Life into Characters in Theatre and Film*.

the room so that we all got to spend a few minutes chatting with them. The first coach to sit down at our table of eight was Jean Louis. And he sat opposite Andrew. All of us were a little bit 'fanboy', to be honest. We were all a little bit desperate to talk and didn't get a chance.

Jean Louis spent his time talking to Andrew about food, talking with Andrew about the power of food, and how primal food is. After about 10-15 minutes, the organiser came around, shuffling the coaches to the next table. Jean Louis kindly brushed them off; he kept talking to Andrew sharing experiences with my little boy.

Another 10-15 minutes passed, and it was time to move around again. And again, Jean-Louis just brushed them away. By the end of the evening, no one else, and that included the other six of us at the table, got any time with Jean Louis. He spent his whole evening giving his experiences back to Andrew, and this was life-changing for him.

The following morning, we were all on stage again doing our warmup exercises—being animals again—led by Jean Louis. No longer was Andrew hiding at the back unshaven, shoulders stooped—not today, NO WAY—he was right up at the front in the form of his animal, a black bear. He was standing at the front of the stage, facing Jean Louis. All 150 people were just really watching these two people warming up; we were doing the work too, but it was all about those two.

The generosity of Jean Louis during the event, and especially the dinner, shifted my son from being interested in the idea of storytelling through food into a whole new universe. He is now developing personal menus based on the diner's individual experiences. The very first menu he created, in thanks for his generosity, was for Jean Louis.

<u>Jean-Louis' menu</u>

Black bear in Spring

> Canapes of three berries

Black bear in the Fall

> Salmon tartare

Return to Italy (Jean-Louis worked as a chef in Italy)

> Spaghetti Carbonara with wild boar lardons and a parmesan tuille.

Wild New Zealand

> Crusty sourdough with a native pesto, kawakawa berries, oven-dried, and crumbled tomatoes

Wharekauhau

> Lamb rack with a red wine jus parsnip puree and charred broccoli

The First Time We Met

> Fruit bowl with orange panna cotta, vodka compressed watermelon, mango sorbet, fresh kiwi fruit, and a kiwi fruit tuille.

This shift started with Andrew's willingness to travel to California but without the 'ultimate sacrifice' of Jean Louis Rodrigue that evening, the potential might still be just that. He recognised Andrew's uniqueness, to the detriment of everyone else, gave of his genius and in doing so changing a life.

The changes haven't stopped there. Within two months of our return from California, Andrew was promoted … twice. The lodge has created an experience called 'Chef in the Wild' for guests where Andrew takes them to a location of their choice, farm, forest, or beach, and he creates a two-course lunch for them. He is now mentoring junior chefs and he has reached out for help, is tee-total, and as he puts it, "There are no mind or body altering substances in my system."

All because of one man's sacrifice. This is the Unstoppable Force we can unleash when we choose to become more than our environment.

Scared? Good!

As high performers, as *Unstoppable* individuals, we must stop being frightened of putting our genius back into the world.

We must understand how to communicate our genius into the world with one another and with our families. That's a true sacrifice; and, when we're living a truly sacrificial life, we feel fulfilled. And when we feel fulfilled, we are an Unstoppable Force. Why? It's because we are just operating at a different level from the rest of the people out there. We are on fire all of the time because we know that we are making a difference out there.

We sit in shame of our greatness. On my return from California, Liz and I sat down to debrief about my experiences and what was likely to happen over the course of the following twelve months. Towards the end of our conversation, I could see a tear forming in Liz's eye. I asked her to share it with me. "What's up?"

She said, "I think I'm a little bit afraid. I'm a little bit afraid that our plans for 2023 might actually work."

That statement reflects what we see across society. We are frightened to release our genius into the world in case our truth is ostracised. That's why society is broken; The 'stupid' uninformed are too loud and the wise are too circumspect. As children, we were told: "Pride comes before a fall."

That's total BS! Arrogance comes before a fall. It is our responsibility to have pride in everything we do. We must live with humility and vulnerability and share our genius generously with the world. That is living with pride, not shame.

Park shame. Shame stops us from giving. Living with pride allows us to grow in the world and not only be *Unstoppable* but also create Unstoppable Forces in others and within society.

This next part of *Unstoppable* shifts the lens. We started by creating an unreasonable level of certainty within ourselves, resulting in a life of self-belief. Then, we took that increased sense of self-belief, used it to move away from fitting in and progressed to finding and creating a place where our higher standard belongs. To a place where we not only love to a higher account but also lead others from a higher account. Next, we will take these experiences and learn how to use them in society. To be generous with our self-belief and standards to repair society through love and generosity.

Rather than complaining or wanting to change the past, we will start from where we are, resolve what is broken, de-stress our communities, and create a lasting evolution for good. We will use our Unstoppable Force to shape a positive, loving, and conscious future for Humanity.

We've Done It Before

There is a small nondescript village in Northern Greece, near the city of Thessalonica. It might be non-descript now but, in its day, it changed the world. Around the year, 350 BC, Pella in Macedonia, was the birthplace of Alexander the Great. From his provincial Macedonian beginnings, Alexander united the Greeks as a nation, defeated the Persians, and set about creating the largest empire the world had ever seen, across Europe, into the Middle East, and onwards to North Africa. But the end goal, the jewel, would always be the great empire of Egypt. Alexander's Army invaded in 332 BC, but not in the traditional sense.

Alexander knew an invasion by force would not work, Egypt would take a hearts and minds operation. This ingenious approach led Alexander to become associated with the religion of Egypt, to make offerings to the priests and, in time became loved by the Egyptians. The result of this 'regime change' was Alexander being revered as a living God in Egypt. For Alexander, this was still not enough; he didn't want to be just another pharaoh. He wanted to dominate the country.

Up until then, Egypt had been an inward-looking empire, looking to the wealth created from the produce of the Nile Valley and the trade brought from deeper into the Nubian Desert and beyond. Alexander wanted a new city, on the coast, and to trade with the remainder of the known world. This new city was to become the busiest port in the world and that port, the gateway to the richest and most multicultural city on Earth. In the ancient world, only Rome was more powerful.

The city of Alexandria traded in more than goods and money; it became the intellectual engine room of the ancient world. It was where its founder was buried, where Cleopatra seduced Mark Antony, and became the crossroads of Greek, Roman, and Egyptian design.

Alexander knew that to truly dominate his empire he needed wisdom because wisdom meant power and so he welcomed and sought the knowledge of the world. The city became a place where writers, artists, and scientists met to debate and share thoughts. It was a repository of all knowledge on Earth with a copy of every single book in the world to be stored there. All the mathematical and scientific treatises, the works of literature, and philosophical fancy were copied, recorded, and stored in Alexandria's great libraries. The Hebrew Bible was first translated into Greek in Alexandria.

It was an environment where new thoughts and ideas could evolve. Anyone from anywhere could voice their ideas. It was an intellectual powerhouse of the great thinkers of antiquity like Galen and Hypatia.

It was Galen who advanced medical science further than any time before in human history. As the Egyptians had a more relaxed view of death and the human form, he was free to conduct more invasive experiments on the human cadaver than was allowed in Europe. And it was through these experiments that Galen developed the hypothesis that the brain was not, as previously believed, the cooling system for the human body, but the seat of intelligence, interpreter of the senses, initiator of body movement, and controller of behaviour—the source of all the qualities that define our humanity.

Hypatia was an early scholar of psychology and science. One of her inventions, the Astrolabe, changed the world. For the first time, humanity could tell the time, accurately measure distance, and know the height of mountains. This invention had the potential to 'unlock' the world. She is considered such an important historical character that there is even a crater on our Moon named in her remembrance.

After flourishing on the collection of knowledge and sharing of ideas for nearly 700 years, towards the end of the fourth century AD, things began to unravel. It was inevitable that such far-reaching scientific discoveries and inventions would breed conflict.

As a city built on the power and strength of ideas and the ambition to hold all the knowledge of the world, Alexandria was an attraction of emerging beliefs and religions, including the fledgling religion, Christianity. Key leaders of the new religion, including gospel writer, Mark, visited Alexandria in an early attempt to bring Christianity to Africa. This was a place for Christianity to gain a foothold, however, there was a small niggle. Up until then, Alexandria had been a success due to the sharing and collecting of ideas in a multi-faith environment. Concepts of the Egyptian, Roman, and Greek pantheon of gods were accepted and a part of the maturing of the city. This structure did not sit well with a monotheistic religion.

Even back in the first century AD, St Mark was killed by pagans for preaching his faith. This was but a foretaste of the violence to come. For centuries, pagans and Christians lived side by side but when one group wanted ownership over the information to gain not only spiritual but also temporal power; that was when all that tolerance became muddied. The arrival of Bishop Cyril was the finale for Alexandria. He was ordained in the city, resulting in a bloody and violent end.

In spite of her ideas and wisdom, the great thinker, Hypatia, was proclaimed a witch, and her inventions were considered works of the devil. She was dragged through the streets to the centre of Christian worship and flayed to death before her body was ripped limb from limb and burned on the city limits. This personal tragedy led to the destruction of Alexandria's monuments and the desecration of the Great Library. Visiting modern-day Alexandria there is very little to see of the city of antiquity and, shockingly only 1% of Great Library's book collection has survived into the modern world.

So it was that a city, built on knowledge and the sharing of ideas, was destroyed by man's wanton hunger for power over humanity.

Are we on the edge of something similar? Through the internet, humanity has access to more information than ever before. Factions across the globe are trying to control free speech. False news has become a part of the common lexicon. Conspiracy theories are on the rise. We are only beginning to understand the power of AI; how vulnerable might the human consciousness become within an internet and AI-driven world? All of this points to a hunger for control and power. I see very little sacrifice for the greater good being shared in this 21st century power grab.

As we grow into Unstoppable Forces, it is our responsibility to learn the lessons of our past—Alexandria is but one—and do things differently this time.

To ensure this doesn't happen again, we need to learn the lessons of the destruction not only of the Great Library but also of Alexandrian society. What went wrong? Firstly, the inhabitants of Alexandria stopped collaborating, and when this happened, factions were created. Secondly, the high values and standards upon which the city was established began to be ignored. And finally, the city and its people become stuck; change was stifled.

A Seat at the Table

The Dissonance of History

The history of humanity is a story of conflict. From the earliest histories, we hear of fighting. Even the Bible gets no further than Chapter 4 of Genesis before telling the story of the fratricide of Abel by Cain. Much like the story of the rise and fall of Alexandria, history is replete with accounts of man's need for power over another. In early history, those 'spats' were no more than raids on neighbouring villages. However, as populations grew and the ability to travel became easier, warfare spread. The ability to travel by horse allowed combatants to travel further. The invention of the wheel meant we could create supply chains extending the reach of our power. The bronze and iron ages brought the invention of weapons that could be mass-produced if you lived where the ores could be easily harvested from the Earth. Those ores became another reason to fight and win the land.

Swords of iron, horses, and wheeled chariots were the status quo for many generations, and this stagnation created an equilibrium that could only be shifted with the size of armies. The introduction of gunpower was yet another stepping-stone to increase bloodshed. As trade took to the oceans, a need to protect the goods and produce resulted in the first fighting ships.

Cannon and artillery overtook the bow and arrow, swords and shields were replaced with flintlock pistols and rifles allowing the decimation of troops even before the infantry or cavalry 'joined' in combat. In spite of the advancement of weaponry, even up to the 16th century conflict was conducted within regional boundaries.

The advancement of weaponry and warfare remained at the pace of a man and horse on a muddy battlefield in torrential rain until the beginning of the industrial revolution when mass production was a game-changer. Mass armies could be equipped and transported further and further afield. The great Empires had greater and greater reach beyond traditional borders. Over a few generations, modern Europe began to emerge. The British Empire was established across the globe and an emergent country, which became the United States, began a new experiment of expeditionary growth and democracy.

The result was a world shaped by trade, riches, and power—the Victorian Age: Pax Britannica. However, the need for power and control continued into the early 20th century. The difference now was opposing forces had access to global transport routes, factories capable of producing armaments and equipment, on a scale never seen before. Put this together with the lessons and experiences of centuries of expeditionary warfare and a powder keg was lit—the age of Total War.

Prior to the 20th century, wars were fought for land, riches, women, and petty ego-based arguments. This new century brought an ideological element to warfare. While wars had been fought throughout history for conflicting ideologies, the potential scale of modern warfare created the concept of Total War—a war that would be fought, by both sides, to the utter destruction of an idea. Be it capitalism, socialism, communism, or any other 'ism'—warfare became binary, and the result was a death toll in the millions. Twice.

The 'War to end all Wars' ended at 1100 hrs on the 11th day of the 11th month in 1919. It was claimed that that lesson had been learned; let's not do that again. Peace reigned for less than twenty years before humanity was at it again, but this time, the weaponry was far more lethal. A few million more dead … maybe this time the lesson would be learned?

Unfortunately, not. One of the last acts of the Second World War was to 'force' peace in the Pacific region by the detonation of two atomic bombs over the cities of Hiroshima and Nagasaki. Japan surrendered and the world entered the Nuclear Age.

The Nuclear Age bred fear across the globe. Humanity was locked in an ideological deadlock between Capitalism and Communism, NATO versus the Warsaw Pact, and the Soviet Union versus the United States of America. The stand-off was similar to the cowboys of the Wild West. The difference was that the weapons were no longer six-shooters they were an ever-growing arsenal of nuclear weapons, and the result was MAD—Mutually Assured Destruction. But the Cold War also marked a return to regional and proxy wars; the US and Soviets carving up Africa and South America. Oddly, the Cold War, with proxy wars to keep Armed Forces busy, was relatively peaceful—the threat of MAD kept us on our best behaviour, mostly.

With the collapse of Communism, the end of the Soviet Union and the Warsaw Pact, the world entered a new age, resulting in several notable trends in this post-Cold war era.

The collapse of Communism and the Soviet Union marked a victory for democratic ideals and led to the spread of democracy in many parts of the world. Eastern European countries, previously under Soviet influence, transitioned to democratic systems of governance. This trend extended to other regions as well, with democratization movements gaining momentum in various parts of the world.

The end of the Cold War era also opened up new opportunities for economic integration and globalisation. Market-oriented economic reforms and the opening of previously closed economies led to increased international trade, investment, and economic interdependence. This period witnessed the growth of multinational corporations, the expansion of global supply chains, and advancements in communication and technology, facilitating the global flow of goods, services, and information.

The end of the Soviet Union significantly altered the global balance of power. The United States emerged as the sole superpower, leading to unipolar world order. This shift in power dynamics influenced international relations, as new regional powers rose to prominence and geopolitical alliances and rivalries were reshaped. This gave rise to new challenges and conflicts. The dissolution of the Soviet Union led to the emergence of independent states, but it also resulted in various ethnic and nationalist tensions. This led to conflicts in regions such as the Balkans, Caucasus, and Central Asia. Additionally, power vacuums left by the collapse of authoritarian regimes sometimes resulted in civil wars and humanitarian crises.

The post-Cold War era witnessed the rise of non-state actors, such as international terrorist organisations and transnational criminal networks. These groups exploited the new geopolitical dynamics and the increased interconnectedness of the world to carry out their activities, posing new security challenges to nations and the international community.

All of this prompted discussions and debates about humanitarian interventions. The international community became more engaged in addressing human rights violations and humanitarian crises in different parts of the world. This led to interventions, such as the intervention in the Balkans and the concept of the Responsibility to Protect, which aimed to prevent mass atrocities and protect vulnerable populations.

The Military Industrial Revolution that Keeps on Giving

The history of humanity is indeed a history of conflict. It was conflict that led to many of the greatest advances in science. Werner Von Braun, the brain behind the V2 rocket program that decimated London during the Blitz, went on to be an important part of the NASA Apollo program of the United States. His work mate, on the V2 program, Helmut Gröttrup, was captured by the Soviets and assisted them in getting to Space. The need to feed our deployed armies was an expansion point for processed food. Another by-product of every war fought in the history of humanity was the need to negotiate for peace reaching a resolution that was acceptable to all sides, even the defeated.

The power of the spoken word was the weapon deployed at the point in which humanity came closest to self-destruction; the Cuban Missile Crisis of 1963 when the Soviets attempted to site nuclear missiles within striking distance of the United States. While luck played its part, negotiating won the day. The Cuban Missile Crisis shocked the leaders of the Superpowers to the extent that a direct phoneline was provided to the Oval Office in the White House and the Office of the President in the Kremlin.

Whether the chieftains of tribal history who fought over wives and land, despots, dictators, or autocrats who threatened ideological world domination, the endgame always resulted in our ability to negotiate. Warfare is no more than an extension of political will, so in the end, all sides will 'come to the table'. The conflict in Ukraine will end in the same way. When one side loses the will to fight, a credible conversation will begin. When the people of Russia finally find their voice and stand up to Putin, he will either 'sue for peace'—unlikely—or be deposed, with the successor withdrawing Russian Forces and negotiating an acceptable future. To be *Unstoppable*, we might have access to all the weaponry, wealth, and wisdom, but without the ability to negotiate, we will always lose.

Unlike modern warfare which has become far more asymmetric in nature, negotiating can be simplified into a process. That process is the same for a global leader, tribal chieftain, business owner, partner, or parent. It is a process that can be taught and practiced. To be an Unstoppable Force, we must become so comfortable with this process that it becomes a part of our daily life, a subconscious habit. A tool that enables us to see an emerging 'conflict' and apply our experience early.

And Then the Fighting Started

Do you remember your biggest ever argument?

More than likely, it was with your 'significant other' or your kids. What went wrong? I have heard of couples who say they have never argued—how dull. Seriously, how controlling is that relationship?

In nearly thirty years of marriage, we can probably count our 'big' fallings out on the fingers of my two hands. Not to say we don't squabble and harumph every now and again (most of the time if you ask our kids about their childhood memories). We don't even store our venom up for the big subjects, money, sex, and the kids. Those disagreements are generally well-considered, thoughtful conversations. Our 'nuclear moments' are often over very silly things.

One of the biggest conflicts Liz and I ever had was in the car. After a dutiful visit to the parents, we drove from Glasgow into the highlands of Scotland. As the main road meanders north out of the central belt of Scotland, through Perthshire, we left the farmlands behind as the road began to climb into the glens and peaks of the Grampian mountains. As we headed further and further north, the land became more and more rugged. We were entering the wild places of Celtic lore as we headed to my childhood playground on the Cairngorm plateau.

Earlier in our journey, I had slowed the car, ever so slightly, to point out, to my then fiancé, a Golden Eagle in a field near the road ripping chunks of meat from recently deceased roadkill. To my disbelief, Liz, this beautiful being to whom I was devoting the rest of my life, responded to my kind gesture, by demeaning my knowledge of the flora and fauna of my native land and declaring the bird nothing more than a crow!

BOOM, my ego went nuts, shortly followed by Liz's ego doing something similar.

Later in the, now silent, journey, Liz, now buoyed by her naturalist prowess, pointed out a herd of red deer on a mountain ridge on the horizon. My response was, "Those are not deer, not this far north, they are a pack of wild dogs."

Around about now, the 'fighting' really started and remains a 'discussion' point over twenty-five years later. Granted, now we laugh about the road trip.

The positive outcome of this trivial spat is that we were learning about one another. We were able to 'poke the bear' to see how far the conversation could go and where the 'redlines' might be. It didn't matter if the Golden Eagle was actually a crow (it most certainly was a Golden Eagle—just saying), nor whether the deer were in fact wild dogs. Mind you, had we really discovered a pack of dogs running free in the wilderness of Scotland, Sir David Attenborough might have shown some interest.

These arguments are an important means of 'letting off steam' and provide us the tools we require to make sense of where we stand on the big issues. It shows that both sides consider the high stakes in regard to how our competence and capacity are seen by the other side. This is the purpose of debating clubs, water cooler chats, and opinion pieces in the media. All of them allow us to gain experience in the process of negotiating.

There is much to unpack in this short story that enables us a glimpse into why, even the simplest of misunderstandings can erupt into raging conflict and, in our role as an Unstoppable Force, what we can do to minimise the wrath while still empowering free and honest debate. Our goal should not be to stifle any ideas or hypotheses but to create a 'safe' environment that results in a mutually agreed solution—rather than the more usual mutually assured destruction.

We used to call this one 'conflict negotiation'. Listening to the media today, it often seems that, if we have a different point of view or belief system, we have to 'hate' the other person. Well, that got us to a good place?? If only we could remember how to negotiate and collaborate, everyone would be a winner.

We are all different, and every day, we are different. It's no surprise we are constantly squabbling. Even with our understanding of communication, we are still getting it so wrong. Why? Because we all communicate in different, nuanced ways.

The art of negotiation is a step-by-step method to getting what you want—every time.

Watch Your Language

When we enter into a negotiation, especially when we are new to it, we are going to feel stressed. Our opponent is going to feel this energy. We are leaking the pressure we are feeling. Already, we have given up 55% of our power of communication. Our voice might be wobbly, there goes another 38%. And then we fluff our words, and we are completely revealed. This is how quickly any advantage we might have had can unravel. It is the same for job interviews, first dates, and meeting the in-laws. This is why it is so important to be aware of how we communicate.

This is the skill that 'method actors' bring to the stage. They rehearse, rehearse and, if you have a moment, they rehearse. They practice their art until it is perfected. They choose the body language they will use; they address any tone that fails to match the character, and they know the words of their character. The best actors will even go so far as to choose the right clothing for their character. I've heard it said that Robert De Niro will not accept an acting role unless he is able to choose a hat for the character … a hat!

Too many of us stumble into conversations with no real planning and we wonder why we don't get our way. We blunder into them by which time it's over. And we haven't even considered what our opponent is communicating. Those tiny 'tells' in their body language, a re-enforcement of an accent or dialect that might suggest stress, too many 'ums' in their sentences. Or, more worryingly, a strong Superman pose, aligned with calm breathing and confident tone, in which they finish every sentence.

Our Advantage

Our first victory, or loss, in any negotiation, starts long before the first word is uttered. Fortunately, our opponent has the very same challenge. And while our first responsibility is to 'own' our communication, we can also assure our opponent that this is a safe space for you both to decide the fate of the world.

The Sweetest Sound

The sweetest sound any human can ever hear is their own name. Use theirs often, and make sure you get it right. What is right? The way they introduce themselves. Do not shorten or lengthen. My name is Stewart, it is the name with which I was baptised shortly after my birth. My middle name is Matthew; named after the man who delivered coal to our house at the moment my parents were struggling with choosing one. Very few people use, or even know my middle name, and I would be very surprised—and worried—if it was used in conversation. But here's the thing. There are only two people who call me Stewart: my mother as is her right for she chose it. The other is my wife Liz, and in this case, Stewart, is very much used for effect when I'm in the shit!

For very sensible reasons, I call myself Stew, as when deployed on covert work, Stew is easier to be heard or said, over the radio net. I never refer to myself as Stewie, this is wrong, and you will be ignored if you use it … even the spellchecker is saying the word doesn't exist. Choosing to shorten, or add a 'Y' to any name, without permission, is a sign of disrespect. Listen to how you are named in every conversation, and you will learn something about the other person.

Learning to naturally 'mirror' your opponent will also create a sense of comfort for our rival. How are they sitting, or standing? Do they cross their arms or lean in? If you do similarly, the conversation will flow more easily. You will build rapport and your intelligence gathering operation (see below) will be simpler. Don't think that because your opponent is sitting cross-legged, arms-folded, they are an aggressive, arrogant, liar. Use your other tools to better understand them and why their body language is what it is. They might always sit that way—or they might be an aggressive, arrogant, liar—gamify getting to know your opponent and learn their tells.

As I teach in our Body Language Bootcamp Workshop, reading body language is much like reading a sentence. We cannot rely on a single word to gain understanding; we must take the whole sentence to fully understand. Looking for a clue in body language will likely cause you to come to the wrong conclusion; instead, look for a 'sentence' of body language cues.

Everyone is a Liar

No matter how good a poker player, teenager, or spy you think you are, you will have a 'tell'. Everyone does. When we feel uncomfortable in a situation or through telling 'porkies' our bodies will release that discomfort. Become aware of yours. I know that discomfort causes me to touch my mouth and nose more frequently. For many people, their hands or feet will 'flick'. Eye Accessing Cues tell us that looking one-way, or another indicates an untruth, that looking up indicates imagining or remembering an image, and that a horizontal glance informs the watcher we are remembering or imagining a conversation heard. Looking down means we are accessing our feelings. Whole TV show sets are designed to take advantage of these humanity-wide traits. Think about Oprah Winfrey or Jeremy Kyle's studios.

But once we know where to look, or not, this is less useful—better to watch for the 'tell'. And we learn to tell 'untruths' very early in life. As an interrogator, negotiator, and debriefer, our role is to ask so many questions that we get underneath the practiced word. As covert operators we had 'cover stories' and much like the method actors, we practiced and practiced our stories. We lived them as much as was possible so that if ever captured, it would take our interrogators longer to 'break' us. The longer our cover story stayed intact, the longer our 'people' would have to change codes, minimise the threat, and ensure other 'assets' were safe. It's a pretty rude awakening to realise that, as much as our rescue was a priority, everything else was a higher priority.

The more we know ourselves, the more we understand when we are likely to 'leak' our discomfort. When we are comfortable with ourselves, we can expend more energy on gaining a deeper understanding of our opponent's discomfort. We can watch, hear, and feel their language.

He Looked at Me Funny

I sometimes struggle to keep eye contact. This is partly because, even after all these years, I am scanning for threats. I'm not lying, I'm just being rude. In some cultures, it is expected that those with fewer years or lesser social standing look at the shoes of their senior or betters. They are not liars, just compliant. The eyes are indeed the window to the soul, but we must not be fooled by our own biases. Before I ever 'popped' into Afghanistan, I would spend a day getting lost in the 'poorer' areas of Dubai. I walked and watched. I spoke and practiced my minimal linguistic skills. I was dulling down my bias and remembering how the Middle East operates. With these twenty-four hours under my belt, I was less likely to offend or make mistakes in downtown Kandahar or Lashkar Gah.

Only by taking time to understand and practice every facet of how we communicate and by respecting our opponent's communication skills can we be prepared for the negotiation ahead.

Become like a method actor—rehearse, rehearse, rehearse.

Your Red-lines

What do you stand for? What are your views on euthanasia? Should humanity's approach to the problem of drugs be a legal or a health issue? Is a bowl of ice cream okay, if most of the main meal is still on the plate? In all seriousness, what do you really stand for? One purpose of the Values Exercise is to assist you in becoming a bold leader. The mentality of a bold leader is the gateway to becoming *Unstoppable*. Unstoppable Forces know what they stand for and will not back down.

When we back down, we give away our power. We must, therefore, choose which power we are willing to give up, and what we are unwilling to move on. As a part of the New Zealand General Election of 2020, the country was not only voting for the next government, but New Zealanders were also asked to vote for legislation on cannabis and assisted dying. As a father of two twenty-somethings, and a husband to a wife whose mother was facing late-stage Parkinson's Disease, there were many healthy debates within our household. Even on election day, I was torn. As I entered the booth to cast my vote, I was unsure which way things might go.

As I reflect now, I had not done sufficient research; I was wobbly. We must not enter into a negotiation feeling wobbly. Our 'red-line' must be set. Your red-line can be whatever you choose it to be but once crossed, the negotiation is over. Bust. Kaput. Done. The Ukrainian president is quite clear, his red-line (at the time of writing), is the complete removal of all Russian Forces from Ukraine.

A part of your preparation for the negotiation is to truly understand the subject from as many angles and through as many lenses as you can manage. As this process removes your 'blind spots' and biases, you will build a knowledge of the subject and find clarity in your position. It might be that through this research you find areas to 'give up', if necessary. Through this research, you will also harden your red-lines.

Of course, a red-line is also a very powerful negotiation tool if you have chosen it to be so. During the sale of our house, I pushed a potential vendor very early in the process by forcing both of us to reveal our red-lines. As a part of my strategy, I declared first, and the vendor walked away. They returned a few weeks later with another, better, offer. In this example, I used the red-line to create a new negotiation—on my terms. This takes 'balls' and experience but it is so much fun.

Choosing the Environment

It had started as such an amazing day. The sun was beating down on an azure sea as our dive boat manoeuvred through the harbour and set free the mighty engines, powering us to the dive site. Even the water was a balmy 20+ degrees. Very different from the usual 12–14-degree waters of Wellington Harbour where we had started this new hobby. The ride out to the site took over two hours as we crossed the deep ocean towards the Great Barrier Reef off the coast of Queensland, Australia. Dolphins joined us for the trip, leaping and diving ahead of the boat. We swerved around sea turtles and watched as the sea birds pierced the sea in their unending search for lunch. In time, the thrum of the engines dulled, the boat slowed, and we entered the shallow waters of the lagoon.

Andrew and I laughed and joked as we prepared our gear, knowing we would be ready well ahead of most of the group who were seriously engaged in BADMIN.[40] A military career is often spent standing by to stand by. Waiting for the next order. In the world of espionage, it is always better to live ready. Know your gear so well that it becomes a part of you. This skill was at play today as we donned our equipment anticipating the wait. Our Administration (ADMIN) was on point.

We entered the water and, after checks, released the air from our Buoyancy Control Devices (BCD) to begin our descent. Passing three metres, we adjusted the pressure in our ears and continued to the planned depth of twenty metres. As we descended, we passed reefs and colourful corals, fish of every hue, but that could all wait; today's 'prey' was sharks. Not the great white, bull, or tiger sharks that strike fear into the heart of many but the 'slightly' more docile black or white tips. And there one was, in the middle distance, minding its own business. In my excitement, I pushed my hand out with such force to point it out to the others and knocked my facemask, filling it with water. I was blind, and there was a shark nearby.

It's a very simple drill to clear a water-filled mask, one of the very first learned when you are in the pool. On this day, could I remember? Nope. I felt panic begin to rise. I was too deep and had been submerged for too long to simply surface. With everyone mesmerised by the shark, I was unable to attract attention, even if I could see them. I was out of my

---

[40] BADMIN, a military term describing bad admin. Admin being the task of organising ourselves.

environment and felt extremely vulnerable. Breathe, no really, breathe. Think this through; replace the water with air, air is lighter than water. Do I look up or down? After what felt like hours, but was probably mere seconds, I expelled the water, my vision returned, and I re-joined the dive.

Being out of our environment is uncomfortable. Our brains quickly move to fight or flight, cortisol and adrenalin courses through our system, stress builds and we react. We lose the ability to respond until we regain control. If we do not plan the environment in which we negotiate, we or our opponent—or both—will adversely react to the environment, making success less likely. Finding a comfortable, neutral environment is key to a successful outcome of your negotiation.

Give a man shelter, food, warmth, mediocre entertainment, and average sex, and he will succumb to mediocrity. If you question this statement, look in the mirror. If you pass that test, look at society. As Michael Easter reflects in his book, *The Comfort Crisis*:[41]

We are living progressively sheltered, sterile, temperature-controlled, overfed, underchallenged, safety-netted lives. It is limiting the degree to which we experience our one wild and precious life.

Our lives and businesses are stagnating in conformity. We conform because life is comfortable. We get lazy and begin to drift. The pounds and kilos go on, we miss gym sessions, we binge-watch shows on the telly-box. While this is tragic for our societies and families, it is exactly the environment we are looking to create for our negotiation—maybe not with the average sex!

If either of you feels threatened, time and energy will be wasted as both parties work to remove the sense of discomfort. As your experience grows, you might use this time to learn about our opponents 'tells' but in your early days, choose a place of comfort for both. Even that can win

---

[41] Michael Easter (2021), *The Comfort Crisis: Embrace Discomfort to Reclaim Your Wild, Happy, Healthy Self.*

you points as the gratitude of your kindness is reflected by their early gestures and you begin to discover why they feel the way they do. Why have they taken that position?

Make It Interesting

As you look at a globe of our planet, where is the North Pole? Where is the South Pole? Obviously, from our viewpoint, the North Pole is at the 'top' and the South Pole is at the 'bottom'. They can never switch places; they can never come together—they are stuck in that position. If we begin a negotiation so 'stuck' on our position, we are likely to entrench our opponent in theirs. This is where most negotiations fail … before we've even got started.

A successful negotiator will investigate 'an interest' with their opponent. In an argument about climate change, we might believe that the extreme weather events occurring with greater regularity across the globe is the fault of man's activity—anthropomorphic change.

Our opponent might believe climate change is just a natural phase of Earth's planetary cycle. Both of you may well have conducted research to 'prove' yourself right. As long as we hold these opposing positions, we will struggle to find a lasting solution. However, in this example, one of us might suggest that it would be great if our planet will still be capable of sustaining a similar standard of human living for our great grandchildren. It is most unlikely that our opponent would disagree with this 'point of interest' and, as such, we can both now work towards seeking solutions to this 'interest', whatever our original 'positions' might have been. Working towards this point of interest is the most important step in leading a successful negotiation.

Do not seek a pay rise by just, outright, asking for one; this is positional. Maybe suggest that you enjoy the work you do and are very happy in your workplace. Confirm with your employer that they are also happy with your work and would like to stay. You now have a point of interest. It is now time to start gathering intelligence.

Intelligence Gathering

One of the lasting memories I have of 'Spy School' was the 'art of listening'. Much of what we see in Hollywood portrayals of espionage is the bombs, bullets, fast cars, and faster women, and while this does happen in the real world (not much of the fast women, if I'm honest) it is a tiny percentage of the experience. The world of espionage is far more about the gathering and collection of information followed by analysis which, in very simple terms, turns information into intelligence. This part of the negotiating process is important, so important that I'll share the method that spies are taught to gather information from human beings—HUMINT.[42]

The first step in this part of the process is to let your opponent tell their story, in their own words. Your job is to shut up and listen. No attempt to jump in, don't be thinking about your next question as at this stage, you don't have one. Just listen. If you want to take notes, ask permission. After years at this game, I can take mental notes to write up later; this is the standard you are working towards but in the early days, note taking is fine. You might even offer to share them dependent on the environment.

Remember the useful phrases to use:

- Help me to understand …
- I'm curious about …
- Tell me about …

---

[42] Human Intelligence (HUMINT) is intelligence gathered by means of interpersonal contact, a category of intelligence derived from information collected and provided by human sources (NATO Glossary of Terms).

With their 'story' complete, you now begin the clarification stage of the operation. It is time to fill in the gaps in your knowledge. One of the easiest ways to do this is to imagine a blank canvas, every colour of paint you could ever need, and the brushes you might use. Now paint that picture. Your opponent's story will have begun to colour your canvas but there will be gaps. Your questions and clarifications must perfect your image. By the time you have finished gathering your intelligence, you should have created a mental masterpiece worthy of a place in the greatest art gallery in the world.

Let the silence hang. Nature abhors a vacuum and we humans are no different. We are desperate to fill in the gaps. Try this technique in any conversation. Become comfortable with the gaps in conversations; they are sometimes more revealing than words. Our opponent will be only too happy to fill those gaps with their words. Often, those words are the most revealing; as they have not been 'pre-scripted'.

The third and final part of this stage is to tell your opponent their story, in your own words. The purpose here is twofold. First, after sharing their story in your words, your opponent may begin to soften towards you.

Secondly, there may still be parts of the story missing. In using your words, your opponent will hear a different version of their tale. This can be revealing, so be on your guard for new information. It might mean you need to 're-paint' parts of your image. This is also where you will begin to see holes in their point of view. These cracks will come in handy later—do not be too eager to call them out. That comes next as you start to give away intelligence.

Building Trust

Have you ever walked into a car showroom and, before you've even shown interest in test driving that Aston Martin DB5, the salesman offers you a coffee? Or, in this case, potentially something with bubbles? This is not just an act of kindness; it is a psychological sales trick.

Your kind salesman knows that through the act of 'giving' you a coffee, you now feel in his debt and want to respond in kind. Whether you give up your phone number, or email address, or roar off into the sunset hastily checking if the machine guns behind the headlights and bulletproof glass come as standard—you are more likely to give them something because they gave you something first.

Now that your opponent has given 'you' his story, it is only fair that you share yours. Even in the most challenging negotiations of my career, I have always been ready to give something away. During the most tense of interrogations, the goal remains the same, to build a level of trust with your opponent. Interrogation is just a different word for negotiation.

As you let your opponent paint their picture, you have the advantage—you already know their story. Remember the cracks that may have begun to appear when you 'reported' their story back to them? You can now use those to weave doubt. Knowing their story, you can also shape your story to seem less provocative. Don't be coerced into changing your perspective … but you might let them think you are.

If you are facing an experienced negotiator, when they tell your story in their words, do not be tempted by embellishment. Correct them if they are wrong, by all means, but not embellishments. Using 'closed' answers is a useful tool to practice, i.e., only answering 'yes' or 'no', even to open questions.

Do not be tempted to go first. You will have given sufficient information away as you both worked toward a point of interest. If you set the environment correctly, you should be in a position to direct the conversation.

The Red Mist

In the biggest of negotiations, each stage can take time, multiple meetings, lawyers, or senior leadership, but the process remains as sound as when it was first used. Remember, a similar negotiation process was used to bring the Cuban Missile Crisis to a close and avert humanity from the Mutually Assured Destruction of the Nuclear Age. You can use these steps to build greater trust and communication in your teams and families. With experience, you will create a collaborative team.

However, there is a simple way that, no matter your experience and skill as a negotiator, things can unravel.

Every Friday morning was the same. The whole team would gather, under the direction of our Training Warrant Officer. We would deploy in 'a job', but this was training day. The Warrant Officer would always create a devious, gnarly, problem for us to solve. We would still operate in the 'badlands' so our Situational Awareness (SA) could not drop but we would not intentionally be engaging with 'the enemy' or meeting any of our sources. These 'jobs' were purely to test us, to push our limits as individuals and as a team. On return to Zero (our base) after a debrief and much hilarity, normally at the expense of those who had 'screwed up', we headed off to the gym.

The next two hours were brutal, unarmed combat training. As the boss, I enjoyed the attention of my biggest and most dangerous operators. What an opportunity to give the boss a good beating. Looking back, I am grateful to them: they made me a far better (dirtier) fighter than if I had taken the easy option of battling the smaller, more respectful members of the team.

I used to get so frustrated as I was knocked on my ass, yet again, or as yet another fist, elbow, knee, or foot made contact. But one rule stayed with me through every one of those encounters. A rule that had been impressed on me by our Special Air Service (SAS) Operator who had been leading our early unarmed combat training at spy school. Throughout those merciless beatings, he would always say, "Don't let the red mist fall!"

No matter how many times a fist gets through your defence, and no matter if you find yourself on the floor, you are still in the fight unless you lose your temper. Of course, unconsciousness and death also cause you to leave the fight, but our instructor never considered those as options. You always had a chance—as long as you kept your cool. When we get angry, we stop thinking. We stop seeing opportunity and, in that moment, we lose. It might not be the next punch, or even the one after that but as they land, your anger will increase. You start flailing, offering gaps that you would never have offered when you were focused.

It is the same in negotiating. Your opponent may use every opportunity to goad you into losing your cool. It may be that, even once you have painted a masterpiece of their position, you are so irked that all you want to do is throw them in the river. Don't! Stay cool. Your serenity must be sacrosanct, no matter what is being thrown at you.

The good news is, much like my weekly beatings, they can only last so long. Even the strongest get tired, or bored, of hitting you. The negotiators who use this style will see that it is not working and, in the end, go for a more collaborative approach.

This Isn't for Me

I teach negotiation as a part of the Unstoppable Force Communication workshops. Some attendees have commented that they don't really think that 'it's for them' and that negotiation is manipulative. As I wrote earlier in this book, every interaction we have is manipulative, but if we do it from a position of kindness and usefulness—from captaincy—we are not manipulating an individual, we are manipulating the environment. Becoming the best negotiator starts long before we meet any opponent. The best negotiators own every environment they enter and that comes from practice, observation, and learning about every person we might encounter.

The Style of Work

As we've learned, we are all unique, so there are some 'parts' of us that we will only learn once we are in the negotiation. However, many aspects of our character are sufficiently similar so that we can all learn them. Once we are aware of the various working styles, we all have, we become better collaborators and we can create better collaborators on our teams. And as we all become better, we become a formidable adversary, an Unstoppable Force.

Human beings are complex. We are indeed unique, but our collective history means that many traits are common to us all. Those common traits can be learned to help us work more collaboratively. One of the challenges we face is that there are so many different 'personality tests' we can take and so many quizzes we might use that we get lost in the verbiage. Am I an ENTJ or 'Fiery Red'? Is my animal a baboon or maybe I am 'Jupiter ascending'?

I once worked with a business that promulgated a new personality test every Friday. This was fine if only for a 'bit of fun', but this business then 'badged' their employees with their results. The results of any personality test should not be a badge to be worn. They should not be a shield to hide behind. For instance, I'm a 'marshmallow', and you shouldn't talk to me that way, as you 'electric eel' types always do that. Any of these 'tests' should be used as indicators, reflective opportunities to consider personal development and reveal strengths. At Unstoppable Force, we use one Personality Test and one Working Style test, whether you align with them or choose your own, my advice is to find one that works for you and stick with it. Your team will be grateful, your hiring process will be simplified and even the most spangly, blue, Siberian meerkat oatcake members of your team will find peace in their uniqueness.

Understanding our personalities and our working styles empowers us all to create stronger relationships. While the uniqueness of our power can seem scary to others, to begin with, we build relationships by finding common ground. As the relationship grows deeper, we find joy in one another's quirkiness.

There are many ways to describe our personalities and Working Styles and I have used many over the years. The one I currently use in

Unstoppable Force programs and will describe in this chapter is powerful in its simplicity. If you are new to this work, use this as a starting point and research what works for you. I like the DISC model as it, not only assists us with understanding working styles but also, explains how stress changes us. The model was originally proposed by William Moulton Marston, a physiological psychologist with a PhD from Harvard. His 1928 book, *Emotions of Normal People*, established the theories that were later expanded by many others.[43]

It is a popular framework used to understand and categorise different working styles and behavioural patterns. It helps individuals and organisations gain insights into their own and others' preferences, communication styles, and approaches to work. Which type are you?

Dominance (D)

Individuals with a dominance style, tend to be results-oriented, driven, and assertive. They have a strong desire to achieve goals and often take charge of situations. They are confident decision-makers, risk-takers, and are not afraid to challenge the status quo. They exhibit strong leadership qualities and are often seen as decisive and direct. However, they may sometimes come across as controlling or intimidating and their assertiveness can sometimes overshadow the opinions and ideas of others.

Influence (I)

If you have an influence style, you are likely to be charismatic, outgoing, and sociable. You will thrive on building relationships and are highly persuasive. You are often great communicators and motivators, inspiring others to follow your vision. You enjoy being in the spotlight and excel at networking and negotiation. Individuals with an influence style are often seen as optimistic and energetic, capable of rallying their teams.

---

[43] William Moulton Marston (1928), *Emotions of Normal People*, https://internal-change.com/emotions-of-normal-people-book-summary/.

However, they may prioritise maintaining harmony over making tough decisions and can be overly focused on their personal image.

Steadiness (S)

People with a steadiness style are reliable, patient, and team oriented. They value stability and prefer to work in a cooperative environment. They excel at building long-term relationships, fostering loyalty among their teams, and ensuring a harmonious work atmosphere. They are excellent listeners and empathetic leaders, often seeking consensus before making decisions. While CEOs with a steadiness style bring stability and a sense of calm, they may struggle with making quick decisions and can be resistant to change.

Conscientiousness (C)

Team members with a conscientiousness style are analytical, detail-oriented, and systematic. They have a strong focus on quality and accuracy, ensuring that tasks are completed thoroughly and according to established standards. They excel at strategic planning, data analysis, and problem-solving. Individuals with a conscientiousness style are often seen as precise and organised, with a keen eye for identifying risks and opportunities. However, they may sometimes struggle with delegating and may prioritise perfection over speed, potentially causing delays in decision-making.

*

So, on review of the above—which 'type' are you? There was a trick in that question; we all possess a blend of the four working styles, with varying degrees of dominance, influence, steadiness, and conscientiousness. The DISC model helps identify primary and secondary styles.

Too often, this is where we stop. In conducting this exercise, we have sufficiently confronted our ego, so we don't ask the question: What happens when I get stressed? The failure to complete this exercise is the basis of many workplace and relationship stresses. We all see that stress changes our habits and moods but, based on working styles, can we be smarter and maybe see these changes before they become stressors or worse, destroy relationships?

In each of the four styles, acute stress will work as a catalyst. Acute stress, being late, a short notice change, or a pet becoming roadkill; these occurrences will amp up our working style. A Dominant will become a tyrant; a Conscientious will avoid the challenge; our story-telling Influencer will use sarcasm and personal attacks; and our Steady as she-goes colleague will become submissive.

Chronic stress is more insipid. That slow crawl of change that most of us will fail to see until that day that we are 'triggered' by something in their behaviour, our relationship. Chronic stress causes each of the 'styles' to flip. The Conscientious becomes the dictator; the Dominant avoids the situation completely; an Influencer will acquiesce; and the normally Steady member of the team will go on the attack.

One of our responsibilities as 'the captain' is to watch for these changes and create solutions early. As I hinted at earlier, there are deeper levels that we have to plumb to really grasp why we respond and react in certain ways. We are all affected by our past.

Ripples in the River

By the Firelight

Just before I fell asleep last night, I spent some time sitting with my dad. We sit, most nights, beside a campfire overlooking a dark, still Scottish loch surrounded by mountains, with the starry heavens above. He wears the same old navy-blue sweater with brown and white diamonds across the shoulders and his denim cap to keep his head warm. We often talk about the day or week that has just passed or the challenges of the week ahead. Sometimes, we just sit, in the silent contentment of companionship.

On occasion, we invite others to join our circle. Sometimes, Mum and my sister will join us, sometimes Liz, and all of us will share the warmth of the fire and our camaraderie. When he is free, my son joins in and three generations of 'the Darling boys' will share stories, experiences, and every so often tears—some of joy, others of pain. Recently, I was fortunate to welcome my daughter and her new fiancé into the firelight on the very day they became engaged.

When it is time to move on, whoever is a part of the fire-lit gathering, we join in one big hug, and we express our deep love for one another. Secretly, the times I love most are when it is just the two of us, just me and my dad. When it is time to go, we hug and wish each other well; until the next time.

My father 'died suddenly' when I was ten years old, and only recently, have we started meeting at our fireplace. I have come to realise that there are still 'things unsaid' and, rather than continuing the cycle of grief, it is 'on me' to start having those conversations. I realise that the person I have become, and the family I have raised, are a direct result of that painful November night in 1982. I have a choice: to live in the shadow of grief or to move forward. To build a relationship of love and forgiveness that will heal me and the generational pain that exists in my family.

By introducing others to our campfire, I can reinforce healing. I can extend the love that my father and I now have, outwards to my mother and sister and forward to my wife and my children. I can heal the pain of the past and grow freely into a new future. These are the ripples in the river we all must address to break the cycles of our generational past.

Let the River Run

Rivers run throughout our lives. For the most part, they are ignored, although we may at times comment on the bigger ones as we traverse the bridges, but rivers have become yet another collective forgotten from our past.

From the beginning of time, rivers were the means through which mankind communicated. It is not insignificant that most major inland towns and cities grew where tidal washes ended or where rivers became narrow enough to easily cross by boat and later by bridging. Earlier still, the Pharaohs of Egypt used the winds and currents of the river Nile to transport people, goods, and culture to expand their empire. Our ability to navigate rivers opened trade routes across Europe and later North America. The trade in beaver pelt soon became a race to see which of the fabled mountain men could strike a route across the great watershed of the Rockies and find a way to the Pacific Ocean thus opening opportunities across the whole expanse of Canada and the USA.

As the number of travellers increased and the requirement for luxury expanded, these waterways were overtaken by roads, and in time, as our human need (greed) increased, railways accelerated movement across the land mass.

If we reflect, we will all find that rivers have played a part in each of our lives. I was brought up in a small Scottish village that sat on the banks of the Glazert Water, a minor tributary of the mighty River Clyde. For a wee boy, growing up in the 70s and 80s the river was a place of dog walking and little else. At the time, you were more likely to see a native shopping trolley than a trout or kingfisher and the old railway that ran along the riverbank was a place of graffiti and intermittent 'gang' warfare between the 'tribes' of lads from the local schools. In recent years, much work has been done along the river and the old railway.

Now the old railway is the Strathkelvin Railway Path which is used in part by the John Muir Way running from Helensburgh to Dunbar. With the end of industry in the villages of Lennoxtown and Milton of Campsie, along with local interest, the water quality of the Glazert Water has improved allowing fish and other fauna to return to the water and banks.

Back in the late 80s, as a bored, bullied schoolboy desperate to escape and find adventure, I found myself on the banks of a feeder stream of the Glazert studying water quality as part of a senior college project. I seem to remember the project had something to do with the amount of chlorine in the purest natural water available compared to water in the local swimming pool. Being that the Finglen Burn flowed off the Campsie fells before joining the Glazert, it made sense that, other than any additions that sheep, cattle, dead sheep, or dead cattle made, this water should be as pure as the rain falling from the sky.

The Glazert Water is also woven into my first-ever visit to a police station. My father and I had been walking along the old railway and as is the wont of young boys, I was scrabbling through the undergrowth on 'an adventure' when to my surprise I found two one-pound notes—riches and fame were mine for the taking; or so I thought. Dad decided that this was clearly one of those times when a lesson in life was required, and so, off we went to the local cop-shop to report the treasure trove and hand it over in case anyone might turn up to claim this 'Lost Gold of Eldorado'. Returning four weeks later, it turned out that the money had not been re-claimed and so ended up in my piggy bank, anyway. It was a kindly first brush with the law and much kinder than the one in Hong Kong, many years later.

For fifteen years, the Glazert flowed through my life along with that of the Kelvin, the Clyde, and the Forth and Clyde canals. I still take time to run or walk along its banks, and on rare occasions, I find myself visiting. A visit during March 1996 saw me and my best man 'valley bash' the feeder streams from Clachan of Campsie to the Crow Road car park as a precursor to my wedding, later that day.

As I grew, I saw the care for all three waterways improve as industry left, and a recognition of the damage that man had created dawned. By 1990, the year I left Scotland, Glasgow celebrated as the European city of Culture and only two years earlier held the Glasgow Garden Festival both signifying the rebirth of the city and doing much to restore Glasgow to national and international prominence.

The Garden Festival was held on the South side of the River Clyde not far from where the River Kelvin joins the Clyde from the north near Kelvingrove. Kelvingrove holds special memories for most children from Glasgow. It is the home of the Kelvingrove Museum and art galleries along with the Museum of Transport; both school trip regulars.

Also entering the River Clyde around Kelvingrove is the western end of the Forth and Clyde Canal. Once an industrial need of the Victorian era, for most of my childhood was a green slimly strip of water that sat gloomily next to the police station (where my two quid spent a few weeks). Over the years, groups got interested in the history of the waterway and in the few years before I left home there were river barges again plying the waters, and the pathway from the Clyde to the Forth was opened once again.

As Venture Scouts, we walked the 44 miles in a long day out with the plan being to complete a few legs resulting in each of us walking around a quarter of the distance. In a possible hint of things to come, I completed all but one of the legs resulting in a day of over thirty-five miles walking. In more recent years, the work on the Forth and Clyde and Union Canals have continued with the completion of the Falkirk Wheel and the Helix (where the Kelpies live); both true reflections and recognition of the industrial might of the British waterways during the Victorian era and a nod to Scotland's potential in the 21st century.

The rivers that flowed from the Campsie Fells into the Irish Sea and onto the Atlantic Ocean hinted at the adventure that lay beyond. As a child, I had been fortunate to visit the US on holiday, and the sight of Ailsa Craig (Paddy's Milestone) as we climbed out of Prestwick airport seemed a guardian protecting the 'stay-at-home' types while, at the same time, a cheerleader screaming, "GO FOR IT!"

The Clyde always seems to have had a draw on those with restless feet. The great river lined with huge shipyards always hinted at 'something beyond' and once the shipyards rusted away, the paddle-steamer Waverley, delivering holiday makers 'doon-the waater' for holidays in Rothsay or Dunoon, suggested more. Even the short ferry from Largs to Millport held a global surprise—if the traveller were lucky (and we were) they might spy a nuclear submarine heading to, or from, a patrol in the Iceland, Faroe, Greenland gap as a part of the UK's support to NATO's defence. An activity that I would indirectly support in later life.

The banks of both the Glazert and the Clyde gave me opportunities to glimpse a world beyond my childhood in Strathkelvin. In the early 80s, around the time John Glenn and Bob Crippen soared aloft in the first mission of the Space Shuttle Columbia, two other astronauts actually visited our small part of the world. Jim Irwin, the eighth man to walk on the moon, and Bill Pogue, who spent four months aboard Skylab 4, were on an Evangelical tour (both 'found' God while off-planet) across the UK. As a naïve child, I wrote to the local mayor fully expecting an invite to afternoon tea. Sometimes naivety pays off, as only one other kid wrote a letter, and we were both invited to afternoon tea with the aforementioned explorers. To this day, I am deeply honoured to have met both men and, accepting I was a pre-teenage child, kick myself for not realising the depth of the honour until years later.

I was in slightly better form a few years later when I met Sir Edmund Hillary. In 1988, Venture Scouts across the UK were challenged to complete a charity climb of the height of Mt Everest in celebration of the 35th anniversary of Hillary and Tenzing's historic summiting of

Sagarmatha, eastern Nepal. Over that year, I took part in some climbs, notably climbing a scaffold tower in a local car park to abseil off; and repeat.

Glasgow scouting decided that a 'Mt Everest' would be built in the Glasgow Garden Festival site and all groups would be invited to take part in the climb … it just turns out that our allotted time conveniently aligned with the arrival of the great man.

The next stage of my life, away from the banks of the Glazert started aboard a train heading south to become a commissioned Officer of the Royal Air Force, and later the Intelligence Corps of the British Army. As I travelled, I found larger and larger rivers and along with them, bigger and bigger adventures. The deserts of the Middle East played a large part throughout my career and even the sandscape of Iraq has two important waterways: the mighty Tigris and Euphrates.

Rivers can also be analogous. I have always enjoyed the notion of people flowing together for important events. When we got married, friends travelled from far and wide to celebrate; a trickle from Germany and further afield, joining a stream from across England becoming a torrent as the Scots joined the journey. When a soldier for whom I had great respect and had commanded on two separate occasions was killed on the Shatt-al-Arab waterway in Basrah, Iraq, her body was repatriated to her hometown of South Shields.

Like water flowing to the sea, family, friends, comrade-in-arms, and senior officers all travelled to pay our last respects.

That day, we were all a part of a much bigger 'family', a family who truly understood our lineage, we understood our collective past. We came together as one to farewell one of us.

I understand that everything is connected, that all roads meet, and that all rivers flow into the same sea.

—*Paulo Coelho*[44]

---

[44] Paulo Coelho (2010), *Aleph*.

Learning from What's Behind Us

Trying to learn from what is behind you is an emerging science aptly reflected by Master Sam Gamgee as he and Frodo face the wrath of Mordor in *The Lord of the Rings Trilogy*:

> *It's like the great stories, Mr Frodo. The ones that really mattered. Full of darkness and danger they were. And sometimes you didn't want to know the end. Because how could the end be happy? How could the world go back to the way it was when so much bad had happened? But in the end, it's only a passing thing, this shadow. Even darkness must pass. A new day will come. And when the sun shines it will shine out the clearer. Those were the great stories that stayed with you. That meant something, even if you were too small to understand why. But I think, Mr Frodo, I do understand. I now know. Folk in those stories had lots of chances of turning back, only they didn't. They kept going, because they were holding on to something. That there is some good in this world, and it's worth fighting for.*[45]

Our stories matter greatly, like the great rivers that flow through our lives, we are also a part of greater stories. Great epics that began long before our birth and will continue long after we are gone and forgotten. Those are the stories that enable us to belong, to find our place in the world but just as Sam wisely suggests, those stories may be full of darkness and danger. Just like the ripples on the river that last long after the rapid, ripples from past traumas, traumas from previous generations, can cause ripples in our lives. Often, unlocking those hidden mysteries, enables 'the sun to shine clearer'.

A river often begins far beyond where we will first see it. The water cycle confirms that the water we observe in a river is a result of precipitation, which is a result of evaporation. So too is it with our lives, our stories began long before we were birthed.

---

[45] JRR Tolkien (1954), *The Lord of the Rings*.

Human biology has confirmed that the number of ova carried in the female reproductive organs are set at birth. Those eggs await the right point in the female's life cycle to travel the fallopian tube in the hope of meeting a single sperm to create life. This miracle of life is confirming a ripple in our 'river' of life.

The eggs of our grandmother experienced all the joys and traumas of her life. At the moment your grandmother's daughter, your mum, was conceived, the egg that would go on to create you was already in existence and experienced all the joys and traumas of her life until she and your dad hooked up. This means that there are at least three generations of 'ripples'. On your father's side of the family, exactly the same has happened. Now attempt to ascertain the ripples, eddies, and rapids that you are experiencing as a result of your familial history.

In our example, we have only gone back three generations, but the science of epigenetics is now confirming that these 'ripples' can still be evident, many generations later.

As Steve Biddulph suggests in his book, *Fully Human*, humanity is still contending with the horrors of World War I, the Great Depression, and World War II.[46] Some families are still facing the holocaust. Even within our generation, we have seen millions of military personnel experience the regional conflicts of the Balkans, Iraq, and Afghanistan.

The might and actions of the British Empire and the colonisation of the USA are still being 'felt' by indigenous cultures. In my adopted home of New Zealand, the Treaty of Waitangi, signed by Māori leaders and the British Crown is still causing untold pain within the country. Not just in the way in which Māori and other indigenous cultures are still treated but also deep within their very being.

For these reasons, it is important to take time to explore our past and the experiences of our families; to identify the 'ripples'.

---

[46] Steve Biddulph (2021), *Fully Human*.

We have explored the development of the human brain. Importantly, we recognised that before the age of five (approximately), our experience is wholly subconscious. Our brain is operating at such a low frequency, that we are soaking everything in, unable to choose whether something is true or false. This is the age that we start hearing phrases like: just grow up, or you are too old to play like that. It is also the age that we start school and probably begin to hang out with different 'tribes'—you know the ones, folks whom your mum or dad would rather you didn't befriend; so, you did.

I wasn't a great fan of attending school. Until my last year, I diligently attended but longed for the lessons. Playtime and lunchtime were always a challenge. I didn't play sport well and wasn't really interested in the small talk of the schoolyard. The bullying started during junior/primary school and set me on the path to becoming *Unstoppable*. School was a lonely time, even the ¾ mile walk every morning and afternoon were fraught with the danger of 'a kicking'.

After many years, I now look back on those years with gratitude towards that younger version of me who stuck it out. I now consider those experiences as formative for this life I am now living. However, until I took the time to recall that stage in my life, they lay dormant, awaiting a future date when I was prepared to address them. The experiences of that age are so important but also can create some major stumbling blocks in adulthood. Those major 'roadblocks' that we face can often be traced back to our formative years. Roadblocks like:

- I don't fit in.
- Nobody likes me.
- Money is evil.
- I'm a failure.
- I'm not good enough.

We were all told variations of those stories by major influencers in our early years.

On holiday in the South of France in the late 1970s, my sister and I were playing 'war'. Obviously, I was the brave British 'Tommy' searching for the dastardly German—played by my younger sister. With wooden sticks held like rifles and machine guns, we would run around the campsite in gay abandon … until we were told to stop. Not only were we told to stop, but what followed was a tirade from the inhabitant of a nearby tent that we were horrible, thoughtless brats. As two young kids from a small village in Scotland, it had never crossed our minds that playing 'war' might upset German grown-ups to the extent of his Teutonic beetroot-faced rage.

And our parents agreed with 'old beetroot head'. The difference was that our parents took the time to explain why a young boy intent on 'killing' his younger sister in a game where she was portraying the enemy might be unsuitable in a campsite full of Germans.

The next day, we were back at it only this time I was a brave heroic cowboy from the Old West while my sister was the dastardly Red Indian—I know, I know, times and my understanding and beliefs have changed but fortunately, there weren't any Americans (of any sort) in that campsite.

I reflect on that story with amusement, it was well dealt with, but many other experiences at that age are often not. Our parents and teachers may not have the understanding or maturity to guide us through these formative experiences and so these phrases and stories settle into our subconscious.

After we heard them a few times, maybe from a few people, we began to believe them. Worse still, we began telling ourselves those stories. Until we face these 'demons' we will always live as that little boy or girl. Many of us have never 'turned to face the change' and as such fail to reach beyond those limits and never become the Unstoppable Force that sits within.

From a personal experience, there may be events in our lives that can trigger shifts in our self-belief. Catastrophic events happening to us, or within us are capable of changing us. The death of my father when I was ten years old is one of those events. Not least, the vicar, at Dad's funeral who told me, "You are the man of the family now." In the shattered state I found myself in the days following Dad's death, that statement was a defining moment in my life.

When Liz, after a 30+ year career in healthcare and midwifery chose to take her career in a new direction, the experience was sufficient to change her personality. Imagine living with a 'Mediator' for most of your wedded bliss to awaken one morning to a 'Protagonist'. As a lifelong 'Advocate', things were tense as we worked through the changes in our relationship.

Working with Unstoppable Force clients this is often one of the early challenges they face. Somewhere, deep in their past, there was an event or a person that helped create this part of their persona. But we can move on from those childhood experiences and even catastrophic events because the signposts are there. The next time we feel this way—pick any of the 'roadblock statements' above or one of your own—you can choose to meet it head-on and ask the question, "When did I first feel this way?"

This seemingly straightforward question has the effect of moving the experience from our subconscious to our conscious; now we are feeling, and thinking, about the experience. Feel into that time when you 'first' felt like that and once you are experiencing that event ask, "Was there an earlier example of me feeling this way?"

Keep going with this exercise and maybe journal the experience. At some point in this exercise—and there will likely be tears and snot—you will arrive at an event, likely in your childhood, when you first experienced that feeling.

Whether you have been journalling the experience or not, it is now time to get the pen and paper out. It is time to write a letter. That letter will be addressed to the young girl, or boy, who first had the experience. You are writing to the younger you. In that letter, you will thank the younger you for the experience and tell them of the person you have become as a result of their bravery in that experience. Coming to terms with the event in your subconscious will enable you to at least move on from the event that has rippled through your existence.

If the event involved another person, you will, in time, be able to forgive and move on from that trauma. This is the very exercise that enabled me to sit by the fire with my long-deceased father.

What happens if the ripple was created within an earlier generation?

How Could You Not Know?

How well do you know your family history? Are there matriarchs or patriarchs still alive who you can 'interview'? Are there family secrets or stories of shame that might help you to understand the challenges that you or your children face? Seeking those 'ripples,' and calming them, is the subject of the book, *It Didn't Start With You*.[47] Over years of study as a clinical psychologist, the author Mark Wolynn, is proving that those ripples can create major issues.

He delves into the profound impact of generational trauma on our lives and presents a transformative approach to healing the wounds that have been passed down through our family lineages. Drawing on years of clinical experience and extensive research, Wolynn guides readers on a compelling journey of self-discovery, shedding light on the hidden forces that shape our behaviours, beliefs, and relationships.

Beginning with an exploration of the concept of inherited family trauma, a phenomenon that suggests traumatic experiences can be transmitted across generations, impacting the mental, emotional, and even physical wellbeing of descendants, Wolynn offers powerful real-

---

[47] Mark Wolynn (2016), *It Didn't Start With You.*

life examples, ranging from seemingly inexplicable fears and phobias to chronic health issues, to illustrate the far-reaching effects of unresolved family trauma.

He unravels the intricate web of intergenerational patterns, revealing how traumas such as war, immigration, premature death, and abuse can leave imprints on subsequent generations. By examining the science behind epigenetics and neurobiology, he explains how these experiences modify our genetic material and influence our brain functioning, creating a blueprint that shapes our lives.

The book presents a holistic and integrative therapeutic framework that combines traditional psychotherapy techniques with cutting-edge approaches like family constellations, somatic experiencing, and mindfulness. He guides readers in identifying and unravelling the entangled emotional legacies they carry, offering practical exercises, meditations, and guided visualizations to facilitate healing and transformation. The author also emphasises the importance of compassion and forgiveness as essential tools for breaking the cycle of generational trauma. He explores how forgiveness, both towards ourselves and our ancestors, can liberate us from the burdens we unknowingly carry, opening the path to emotional freedom and resilience.

Through his book, the author provides a roadmap to understand the hidden influences that shape our lives and break free from the chains of generational trauma. With its profound insights, practical tools, and inspiring stories, this book illuminates a path toward self-empowerment, personal transformation, and the possibility of a brighter future for ourselves and future generations. This is a healing that transcends individual suffering and offers hope for a world where the legacy of trauma can be transformed into a legacy of resilience, love, and wholeness.

One of the signposts he suggests to clients is to listen to the words they use in describing their stories.

In asking some simple questions we can very quickly begin to understand ourselves, and potentially our family history, more deeply. Try these:

- What was happening in your life when you first felt this way?
- Was there anything significant in the build-up to these feelings?
- At what age do you first remember feeling this way?
- Describe how you feel in these moments.
- What might make these feelings feel worse?
- Describe your life if these feelings persisted day after day.

With these answers journalled, look at the language you have used and ask these questions:

- Do certain words repeat?
- Do these feelings reflect a certain age?
- Are there similar events that trigger these feelings?
- What emotions and behaviours repeat?

When reading the book, I really struggled to engage in the exercises. Possibly frightened of what I might uncover, I read each chapter thinking about how much other people should do the work; I was fine. However, the questions kept nagging at me. I began to think about my answers to the author's questions and discovered my sentence to calm the ripples and rapids of my story.

'I am not good enough' is my sentence. It becomes clear where my *Unstoppable* nature comes from. It comes from my generational belief that I am not enough. In unearthing this belief, I am now able to reflect on where that may have arisen. I can look back over the generations and see where potentially that ripple began. I can look forward and see how it is still manifesting within my family.

Within these answers potentially lie an uncovered story from your ancestry. A ripple in the family history has surfaced. The most likely response is, "Why did it happen to me?" However, working through this past trauma means that you will release future generations from this experience. We all imagine being the first millionaire in the family. How about we are the ones to finally move our family on from past trauma? Of course, the side effect of doing so might even result in you bestowing greater financial freedom for your progeny.

Have the courage to learn about your past. Ask questions of anyone who was (or is) a part of your family or a contributor to your family experience. Studies have shown that we are forgotten within two or three generations. Take the time to explore your past. Where did your river rise? What path did that river take to get to you? What were the major rapids that it survived?

Discover if there are still ripples from those events. Our ultimate sacrifice, in becoming *Unstoppable*, is to remove those ripples from the flow for the generations further downstream.

The Baggage We Carry

The great stories of which we are a part are but tributaries of the river of life. The point where the flow and currents of our story confluence with others can create great stress. This is why it is so important to establish values and standards for ourselves before we arrive at the locations and events where these 'joinings' happen. When our values are not aligned, we have a choice, move on or stay. There are also places where we may not have the luxury of simply moving on. The stress we feel in these places is caused by the ripples of our history mixing with other ripples. The term adopted for this is 'Unwritten Ground Rules' (UGR).

UGR occur when things are not what we expect. Ever wondered why we 'go silent' when we join new groups or start a new job? Over the first few weeks, we will silently listen and watch our new environment. Questioning where the danger is, where is it safe? We will look to find individuals with similar values. We will learn the rules of this jungle.

We drop into survival mode—we are figuring out what the rules really are. We are understanding if our values actually fit into the new 'tribe'.

When we agreed to join this new tribe, accept the job, or go on the second date, we did so because, through the 'interview' process, we felt that it was right for us. We believed that the values and the standard of this new arrangement were close enough to our own. We then return to our more elemental state as we begin to understand our new environment. We get stressed. The reason for so much stress in our reality is because what we are told as 'truth' is often not.

UGR are the actual state of our environment, not what we imagine it to be. In our imagined reality, we would willingly give our ultimate sacrifice as we believe in the cause. But when we are faced with the actual state, we know what we should be doing but stop short because the values and standards we were promised are not there to see.

Organisations can spend eons and thousands of dollars writing values, but most organisations fail to uphold them. There might be a nod to them, but have they become a living embodiment of the organisation. If the answer to that question is "Hmm, sometimes" or a flat "No!", it is the UGR that rules. If this is the situation, return to the values chapter (Turn and Face 'the BUT') and do the work.

Even within our closest relationships, we will sense UGR as we grow and mature at our individual pace. As children grow and our roles change, we will feel the stress. When one of us changes jobs, we will feel the shift. There is a reason why moving house is one of the most stressful events for most people. The reason is UGR.

These unwritten ground rules are the remaining rapids in our relationships.

Now that we have given this stress a name, we can see it for what it is. UGR are a signal that we do not belong, or do not yet belong. It is a signal from our reptilian brain that we are evolving.

The Evolution Revolution

When Gabrielle Visited

In February of 2023, Gabrielle visited New Zealand. This was not some heavenly, winged creature bearing the good news from above. Instead, Gabrielle was the most devastating cyclone ever to hit the Land of the Long White Cloud. Months' worth of rain fell in a matter of hours across the far north, Auckland, the Eastern Cape, and the Hawkes Bay region. Accompanied by ferocious winds, homes, businesses, and agriculture were decimated and the national infrastructure was destroyed. The final death toll was only 11 but the effect on mental health was immeasurable. The initial estimated cost of recovery was at least NZ$15-20 billion.

This was a weather event the likes of which New Zealand had never encountered but one which was only a matter of time in the coming. As our planet warms, more and extreme weather events are being experienced across the globe. How did humanity allow it to get to this state?

We allowed it to get to this by arguing, by nit-picking about the wrong thing. For decades, the developed world has bickered about whether the climate crisis was caused by anthropomorphic change or was it just the natural cycle of Earth. We prevaricated about policies and spoke of guidelines while continuing to change our natural environment like a vengeful greedy god intent on short-termism rather than protecting our futures.

Collectively, we have done what all humans do; we stuck our heads in the sand rather than face change. Now the change is being forced upon us and it will be far more expensive than that which could have been achieved if sanity had prevailed when these planetary changes were identified.

Why do we never learn? Earlier in the book, I wrote about our inherent need for certainty. From the womb, we seek certainty. If we are fortunate to be born to loving parents in a healthy community, our certainty is confirmed and as we grow, we begin to seek variety. This is the first paradox that allows us to grow. But, even for the most fortunate of us, what happens when we are challenged by issues that are so big, we cannot comprehend them, uncertainty roars so loudly, it cannot be ignored. When this happens, we will do anything to feel certain again. And in this world of instant gratification, we seek the easiest path, the path that confirms our certainty, RIGHT NOW, and to hell with the long-term consequences.

This is why real lasting change is so hard. It takes time. Initially, we are unlikely to see any benefit, personally, politically, or economically, so we stop bothering. We get distracted and seek the next shiny penny. How do we, therefore, individually, and collectively, change?

Let's start by extracting the word 'change' from our vocabulary. See what I did there? You probably read that and immediately thought—stupid idea, that wouldn't work, I like the word change, you have no right to remove that word from my lexicon! To be honest, I felt that as I wrote these words. But this is the problem with our definition and our relationship with change. We were always taught that you can't change other people. That might be true but what if it's not? What if we modified the environment to invite them to grow and had a framework that helped them with evolving to their best selves?

Change often feels like an event, a point in time. Change is our one companion. It is always there. Most often, change is a drift in a direction. We don't notice this until we do. Those extra calories or an extra glass of wine … we tell ourselves, it's fine. Until our clothes don't fit quite so well, or we are drinking every day rather than just on the weekend. Our visits to the gym become less frequent, which is fine until we can't walk up the stairs without wheezing.

Change occurs in families, and too often we don't take time to notice. We remember the big events, birth, crawling, first undisturbed night, potty training then, all of a sudden, the kids left home, and we are empty nesters. How conscious were we during those years? Life is a constant transition through which most of us drift. Imagine being more conscious, every day, and how much more would we feel blessed?

Then change happens, and it normally happens to us. Too often, we swerve well clear of making that shift ourselves. And, because we didn't notice the tell-tale signs that modification was necessary, God or the universe steps in, and the activity is directed. And let's face it, no one likes change being done to them. We love change, for the other person. Why, because, we are perfect; are we not?

If you've got this far in your quest to become *Unstoppable*, you will be long past the belief that you are perfect. You are perfectly on the road to Unstoppableness but there are always roadblocks and on our accelerated road trip of Unstoppability we will often feel that those roadblocks are other people. It must be other people because we are the *Unstoppable* ones.

This happens to me all too frequently. During a period of massive growth, I go deep inside myself thinking no one else can help. As I look back over life, I can see all those periods of acceleration and they are matched with frustration … towards other people, especially those close to me. I'm moving forward, they are not—it's their fault!

But we all evolve at our own pace, and we must have patience to allow others to catch up. Some others will be left behind. This is why, as Unstoppable Forces, it is important to empower transition rather than expect change. Transition, along with its many definitions and connotations that the 21st century has required of the word, creates a constancy of change. Transition is an iterative process. I will, for the most part, always be a human being. During my time in this Earthly Suit, I have transitioned from a foetus to a baby, through toddlerhood and teenageness to adulthood. Ahead of me, I have old age, and then, in that final moment, when I remove 'The Suit' for the last time, Spirit. Life is transition and we should embrace it.

We fail because we fight the transition. We are comfortable with where we are and what we are doing, so we stagnate. If you have ever walked past stagnant water, what does it look like, what does it smell like, and if you were brave enough, how did it feel? It's slimy and stinky. We increase our pace to get away from it. But that is how most of us live our lives. Living in that unhealthy stagnant fug and telling ourselves we are happy about it. Our governments, media, and employers reinforce how grateful we should be to have these comfortable (stagnant) lives.

We are so desperate to protect our comfort we have stopped growing. On our quest to be *Unstoppable*, we have left too many behind. If humanity is to survive, we have a responsibility to bring others along for the ride, or at the very least, introduce them to the concept that there are bicycles for hire. Too many, at the first feeling of resistance, give up and melt back into their mediocrity.

In his book, *The War of Art*, Stephen Pressfield, asked the question, "How many businesses would have to close if we all took one step towards our dreams?" [48]

Just think, prisons would empty, the tobacco industry would go up in smoke, and the alcohol industry would dry up. Fast food industries and big pharma would have few customers or patients. And that is with just one step towards dreams, one step away from mediocrity. But as Pressfield's whole book surmises, too many are crushed by the Resistance that the idea of change introduces.

We commit to modifying a small part of our lives and resistance comes roaring. We choose to drink less, but there's a bottle of 'white' in the fridge. Our diet is going so well but ... that chocolate cake. We commit to writing a book (ahem) and even get started, but then one day,

---

[48] Steven Pressfield (2002), *The War of Art*.

the words don't come, so we stop for a few days convincing ourselves, *that's okay, I'll go back to it*. Then, another idea gives us an excuse not to write and the book dies. Resistance wins.

To change, we must embrace resistance, accepting that, in a way, it is a part of us, and in another, it is a very different beast. We 'beat' resistance by living a life of transition. Becoming comfortable with the discomfort of change. When resistance rises, we lean in and welcome it as a part of the process. When we welcome resistance as a part of our growth, it loses its power, and we can continue on our path.

Don't be fooled, resistance will not give up. Resistance will come at you again and again and every time it will be smarter and 'badder' than the last time. This monster will not stop and the closer you get to your goals, the harder it will charge at you. Be ready and learn to walk with resistance as if it is your very own, hungry, bored, tired toddler in a sweetshop. We must love resistance into submission or face a stagnant life. Resistance feeds off every endeavour we commence and, as it will not stop, we must get used to it and use its power for our growth. This is how we transition to *Unstoppable*.

How is it that some organisations succeed with the transition while others fail? Why are most businesses at a standstill while others flourish? The answer lies in the definition of the word evolution.

Survival is the Exception

Evolution refers to the gradual process of change and development over time, typically involving the accumulation of genetic variations within a population. It encompasses the diversification of species, adaptation to environments, and the emergence of new traits and characteristics. In simpler terms, evolution is nature's way of saying, "Hey, let's try something different and see if it works."

My first ever business began before I was ten years old. At that time, in Scotland, fizzy drinks were all the rage. Beyond the popular dark brown-coloured soda drink and lemonade, new flavours were coming onto the market. IRN-BRU, made in Scotland by Girders, was our national drink. The Bon Accord lorry would even deliver glass bottles filled with your 'nectar' of choice once a week. I know, imagine getting your groceries delivered every week, just like the milkman.

Long before the realisation that, as guardians of this planet, we should be managing our waste, the purveyors of our 'ginger' as it was colloquially known in the West of Scotland, wanted us to return the bottles for re-use. For every bottle returned, we would be given ten pennies. Our weekly consumption of 'pop' was never going to make me rich, even if I'd managed to get my hands on the bottles. However, not everyone was interested in making the effort to take the glasses back to the shops. What was needed was an enterprising young man to take these bottles off the hands of our neighbours and return them to the shops.

The money started rolling in; well, when I say rolling in, I was making more through this enterprise than from pocket money. And then the opportunity to mow people's lawns came along. Within a year, I even hired my first employee. He only lasted one garden, but it did teach me some leadership and human resources skills, so probably worth his wages. The grass cutting was hard graft, but it was good money, better than the paper round, which paid one penny per paper delivered.

With every step, I was evolving, learning from each experience, and applying those lessons to the next endeavour. It is the same within the British Army. Learning to clean a weapon has a 'drill', and learning to fire that weapon has a drill. Every activity has a 'drill.' Learning to march has a 'drill'—this is considered so important that armies even employ psychopaths known as Drill Sergeants to ensure we get the basics right. The American Forces now use the term 'evolution' to describe the activity of drilling. The idea is that every time the exercise is practised the student evolves into a higher version of themselves. If at first, you don't succeed, try and try again.

In time, with practice, that 'drill', or evolution, becomes second nature. It becomes embedded in our subconscious so that, no matter the situation or level of fear or stress, we will still carry out that action; perfectly. This is no different from the activity of learning to drive. Our instructor 'drills' us until we can safely control the vehicle. Only once we can prove we understand the basics can we move on to the next level— actually driving.

Weapon handling always requires a level of attention, rightly so, as the end of a rifle can do lots of damage. Weapon stripping and cleaning drills, followed by dry-firing drills —where there are no bullets present—lead on to range firing. On exercise, blank rounds are used to allow soldiers to become comfortable with fire and manoeuvre drills. Every step is a building block for the next step.

After a tour of duty sitting behind a desk—staff work was never my choice but necessary for promotion and advancement as an officer—it was time for me to go back into the field. Staff work requires writing papers, doing analysis, under using my trigger finger with mouse clicks as I stared into a computer screen. Losing that muscle memory and replacing it with the mundane. Working on my fitness was relatively straightforward as I always ensured my fitness was above average, however, my weapon skills were rusty, to say the least. I requalified on the Heckler Koch 53 Assault rifle after a day on the firing range, but my pistol skills were rubbish.

I organised with the senior small arms instructor to open the firing range for one morning. It was a beautiful blue-sky day. Most range days are planned for driving rain and gale-force winds, so I was already running out of excuses for missing the target. My instructor checked my Sig-226 pistol as I entered the range and then picked up a full ammo box of 9 mm rounds. After checking that I could remember the dangerous end and watching me firing off the first few magazines, he turned to me and said, "You know what you're doing; you just need to practice now. Come find me when the box is empty."

That box contained 1,000 rounds of ammunition. That equates to seventy-seven reloads of magazine clips. But there are no shortcuts to rebuilding that muscle memory. With the firing of each magazine of thirteen rounds, I would walk to the target, and analyse my shooting. Was the grouping tight enough, was it in the right place? Was I snatching as I pulled the trigger, and was my finger placed correctly on the trigger with every shot? And with those seventy-seven reloads, had the rawness on my thumb from the reloads caused me to shift my pistol grip? Before returning to my firing point, my last task was to patch the target, and then repeat.

After seventy-seven evolutions, the back and forth to the target, my shooting had improved! It was then time to clean my weapon: the striping, cleaning, and oiling should always be the last activity. Look after your weapon and it will look after you. Like riding a bike, once the basics are 'locked in', no matter how long it's been, getting back to 'drill', or the evolution, is all it takes.

However, when we are trying to figure out something new, where we think no drill exists, we need to get imaginative. We need to 'down, test, and adjust". This is another weapon-firing principle we can use until we settle on what is right.

My first 'post-uniform' business was called 80 Summers. After trying out building a software business, which was successful but not my passion, I committed to creating a business that focused on my passion, a business where I was doing what I loved. 80 Summers was my first attempt at a coaching business. It was a side hustle, as I figured the basics out. The name, 80 Summers, is the average life expectancy in the developed world. We have only eighty trips around the sun to ensure that we have truly lived. My coaching business provided clients with the tools to embrace life to the full. That business set the foundations for business number two, Stew Darling Limited, and resulted in me authoring the book, *Lead through Life*.

Over the following three years, I continued to fix the bugs, recorded online courses, began keynote speaking and delivering one and two-day workshops, and began my radio show. Throughout the pandemic lockdowns, I shifted the whole business online and continued to operate. During 2020-21, I assisted businesses in doing the same using a simple planning tool that I had developed during my years in the field. I call it Dominate the Ground.

Every evolution has created more challenges, but they have also readied me to face those challenges. Everything that Unstoppable Force is becoming is based on learning from these 'drills' and evolving as the environment requires. Using Dominate the Ground has been key to this work.

Dominating the Ground

On a rather damp Sunday in 1815, the decisive battle of the Napoleonic wars was fought. The result caused a shift of power from the vast empires of Europe to a time known to historians as Pax Britannica. This period in history saw peace due to the growing power of Great Britain on the world stage. Not just in military terms, but also in trade, democracy, and global influence. Pax Britannica lasted until the end of World War II when it is generally accepted that the world order shifted again to Pax Americanus. That rainy day saw the defeat of Napoleon's army by the combined armies of Arthur Wellesley, the First Duke of Wellington, and Field Marshal Blücher.

The place was a small town called Waterloo. Knowing an engagement was inevitable, Wellington gathered his British troops on a sloping ridge near the Hougemont farm. The reverse slope enabled Wellington to 'hide' his forces from Napoleon, thus utilising the element of surprise. The, late, arrival of Blücher's Prussian forces resulted in the outcome. However, it was Wellington's strategic preparations that were the 'hinge factor' of the battle. The hinge, or deciding factor, of the battle, had taken place over a year earlier. As Wellington's troops moved south during 1814, he had reconnoitred the lie of the land around Quatre-bras and Waterloo commenting to his generals that the land in front of the reverse slope would be the place to close with his enemy.

The hinge factor—certainly one of them—was that Wellington's troops, the British, held the high ground. They could 'dominate' the ground.

The sound of that cannon fire over that farmland of Northern France still ripples around the world. The end of the great European empires, the outbreak of two world wars, the Great Depression, and the Cold War can all be linked to that day. Humanity evolved as a result of Wellington's choice of ground.

A few decades later, on a different continent, Lieutenant Colonel Joshua Chamberlain found himself and his 20th Maine Infantry Regiment in a precarious position. They were the end of the line. Responsible for protecting the left flank of the whole Army of the Potomac. If Chamberlain's forces were destroyed, it would start a ripple effect that could result in a very different end to the American Civil War. In the days before the battle of Gettysburg, the Army of the Potomac and the Confederate Army were advancing towards one another.

On the second day of the battle, Chamberlain, a quiet-spoken schoolteacher, had his worst fear confirmed. The enemy was advancing toward his position on Little Round Top. Like much of the rolling countryside of the northeast United States, Little Round Top is a wooded, rocky feature. Standing there many years after the battle, I could imagine those soldiers, miles from home, digging into that rocky soil. Scraping away the dirt to secure their position as much as possible. The cold and damp of the hours of darkness, unable to light fires for fear of giving away their position. The constant threat of an enemy incursion—knowing it would come, but when. The hunger and the thirst.

Aware of the danger to his troops, aware of their location and situation, and the strategic importance of his orders, Chamberlain launched an audacious bayonet charge down the steep side of the rocky outcrop. The courage of the decision and his men's action was the beginning of the end. The battle would continue for another two days but the left flank was secure. General Robert E Lee's army was defeated and in time, the Army of the Potomac would be victorious. It might be said that the modern-day United States had its faltering birth in that Bayonet Charge. Chamberlain held the high ground, and he used it to his advantage, dominating the ground and the enemy.

How would humanity have evolved without the bravery of Chamberlain and his men? What could have been our history? Would the Gettysburg Address ever have been proclaimed? Would Abraham Lincoln fail as a president? Would slavery continue for another generation?

Military history is replete with examples of battles being won, or lost, by 'the ground'. That might be the physical ground on which it was fought, or it might be dominating the thought space of the environment. Having such self-belief in ourselves or in the ability of our people that victory was achieved before an artillery shell was even fired. This superior thinking and execution are at the heart of Dominating the Ground.

Any organisation that creates a plan and slavishly follows it is destined to die. Any business plan is out of date before it is even signed off by the board; that business is already living in the past. We need a more dynamic tool to manage the pace of life. The solution comes back to mission command; what to do, not how to do it. The tool I have used to assist clients out of the stagnant morass that has been suffocating their business is based on the British Army planning process. On the battlefield, everything changes all of the time and at every level. The British Army developed a planning process that is so simple that the most junior soldier can understand and use it for the tiniest of tasks while that same tool is utilised by vast headquarters to plan major campaigns. As it is the same tool, used across the ranks, as the soldiers promote through the ranks, they become more and more proficient with the tool.

While the British Army planning process may not be best suited to the civilian/corporate world, with a few tweaks, it is still powerful. The Unstoppable Force, Dominate the Ground planning tool has a proven success rate, from keeping me alive during my years in the field, through single-employee businesses, to multimillion-dollar enterprises. Why does it work? Because it does not focus on change, it focuses on prioritising the tasks that enable evolution to occur. Through a constant reflection and review process, the whole team holds one another accountable and so the business accelerates. The reflection and review process are dynamic and happens at all levels of the organisation every day. We have not yet found a business in which Dominate the Ground does not work.

At the most basic level, the reason I am comfortable making this statement is that Dominate the Ground reaches into our deepest needs. It creates a certainty in the process, removes the fear of change, and introduces the enthusiasm of variety. This is the answer for us all. Fall in love with the process and the evolution will happen. Consider your Little Round Top moments—what could be the alternative if you chose not to evolve?

What Next?

When it became clear that my military service was coming to an end, Liz asked me, "What next?"

My reply, much like the vultures sitting the tree in Disney's version of *The Jungle Book*, was to respond "Donno; what do you what to do?"

Both were serious questions that would have repercussions for the rest of our lives but my offer to allow Liz the decision was in no part lazy. Throughout our married life, Liz fulfilled the traditional role of a military wife. Giving up her career, and some might say, her identity to support my career. It was she who faced the stress of raising two children while I was off in the sandbox. As I was promoted, she assumed whatever role was required. All this without complaint (well, not too often anyway).

It was only right that a decision about our post-uniform life was offered to her. About a week later, Liz bounded into the kitchen, magazine in hand, and said, "How about moving to New Zealand?"

I looked at her agog and stuttered some sort of reply.

Before Liz and I became an item, she had written to hospitals across New Zealand looking to gain midwifery experience overseas. She heard nothing and joined the British Army instead. In the middle of this process, enter, stage left, the love of her life, a certain Pilot Officer Darling. As our relationship deepened, she 'parked' her dreams of New Zealand and commenced a successful military career, and then we got married.

That evolution died. Or did it? Her hankering for travel, specifically to New Zealand, obviously sat quietly in a corner of her brain, until the right time. This was the right time. Who was I to say no? So, my response was, "Let's start the process."

That process took over two years. The initial excitement of the idea soon wore off as the bureaucracy of the process took over. That it didn't fit into our perfect schedule (and the school calendar) didn't matter to the process. The fear of a negative response from the medical checks, Liz's new employer, or New Zealand Immigration grew and grew.

The thought of home-schooling our two teenagers as the timeline slipped caused stress in our relationship. Liz was then informed that the medical check had discovered a health issue that might ruin our plans. Every step of the way, we were hit by the negativity of the process, but we stuck it out. Each roadblock made us stronger for the next, and we soldiered on.

The home-schooling actually became a thing for a few weeks. Biology was studied with a visit to Kew Gardens in London. Music studies were completed on a trip to see *The Jersey Boys* in London's West End. Physical Education was achieved when the kids joined me for my morning routine. The day home schooling finally came to an end we were studying Physics at Alton Towers theme park in England. In the queue for the biggest roller coaster discussing the merits of centrifugal force, I got the call. Our visas had arrived, and we were off to a new adventure in New Zealand.

Throughout that whole process, from Liz's first letters to the arrival of our visas, we had lived the roller coaster of change. The benefit of those years was that we had evolved into the people we needed to be to make our new life a success. Over those years we had become anti-fragile. The start-stop of change takes this lesson, this evolution, away from us. Recognising that it is the evolution that got humanity here, embracing this and using drills and evolutions will get us 'to next'.

How do we solve climate change and every other major issue facing humanity in the 21st century? If I had the answer to that question, I'd likely have more media coverage than Elon Musk, but here are a few ideas. We can all begin to treat life as an ongoing evolution. Using every experience as an opportunity to learn. If we move away from a mind of success and failure to a growth mind of everything is a lesson, we can all lead more content lives. At the family level, teaching our children about failure as a lesson, about standards and values as key to growth will result in a society that embraces the best of us rather than sinking to the lowest level. Humanity will meet this challenge—it always has.

Governments and big businesses take note of shifts in societal thinking, so we must not believe that we have no voice. There are so many examples of grassroots organisations creating lasting change. Rosa Parks not moving from her seat on the bus and Nelson Mandela's belief in freedom, are but two, and if we choose to look closer to home, we will see examples everywhere. We can all change our world, this world, if we start. Evolution is inevitable even if we dislike change. It is our responsibility to choose the direction in which we evolve.

Waiting for Superman

There is nothing better on a rainy afternoon than heading to the cinema or cuddling up on the couch to watch a good movie. Obviously, my genre of choice is the Bond franchise but sometimes for a break, we will watch either a Marvel or DC superhero film. The escapism is fun.

The nod to our childhood is comforting—who was the best Hulk, the Lou Ferrigno version of the 1970s or the more modern CGI?

However, I see a negative to the superhero genre that is sweeping our screens. Are we waiting for our Superman (insert other superheroes if preferred)? Do we sit in expectation of someone else solving humanity's problem? Do we blame the lack of activists for the direction of society? Do we look at the activists and claim it is their fault? This is living in lack (of energy). This attitude has led to the current zeitgeist that plagues our society.

We see it in the gathering anxiety of our children and grandchildren. We see it in the apathy toward the big issues of this century. We fight our responsibility to change and blame someone else. As was revealed toward the beginning of the book, we don't have to wait for Superman (or woman); they have been here all along hidden in the only place we fear to look. Our superhero looks back at us every time we look in the mirror, but society has hoodwinked us into blindness.

We watch these films yearning for our superheroes or superpowers and are left bereft. Sure, we might not fly, see through walls, or shoot laser beams from our arse, but humanity never really needed any of those powers—although that third one might come in handy—all we need is to evolve, little by little, every day. This is how we all become *Unstoppable*.

I Am Enough

There were over fifty of us, all 'on parade' in our sports kit. I was breathing as if my left lung had slipped out of my backside and been left somewhere on the route along which the physical training instructor had led us. It was lovingly known as 'THE VOMINATOR', a hilly circuit through the forest. Our challenge was to complete each circuit faster than our last attempt. No one told us that on the first circuit or we might have attempted to slow the pace a wee bit. Failure to stay with the group resulted in an unsuccessful grading—and a train ticket home, joining the hundreds of applicants who hadn't even received the invite to throw up. Throughout the physical training epic, there were cerebral tasks to be completed too, and failure to meet the standard received the same result, a train ticket home.

Having prepared for over six months for this week, I still found myself wanting … a lot! We all did, that was the point. We had volunteered for one of the most challenging selection courses in the world but the prize at the end might be a coveted place at 'spy school', a step closer to covert operations.

These four days pushed us all mentally and physically beyond ourselves. The discomfort required us to go well beyond motivation. It took the few of us to a place of discipline—where the dream far outweighed the discomfort. It took us to a place of self-belief that we were good enough—even when the pain came—that we could meet it head-on and come through the other side. We were ready to give our ultimate sacrifice, again and again, for a cause that was bigger than ourselves.

By the end, over thirty-five had boarded that train, returning to their units. Those remaining were loaded on for the main course. Most of those courses resulted in a low-single figure pass rate. Why? Because the standard had to be high. Only those who were capable of giving their most again and again in the harshest of environments and still have the capacity to give the ultimate sacrifice, day after day, we were fortunate enough to receive the prize. The prize of fulfilment. The prize of realising that, "I Am Enough."

There is a gift hidden deep within your ultimate sacrifice. I get it, giving of yourself day after day can feel thankless. Sometimes, it feels that no one is recognising that extra mile. Maybe we even feel we are being taken advantage of. When we feel like this, we are not giving our ultimate sacrifice. We are being selfish. Deep down, we are still thinking about what we will get out of our service.

When we shift focus to the other person, all these feelings of inadequacy disappear. The great thing about this shift is that we will physically feel the energy flowing from us and back to us. This is the gift of truly giving our ultimate sacrifice—we feel fulfilled.

No longer will we seek happiness in things. The happiness that the developed world seeks is always in more things. Bigger TVs, faster cars, more luxurious holidays and while the event of the purchase releases high levels of positive energy, we are still left wanting. Those holidays are amazing but the return to reality comes with a heavy bump, and we are already looking for the next 'hit'. This life cannot lead to fulfilment.

Fulfilment comes from addressing our deepest need, to have certainty. Certainty comes from the self-belief that we are enough. The only statement we need, to move beyond the selfish, instant gratification of our world is, "I Am Enough." Not only does our self-belief flow from this statement, but our choice to hold ourselves to a higher standard and to make our ultimate sacrifice also flows. When we know, 'I am enough', we receive the gift of giving. We are enough to share our experience.

You have learned the 'how to' of negotiation. We have introduced the ideas of how our collective, and individual, past is adding to our stresses and keeping us 'locked' in stress. With both these tools we are better prepared to see where and how we can assist our fellow travellers on humanity's journey. In the previous chapter, we plunged into the challenge of why we find it so difficult to change. This is the paradox earlier introduced—humanity is desperate for certainty. Once we have accepted that 'I am enough' we become the certainty for our family, our team, and the world. By providing that 'crutch', our gift to these communities is that, in time, they will see a deeper and deeper level of self-belief within themselves.

In the early days of giving your ultimate sacrifice, it will feel like the flow is away from us. Lean in, and you will feel that flow returning. It will not always, in fact seldomly, come directly from the person or group to which you are giving your ultimate sacrifice. Look for the moments of coincidence when you feel energised and when you feel joy. In those gifts that you unexpectedly receive. God is listening and responding to the positive vibes you are manifesting. Now you know you are giving the ultimate sacrifice. There is no such thing as coincidence; it is a word that humanity has coined to answer the gifts God and the Universe provide when we are giving of ourselves. What we are experiencing is synchronicity, a true fulfilment, and it can only come from freely giving of ourselves.

A fulfilled life is available to every one of us when we freely give and are always on the lookout for opportunities to raise society's standard. The accountability will not be accepted by everyone in the first (or forty-first) instance—that's okay, they are not yet ready to receive. Make the sacrifice anyway, sometimes we can be surprised.

Giving the ultimate sacrifice, when done from service, is self-fulfilling. By helping others, we are ultimately helping ourselves. We build that muscle of self-belief and can give more and more freely. The ultimate freedom is a life of fulfilment, built from within. When we move closer to this state, we begin to live from the centre. In living from the centre, we are truly *Unstoppable*.

Discovering Wholeheartedness

Just outside the gothic doorway of St Giles cathedral, Edinburgh, Scotland, there is a heart. The mosaic was created within the cobbled streets of The Royal Mile and this tourist attraction marks the entrance to the now demolished tolbooth. In Scotland, a tolbooth was the courthouse, meeting room, and jail in each town; the 'centre' of the town's activity. This heart is known as the Heart of Midlothian and in Scottish folklore, the phrase, 'to touch the Heart of Midlothian' refers to a tradition where individuals would spit on the heart-shaped pattern as a gesture of contempt for the former prison and its prisoners. I'm still amused when I remember the look on Liz' face, my wife of fewer than thirty-six hours, when I 'hocked my loogie' and spat it into the heart. Even after my explanation, she refused to do the same.

Tradition states that those who partake of this gross activity will be granted good fortune, unlike the poor souls who were historically executed on this spot in the past. That act of gobbing onto this street reminds us not to give up on our lives. That, to live a fulfilled life, we should all live from our Centre, we must all live, as the towns of ancient Scotland did, from the heart.

The Standard of Man

We have a toast in our family. It is based on an old Scottish saying from the era of the Scottish poet, Robert Burns.

Wha's lik us? (Who is like us)

Naebody (Nobody)

An' their all deid! (And they are all dead).

The writer was suggesting that, even back in the 18th century, humanity was falling short of the standard of man. Worse, the third line of the toast proposes that there was no one left to remind us of that 'standard of man'.

I choose a more positive view. In spite of the seven generations that have passed since these words were written, I believe The Standard of Man is still there. It is still there and screaming to many of us to be set free. The Standard of Man is the reawakening we are experiencing in society, and concurrently being crushed through conformity. We have only been fooled into looking for the Standard of Man in the wrong places. When we finally choose to turn our view inwards, we feel the Standard of Man patiently waiting for our attention. Recovering the Standard of Man is to become *Unstoppable*.

I love the unattributed quote: "Step into the Zone of the Unknown."

I love it so much it adorns the wall of our toilet at home. This quote means so much more than the more common, step out of your comfort zone.

Stepping out of our comfort zone suggests leaving something we love, a place where we are, err, comfortable. But we can only be comfortable with something we know. And this is the crux. Our comfort zone comes from a head position. Leaving our comfort zone causes us to think of everything we will miss as we set forth on our adventure. Every Friday morning, when I hoist my 60lb (27 kg) pack on my back and set off on an 8-mile Tab, I am not thinking about the weight or the distance, I am thinking about leaving my warm snuggly bed. The discomfort will come, and trust me, it does every week.

Tabbing—the Tactical Advance to Battle—is a part of military training. It is a means by which infantry soldiers can move rapidly on foot towards the objective. United States Armed Forces studies from Afghanistan have shown that a physically fit soldier has the ability to fight, manoeuvre, and survive carrying up to ⅓ of their body weight.

Every Friday, it is the anticipation and excitement of the Tab that causes me to drag my sorry ass out of bed. The memories of 'those days', and the camaraderie of the joint effort.

This is a reminder of my time in Command when I was honoured to join my junior soldiers and officers under training as they were 'tested' by my physical training instructors. Even the iconography of the British soldier tabbing across the wastes of the Falkland Islands strikes a chord despite that campaign taking place nearly ten years before I took my oath of Service. I should note here that the activity being undertaken in the image of those soldiers, with the radio operator in the rear flying the Union Flag was actually called 'yomping'. Yomping is very similar to tabbing, the only difference is, it is what the Royal Marines do. Why have one word when three are available? The US Forces call it Rucking.

Tabbing has no interest in rank, Lance Corporal or Lieutenant Colonel. The weight of the pack is the same, the distance is the same, and the time limit is the same. It is a simple pass or fail. This is the reality that meets me on the trail every Friday. Each week, as I hoist that pack, I enter my Zone of the Unknown. How will my body respond? What about 'the voices' in my head? Will it be one of those mornings when I embrace the dark, the scent of the trees, and the sound of the ocean, or will it be a day of mental violence?

Will it be one of those days when 'Negative Nelly' has the upper hand? These are the best days. The two-way flow of words all suggesting that I only tab half the distance, or for half the time, or, my favourite, throw my pack altogether and sort it out later. On those days, the battle is never the physical pain, it is always the head games that create the fire fight. If I spent those tabs in my head, focused on my comfort zone, I would always lose. Leaning into the head games and pushing harder, rather than listening to them, takes me further and further into the Zone of the Unknown. How hard can I go?

The comfort zone is about looking back. The Zone of the Unknown is about looking forward, about seeking new challenges. This is a true heart position. What our brains are telling us or reminding us of no longer matters, we have become primal. We are predators once again and we are on the hunt. We are living from the heart.

When a mammal is developing in the womb, as the foetus is nurtured by the host (mum), the heart is one of the first organs to form. Until recent scientific discoveries, it was thought that the sole purpose of the heart was as a muscle to pump blood around the body. However, we now know that the heart is so much more. In the ancient Greek world, the heart was 'the seat and centre of human experience'. It was understood to be the centre of the personality, and included the intellect, emotions, and will. The electromagnetic field of the heart is so much more powerful than that of our brain—but we ignore it.

We fall in love and send images of the heart to our intended. Iconography of Christianity often displays Jesus surrounded by a heart or the artwork may even focus on His heart—maybe they knew something we've forgotten. When you last fell in love, was it a brain activity or did it come from the heart? When relationships end, we do not say we are brain-broken but heartbroken.

Living from our hearts is a vulnerable position, it is where we can really move the needle towards becoming *Unstoppable* and that is why we don't do it. We must become comfortable in this discomfort. It is also why I 'Tab' every Friday.

The Zone of the Unknown I enter every week causes pain and discomfort, but over time, I have learned to lock that sensation away. My brain has learned to stop whinging, well, for most of the time. Tabbing has taught me that there is more within me than my brain gives credit for. Living from the centre enables me to be *Unstoppable*. Not only in the pre-dawn light but throughout my day. When business challenges arise and my head explodes, or there is a 'tender moment' with a friend or family member. The muscle I have developed through tabbing reminds me that all I have to do is go deep and live from my centre.

Our brains are trained to keep us playing small. As we have read throughout this book, our brains have developed over thousands of years to keep us safe. Whether from sabre-tooth tigers or the bogeyman, our brains will remind us of our limitations and hamper our growth. It is doing its job too well. Unfortunately, as humanity has matured, and we live in a more and more comfortable world, our brains are causing us to stagnate.

If we let them, our saddest and most joyful moments can teach us to live from the heart, from our centre. We can use those emotions to learn more about what is important to us. Instead, we have been taught to lock those emotions away, and not to show our vulnerability. I shared my happiest and saddest moments at the very beginning of this book. Where might yours lie?

We now know that we can revisit those moments and feel the emotion. With years of maturity maybe we can see the event through a different lens. Not to change the event but maybe see it from another's perspective. We can meet those friends and family members long dead and have those conversations, those arguments that we thought were left unsaid. To look that person in the eye and wish them well. To thank them for the person we became because of their input in our lives. This is a heart position, and it is a place from which we must learn to live if we are to make the most of our time in this earthly suit.

To understand all that is going on in our brains and bodies from before the moment of conception to our last breath requires us to listen to our hearts. To feel the shift from the highest frequency of brain waves to the calm restorative state of deep sleep we sense the flushing of cortisol and adrenalin from our systems and in doing so we relax into a heart position, into our centre.

By removing the 21st century focus on money and financial wealth and challenging ourselves to refocus on what wealth truly means to us returns us to a place of love, for ourselves and our communities. We have become greedy. This instant gratification mindset is destroying our health and our relationships; it is destroying humanity's opportunity to live in harmony on the planet that sustains our lives. It is our responsibility to review our relationship with wealth.

To realise that money is not the root of all evil, but our relationship with it, can be unhealthy. A healthy relationship with money should consider our relationships with other parts of our lives. Is our health a priority or something we take for granted? How can we deepen every relationship? When will we address the spirit that exists deep within us all and allow it to guide us, rather than existing in the rat race? Have we considered our uniqueness and what we will do with the precious time in our Earthly Suit? When will we give ourselves the permission to work more smartly and in doing so reward ourselves with the time to grow in other areas? Once we have addressed all these areas of our lives, when will we be courageous enough to ask, how can I become more 'me'? In this question, we engage in Personal Development, becoming *Unstoppable* and growing from our hearts.

Like the houses in which we live or the vehicles we drive, our Earthly Suit requires regular maintenance. From before we are born, we are under attack from our environment. The air we breathe, the water we drink, the food we consume, and the medication we require are all accelerating our Earthly Suit's journey to the scrap heap. So, when will our health become a priority? When will we holistically review our lifestyle? Is it time to 'rest our heads upon the grass and listen to it grow'—a quote from the American poet, Walt Whitman (or the band, *Pink Martini*). [49, 50]

When will we consider sleep as a necessity rather than wasting 'precious' time? Will we ever return to the days of eating 'real' food to protect our liver and feed our gut? How long will it take us to realise that in doing so, our need for drugs and pills will decrease? With those

---

[49] Walt Whitman (1855), *Leaves of Grass*.
[50] Marashian and Lauderdale (2009) *Splendor In The Grass*.

additional hours of sleep and a well-fed gut, when will we feel the energy to get out and exercise? With sleep, sustenance, and exercise, our hearts will reflect the love that we are giving to ourselves, and every facet of our existence will shine. Taking care of ourselves shall empower us to be more within our families and throughout every relationship. By looking after our Earthly Suit and the heart within, we will live from our centre, and become a centre for those still seeking the path to *Unstoppable*.

In addressing these first three aspects of our lives, we harness what it means to be unreasonable on our terms. To question the world around us through self-reflection and return to our unique selves. Through a new deeper understanding of ourselves, of our wealth, and of our health, we come to a place of self-belief that no one can take from us. We are becoming *Unstoppable*.

What use is self-belief if we have no one with whom to share it? How do we grow? How do we find where we belong and stop just fitting in with a world content with mediocrity? We must face ourselves. Question the values of our ancestry, our country, our religion; or anything from our past that doesn't make sense. We should cast off that backpack, overloaded with pointless emotional baggage, and address our values and our standards.

Do the beliefs of our history still stack up based on our experiences or should they be the basis of the next level of our metamorphosis? In addressing our values and standards, we take the next step into our uniqueness however this can feel scary, as we are allowing ourselves to be vulnerable. Without this vulnerability, we cannot live from our centre. It is our heart that will tell us if we are truly living our values to the full.

Living our true values is how we then lead those around us. To boldly 'captain our ship' we required those values. It is our values that are the foundational level of our ability to lead. Without those values, we have no chance to live with boldness, as we will 'roll' with whim or suggestion. Without that foundation of boldness, how will we ever reach the pinnacle of leadership? Building relationships with everyone we meet moves us beyond the common concept of leadership into the world of captaincy. We deepen those relationships with vulnerability. Without values, relationships, and vulnerability, how can we ever lead without embracing the service mentality of every great leader? And only through our faith that to serve is to lead can we achieve that true leadership position of love. To truly lead through love is to live from our heart and our true centre.

Were I to develop the Lead Through Life Framework again, it would begin with a new foundation level. Before even considering our boldness or the art through which we might adapt and move through the three leadership styles, and long before I began to mature through the leadership principles, I would dig those foundations through relationships. As pack animals, we seek relationships but too often we are fearful that our vulnerability will be used against us. Other humans see that fear through our body language, and we sense their nervousness. The result is that we remain closed to that new friendship. If nervous, the tone of our voices will be all over the place, so our 'pack' grows no further. To be *Unstoppable*, we are to lean into this discomfort and build new relationships. Our world can seem a lonely place and it is too easy for us to feel alone. By recognising this malaise in society, we should see an opportunity to grow, to become *Unstoppable*, and to live from our centre.

Our values, captaincy, and ability to grow and deepen relationships through communication result in a more profound sense of belonging. That belonging requires us to be accountable. This accountability is necessary to ensure that we are no longer comfortable with just 'fitting in'. We are prepared to live in a constant level of discomfort (a little bit anyway) to assure ourselves that we are living to a higher standard. We accept that this belonging, accountability, and our new standard might result in a period of change where old relationships might end before our new tribe emerges. We accept this because we know it is but another stepping-stone on our *Unstoppable* path. Leadership is a heart-centred activity.

It's not that simple, I hear you cry. There are people and views out there that I simply disagree with. The world is unfair. There is so much conflict. To be *Unstoppable* means to rise above the pettiness that surrounds us. We are to change the narrative of conflict. Our role in conflict is to ensure that every party feels they gained some success through the conflict and grow as a result. Rather than facing off for the fight, we create an interest that we can work towards, side by side. Painting a beautiful piece of art to see our rival points of view and giving of ourselves sufficiently for them to understand our passion thus building a mutually supportive relationship. This process empowers everyone to succeed; the result is a win for humanity, and conflict becomes an opportunity for growth. When we think about conflict in these terms, not forgetting that our redlines are only a stage in the process, we remove the contentious issue and replace it with the new relationship. We negotiate from our centre.

Anyway, these conflicts are nothing more than the confluence of many rivers. The ripples, eddies, and rapids of many lives coming together in an ever more connected world. But we now know that these ripples didn't just begin within our generation. Our pains and anxieties might be the result of the lives and experiences of long-dead ancestors. Science is now revealing the reason why many struggle to become *Unstoppable*, to live this truly unique existence. Science is discovering what many ancient texts have said for millennia: "The fathers have eaten sour grapes, and the children's teeth are set on edge."—Jeremiah 31:29.

The emergence of epigenetics is not only revealing these generational experiences to be, at least in part, responsible for many of our challenges, it is also guiding us towards a solution. That solution, if we have the courage to embrace it, allows us to not only create an Unstoppable Force within our own lives but also for the lives of generations to follow. Living from our hearts has become out of time.

And why should we not live out of time? Quantum physics has proven that we do. It is humans who have put this limitation on our existence. Timelines and deadlines exist but living out of time is an opportunity to embrace growth. Change is our one constant, but we fight it. We fight the demise of our Earthly Suit; we battle the path of society. We abhor the change agents who tell us what we must do. We forget that all of life is an evolution. From the primordial soup from which we came, throughout the mutation that resulted in our current form, there has been a slow and constant transformation. Recognising the inevitability of change released us from the demands it has created on our lives. Living as a part of the evolution that is humanity is an honour. This accepted, now we can be excited about our part in the experience. Our *Unstoppable* nature is a right, not an ambiguity. Our nature is to freely live from our endless centre.

And so, just as our journey through this book is coming to an end, our path to remaining *Unstoppable* is just beginning. And, if we choose, may it never end. Sure, there might be times when we will lose our way. Times when we will be too reasonable and give way to the pressures of society. The loneliness of this path might, on occasion, cause us to hang with the 'wrong uns'. Hardship might harden our hearts and we will step away from the vulnerability that our ultimate sacrifice requires. But those of us who are pulled by a deep sense that there is more, that we can be so much more than the standard and behaviour we see all around us, will always feel the pull of our *Unstoppable* future.

We will awaken once again and discover, every time, that we can reverse our stagnation. We deeply feel, and when living from our centre, that we are *Unstoppable*. We know our heart knows no bounds. This is the freedom we once knew and that we will always seek. Our awareness feels our Unstoppable Force has been within us all along, quietly waiting to be recognised, always guiding us on a unique path to ourselves. A 'Standard of Man' for a future that the rest of humanity is silently, desperately willing us to take. A path upon which society has little choice but to embark. It is us, the *Unstoppable* ones, who will show the way.

The Unstoppable Muscle

A wholehearted life requires grit, tenacity, conflict, and a higher purpose. When all this comes together, we are truly *Unstoppable*.

It was a late fall morning. The sky was the bluest blue. The sort of endless blue that reached forever but it was cold. It was a beautiful biting, dry cold, and my hands were feeling it. I had left the sandstone edifice of Canada's Parliament buildings that sat resplendent on the bluffs overlooking the Ottawa River and considered a quick coffee at the Chateau Laurier hotel, but I needed to keep moving. I made my way past Canada's National War Memorial towards the bridge across the Ottawa Canal and back to the office in one of the twin towers of the National Defence Headquarters building. My hands might have been feeling the cold, but within, I was warmed by the heat of rage.

I had just received by far the best bollocking of my career to date. And that's saying something, I once held the record for the highest number of speeding fines across the battalion, and the Commanding Officer, quite rightly, saw fit to increase the ferocity of my dressing down with each fine. There was a sort of perverse pride that I had succeeded in three fines from three different countries; Germany, Austria, and The Netherlands, all in the same month, but 'the boss' was right to remind me of my responsibility. The most intense of those one-way conversations was a result of me informing 'the boss', when asked why I wasn't learning, that I knew my soldiers would respect the bollockings I issued all the more knowing that I was often on the receiving end too.

On this Canadian morning, the redress was different. It had been delivered by a civilian. My chilly walk that morning was returning me from a visit to the Canadian Parliament building where my presence had been requested, nae required, by the Chief of Staff to the Minister for National Defence. For months, a small team, led by me and a senior lawyer from the Canadian Defence Force Judge Advocate General's (JAG) office, had been drafting a new piece of legislation to allow the deployment of specialist troops into Afghanistan. This was important work, as the wars in Iraq and Afghanistan dragged on all countries in the coalition were struggling to meet the manpower demands. This legislation would have the double effect of not only deploying much-needed Canadian capability but also lessening the manpower drain on the UK Armed Forces.

I was a man possessed, but I had overstepped the mark. This one-way discussion was deserved but I was still mad. Why were the Canadians dragging their feet? Did they not see what I could? Their aversion to risk was actually increasing the risk. The longer this legislation might take, the greater the risk was to our soldiers on the ground. A lack of legislation risked Canada's good name on the international stage.

At the time, I was reading Lieutenant General Harold G Moore's book, *We Were Soldiers Once…And Young*, which was made into a Hollywood blockbuster with Mel Gibson playing the part of Moore.[51]

Lt Gen Harold Gregory Moore Jr, known as Hal Moore, was a remarkable military leader whose career spanned three decades and left an indelible mark on the United States Army. From his distinguished service in the Vietnam War to his unwavering commitment to his troops, Lt Gen Moore exemplified the qualities of valour, leadership, and dedication. Hal Moore's military journey began in 1945 when he enlisted in the United States Army. Rising through the ranks, he distinguished himself as a talented officer, demonstrating exceptional leadership skills and a keen understanding of tactical warfare. Moore's combat experience started during the Korean War, where he served with distinction as a forward observer. His courageous actions and strategic acumen earned him several commendations, including the Silver Star.

His most renowned contribution to military history came during the Vietnam War. In 1965, as a lieutenant colonel, he led the 1st Battalion, 7th

---

[51] Lt Gen Harold G Moore (and Joseph Galloway) (1992), *We Were Soldiers Once… And Young*.

Cavalry Regiment, in the Battle of Ia Drang, the first major engagement between American and North Vietnamese forces. Facing overwhelming odds and a fierce enemy, Moore displayed exceptional leadership, effectively coordinating air support and employing innovative tactics. His resolute leadership and dedication to his men became the hallmark of the battle and showcased his exceptional command abilities. It was this unwavering commitment to his troops that led him to co-author the book I was engrossed in. It is a gripping account of the Battle of Ia Drang, immortalising the heroism and sacrifices of the soldiers who served under Moore's command. It introduced Moore's leadership style and his dedication to the principles of honour, duty, and sacrifice to a global audience.

General Moore's military career stands as a testament to his unwavering dedication to duty, leadership, and the welfare of his troops. His innovative strategies, fearless approach to combat, and relentless commitment to excellence have inspired me throughout my military career (and still does). A copy of his book is still frequently taken from its place on my bookshelf as I reflect on the situations that caused me to turn down many page corners and even add side flags to wisdom-giving paragraphs and seek further guidance.

There is, however, one phrase in the book that I have committed to memory. It resurfaces when I feel challenged. Throughout Moore's career, especially when things got tough, he had a mantra, a mantra that, on that day in Ottawa, I was borrowing: "There is always one more thing I can do to increase my odds of success."

This mantra was feeding my Unstoppable Force to get things done. I was being unreasonable, I was expecting the highest of standards, and I was giving my ultimate sacrifice day after day to bring this legislation to life.

Four years earlier, I had been sitting in my office overlooking the river Clyde in Glasgow, Scotland. At the time, I had been responsible for the careers of all junior officers serving in the Intelligence Corps of the British Army. Next to me sat an officer, and friend, who had responsibility for my career. The opportunity for an exchange tour with the Canadian Forces had come up and it suited my skill set. I phoned home and suggested that Liz think about another overseas posting—she didn't need much convincing.

A 3-year exchange tour, in Canada, versus the inevitable two years in the grey drab building of the Ministry of Defence in London or the bunker of the Permanent Joint Headquarters. The chain of command had been clear, the latter options would be better for my career (if I did a good job). I was clear that if I took the exchange post, I would do an awesome job, which would be better for my career; and it was an exchange job. As a family, the idea had been to take those three years and experience as much of Canada and the US and, for Liz and the kids, it would be an opportunity for me to rest, recuperate, and spend some time in recreation.

But life is seldom like that. Canada was an amazing experience for the family, and we did everything we had planned and so much more; Liz and I even ended up in *Hello* magazine. But my *Unstoppable* nature is never far from the surface. Along with drafting this legislation, I was involved in the creation of a new training establishment and the course content that the students of 'said' seat of learning would undertake. My experience was also being extensively used every 2-3 months on Operations in the Kandahar province of Afghanistan.

For some of us, our Unstoppable Force seldom rests. We sense it, just below our consciousness. That *Unstoppable* muscle is restless. When we have been stagnant for too long, we lose momentum, a level of misery sets in, or we become restless. Our restlessness is our Unstoppable Force seeking the next 'thing', the next adventure. That bollocking, in the midst of the wood panelled rooms of the Canadian Government, was the reminder that I needed. I was *Unstoppable*, that legislation had to become *Unstoppable*; the lives of soldiers across the coalition required this of me. A few months later, the legislation was signed and the first group of Canadians with this specific skillset commenced operations in Afghanistan.

Maybe you've never felt that drive to be *Unstoppable* but, if you reflect you will see glimmers of your Unstoppableness. Unconsciously, you are likely to have been Unreasonable, to have improved on your standard, believe it or not, you will have committed to your ultimate sacrifice. You have survived every experience so far in your life—even getting to the end of this book. There is evidence that you are, or at least can be, *Unstoppable*. Take time to reflect on the big growth moments of your life.

Those moments in your life, those occasions when you were living from your centre. You did everything with a whole heart. No matter the challenges you faced, you went in wholeheartedly. You went all in, and you flexed the muscle.

With those experiences in mind, take time to remember how it felt. How did you feel when you were in the act of being *Unstoppable*, what about in the days and weeks leading up to your action? And, how about the days following your Unstoppableness? This exercise will help you to exercise the *Unstoppable* muscle within. This book is about becoming more conscious of your Unstoppableness. As we move this sense of Unstoppableness from our subconscious into our conscious, we discover that it is never too late to start.

There are many examples of the birthing of an Unstoppable Force in every phase of life. Our first decade is a litany of Unstoppableness, we crawled, we walked and talked, we started school, and had so many first experiences. We hear of fellow humans breaking the mould:

- Malala Yousafzai, the education activist, was awarded the 2014 Nobel Peace Prize laureate when she was seventeen; the world's youngest Nobel Prize laureate, and only the second Pakistani and the first Pashtun to receive a Nobel Prize.
- Mark Zuckerberg was not much older when he invented Facebook.

- JK Rowling birthed *Harry Potter* in her thirties.
- Julia Childs was fifty-one when her French style of cooking hit the US airwaves.
- Ray Kroc didn't buy his first McDonalds from the McDonalds brothers until he was fifty-nine years old, and staying with fast food …
- Col Sanders hadn't coined the phrase *"finger lickin' good"* until he was well into his sixth decade.
- The American astronaut, John Glenn, flew aboard the Space shuttle aged seventy-seven.
- In 2014, Yuichiro Miura became the oldest person to reach the top of Mount Everest at the age of eighty.
- Australia's first cowboy and pioneer of Western music, Smoky Dawson, became the oldest person to compose, record, and release a new album at ninety-two years old.
- There are even examples of 'athletes' finally finding their stride and completing their first marathons after they have received their birthday card from King Charles.

These examples do not have to be the exception, they are but evidence that we can be *Unstoppable* in every decade of our life; so why should we stop?

We live in a world of the status quo, of greed, and of mindless and mediocre living. This is a world where living wholeheartedly is missing, evidenced by the escalating dangers of overpopulation, climate change, gun and gang violence, and every brand of fear. Now more than ever, let's wake up … be unreasonable in your thinking, stretch your imagination, set the highest possible standards, and be prepared to serve the common good with real sacrifice.

In living from your centre—wholeheartedly living—there will always be opportunities for us all to become, be, and remain *Unstoppable*.

This world remains desperate for your input. Even if you feel you have not had an *Unstoppable* experience, whatever your age, there is no reason to limit yourself to a life of mediocrity. You are not here to live a reasonable, mediocre, self-serving existence.

Starting now, go into the world as an unreasonable force for good. Look for ways to lead by raising your standard every day and always give your Ultimate Sacrifice. Go out and live beyond your limits.

You are *Unstoppable*.

A Final Word

On our *Unstoppable* path, good enough is never good enough. And, if there is any doubt, there's no doubt.

Keen for more? Watch out for podcasts and newsletters from Stew and the Unstoppable Force team.

Use this link to receive downloads of worksheets mentioned throughout this book: **https://unstoppableforce.co.nz/worksheets/**

A Note from the Author's Wife

I sometimes wish this book was titled *Let's Be a Little Bit Brave Every Now and Again*. But then that wouldn't reflect me, nor the man I met and married. I have been an active bystander in this *Unstoppable* experiment for the last thirty years. I have watched as my husband has been broken physically and mentally and worked his way back. I have seen him battle with alcohol and his other demons often tending his scars with him. While not always aware of the detail and danger of his work, I have seen the toll that, on occasion, these operations took. Stew is passionate about his life and so protective of the people around him that his sacrifice has often gotten him too close to making the Ultimate Sacrifice.

None of this would prepare us for the challenges faced in the writing of this book and the emergence of Unstoppable Force. Stew was recently asked if there had ever been a time when he discovered that he was, in fact, Stoppable. This book was nearly it.

Early on, I came home to find Stew collapsed on the floor, unable to move; it took months of medical support to get him back to health.

We have been let down again and again by people who said they had our backs.

After pouring our life savings into our new business and beginning to see the fruits of our labour, we watched dumbstruck as, on a Friday afternoon while doing our banking, all our accounts were hacked, and we were left with nothing.

With each challenge, Stew has doubled down, remembering the three steps that have kept him and our family safe, whatever the threat. He has become even more unreasonable, raised his standard yet again, and continued to give his Ultimate Sacrifice.

When we first met, Stew suggested that our life would not be boring. We still often joke: *Are you bored yet?* Not a chance, there is no time when living this Unstoppable life.

Far from boring, our lives together are full of love, fun, adventure, and laughter.

I have watched as our two children have begun their own *Unstoppable* lives, proof of the benefit of 'proximity' to an Unstoppable Force. Personally, I have seen my own life change in unimaginable (positive) ways … I'll keep that for my book; maybe!

Take it from the one who has been alongside the author throughout this rollercoaster ride; Stew lives every word of this book, and you can too.

With love,

Liz

With Gratitude

This book is a direct result of the completion of my first book, *Lead Through Life*. I felt there was so much left to say. It took this long as I navigated many changes and I recognised the many people who endured what must have, at times, seemed like a fantasy.

To my coach, Bo Eason, and the whole Warrior Mastermind team, and my accountability group, who finally got me to sit down every day to write. To Keiran, and the whole crew at The Appleshed Restaurant in Mapua, New Zealand, who kindly provided the seat, table, and electricity that allowed my imagination to focus. The whole team made me feel at home but a special shout out to Lani Hopkinson, who always ensured my table by the power point was reserved, with water and a cappuccino (with cinnamon) was at the ready.

To the team of reviewers who took the time to honestly provide feedback to sharpen the message. And to Roxanne McCarty-O'Kane of Ignite and Write Publishing for the assistance in Edition 2 of the book and all that was required for me to become a self-published author.

To Liz who, as I said in the first pages, is the believer behind this dreamer.

Finally, to all the people referenced in this book and many more, who have assisted me in becoming *Unstoppable*. It was never about me; it is about all of you.

He aha te mea nui? Make e kii atu, he tangata, he tangata, he tangata.

What is the most important thing in the world? Well, let me tell you.

It is people, it is people, it is people.

About the Author

CEO and Founder of Unstoppable Force, Stew, is a former Lieutenant Colonel in Military Intelligence with a 23-year career in the British Army running security, intelligence, and counter-intelligence operations around the world. Stew worked with all three UK national intelligence agencies and was responsible for thousands of lives in high-stress environments including operations in The Balkans, Iraq, and Afghanistan.

After leaving the Army, Stew and his wife Liz emigrated to New Zealand, where Stew became CEO of a software start-up.

Since launching Unstoppable Force, Stew has applied his extensive skills and experience to make a difference in the lives of individuals and organisations. His events and workshops are often sell-outs, his books and online programs continue to inspire around the world.

Also by this author:

Lead Through Life (2020)

The Cave (2026)

Ready for What's Next?

If this book stirred something ….
Not a desire to *do* more, but a pull to become more.
You've already felt the first signal.

I don't offer coaching, I offer recalibration.

For founders, CEOs, and leaders who've outgrown their identity…
and are ready to step into the version the world hasn't met yet.

You've built it all. Now build yourself.

Work with me privately, with a high-stakes, identity-level experience designed for the powerful, the restless, and the unfinished.

WORKSHOPS AND KEYNOTES

Want to make your next event unforgettable?

An Unreasonable Life Workshop is a one-day experience designed to challenge the status quo.

Reset your mission so it moves people, not scares them.

Rebuild values to match how you actually want to work.

Redefine what wealth means beyond profit and why it matters.

For more information about becoming an Unstoppable Force:

   www.unstoppableforce.co.nz

   stew@unstoppableforce.co.nz

   @Unstoppableforcetv

www.ingramcontent.com/pod-product-compliance
Lightning Source LLC
Chambersburg PA
CBHW071952070526
44583CB00015B/1165